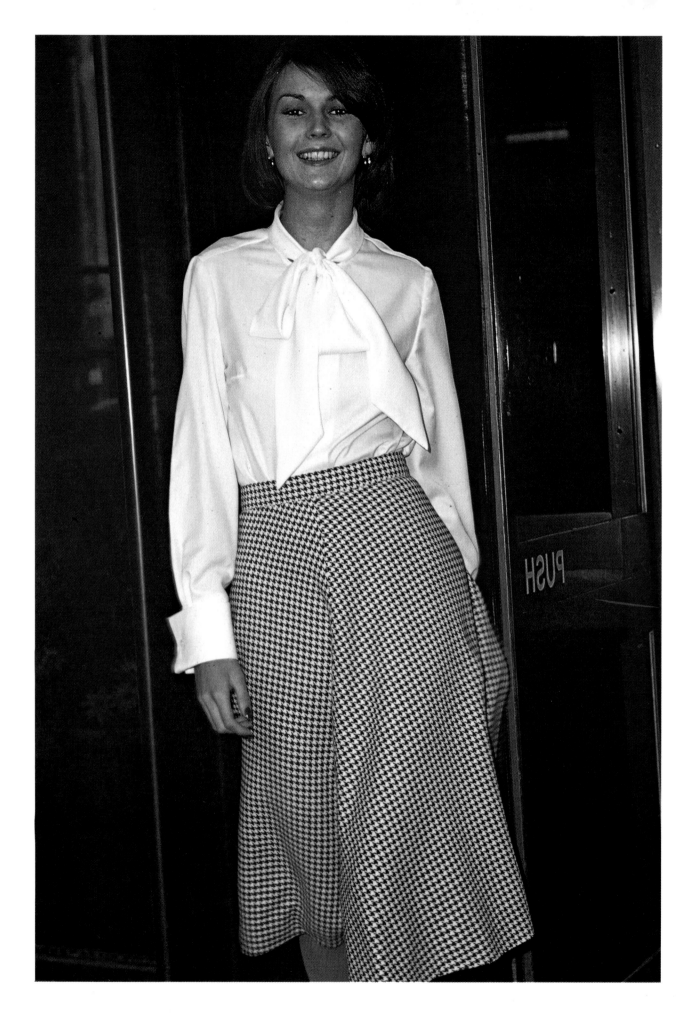

The Complete
DRESSMAKER

Peggie Hayden

Marshall Cavendish

Published by Marshall Cavendish Limited
58 Old Compton Street
London W1V 5PA

© Marshall Cavendish Limited 1974 – 83

First printing 1976
Second printing 1977
This printing 1983

ISBN 0 85685 194 9

Printed in Hong Kong

Introduction

The joys of dressmaking are often lost to the fashion-conscious today. You may have started to make a garment and gave up because you encountered difficulties, or the design you had in mind was unobtainable in pattern books. Now you can start afresh with *The Complete Dressmaker*. A really comprehensive book, it is ideal for today's woman who wants to dress in an individual style at a reasonable cost. All the basic techniques of dressmaking are discussed in a step-by-step course which takes the beginner from the most basic stitches and shapes right through to intricate seams, tucks and pleats, tailoring and pattern making. It helps you to become creative and adventurous, as you acquire the know-how to make original clothes and accessories at rock-bottom prices.

Every stage is illustrated with bright, clear diagrams — you can see what you are doing, and progress at your own pace. Don't worry if you are not a standard size — directions are given for adapting basic shapes to other designs, and with practice, you'll soon learn to make patterns to your individual requirements. You can use lengths of leftover fabric to make mix-and-match outfits right up to date with modern trends. Included are a variety of collars and cuffs, together with different styles of pockets, sleeves and belts. Why not brighten up a coat or jacket with fur fabric collar and cuffs? We show you how to work with this and other special fabrics such as lace and luxurious velvets, as well as leather and suede.

Finally, we provide lots of invaluable advice on choosing, caring for and cleaning fabrics, plus hints on how to press your work so that it has a really professional finish. All the latest information on sewing machines and handy accessories is given, to save you time and labour. Whether you sew for yourself or others, *The Complete Dressmaker* will inspire and teach you at the same time, so you'll step out in style with complete confidence.

Wishing you many happy, constructive sewing hours,

Peggi Hayden

Above and previous pages: *beautifully tailored trousers like these, well-cut skirts and blouses, even a smart coat – all these are easily made at home once you have mastered the range of dressmaking techniques.*

Contents

Equipment and general advice

Know your tools 7
Helpful accessories 12
The art of pressing 14
Choosing cotton fabrics 16
Caring for cotton 18
New age fabrics 20
Fabrics and you 23

Basic skills and techniques

The dressmaker's stand 27
A bodice and sleeve toile 30
A skirt toile 33
Commercial patterns 35
Altering patterns 39
Striped and checked fabrics 43
Basic sewing techniques 46
All about seams 50

Advanced techniques

Advanced sewing techniques 55
The art of quilting 59
The art of smocking 63
Basic facing techniques 67
Know-how with collars 71
Ways with necklines 75
Fun with flounces 79
All about sleeves 82
Stylish cuffs 86
Sleeve openings 90
Ways with waists 93
Ways with zips and plackets 97
The useful bias 101
High fashion belts 105
Loops, tabs and cummerbunds 109
How to make fastenings 112
A variety of buttonholes 115

Pretty pockets 119
Pockets with a purpose 123
Techniques for linings 127
Ways with hems 131
Pretty pleating 135
Decorative braids and cords 139

Problem fabrics

Jersey polyester fabrics 144
Sheer know-how 148
Working with lace 151
The luxury of fur 155
Fur collars and cuffs 157
The leather look 159
More ways with leather 161
Using velvet fabrics 163

Making your own patterns

The basic block 166
Making skirt patterns 170
Planning for pleats 174
Making a pleated skirt 177
Bodice and sleeve block 180
Altering bust darts 192
Other ways with blocks 196
Quick slip pattern 199
Patterns for shirt sleeves 201
Close fitting sleeves 204
Gathered sleeves 207
Basic collar patterns 210
High style collars 213
Patterns from circles 215
Capes and ponchos 218
Patterns for trousers 221
Making up trousers 223
Extra hints for trousers 227
Index 231

Opposite: *learning how to make clothes at home is a valuable skill for today's teenager. Even a beginner can make a pretty summer dress like this without difficulty.*

1

Equipment & general advice

Know your tools

You will need

A sewing machine There are three main types: straight stitch, swing needle (zig-zag), and swing needle automatic.

Straight stitch. This type will sew only in a straight line. It is the least expensive and is perfectly adequate for basic sewing. It is also possible to buy attachments, such as a piping foot for stitching close to a zip.

Swing needle. As well as straight stitching this machine does zig-zag stitching which is useful for neatening seams and hems, for making buttonholes, for stitching stretch fabrics, and for sewing on buttons. It is also possible to do simple embroidery stitches. Swing needle machines are in the medium price bracket.

Swing needle automatic. This machine does embroidery as well as the stitches which the other two types offer. But this type of machine is the most expensive and rather a luxury unless you intend to do a good deal of decorative stitching and embroidery.

Note Make sure that the machine you buy has a clear instruction book. It is also important, particularly with a more complex machine, to have it explained by an expert and if possible to take a few short lessons in its use. In order to get the best possible results, it is essential to get to know your machine really well.

Machine needles Use size 70–80 *(11–12)* for medium fabrics, size 80–90 *(12–14)* for heavy cottons and blended cloth, and size 100–110 *(16–18)* for heavy coatings and plastic. Continental sizes are given first here followed by British sizes in brackets.

Ballpoint machine needles should be used for jersey fabrics to prevent cutting the thread and laddering.

Sewing needles Use size 8 or 9 for most fabrics, size 6 or 7 for fabrics such as heavy linen and for stitching on buttons, and size 10 for fine work.

Pins Use steel dressmaking pins, at least 2.54cm *(1 inch)* long. Nickel-plated pins sometimes bend during use and could damage fine cloth. Glasshead pins are very sharp but have limited use as the heads easily break.

Tape measure Buy one with centimetre and inch markings. The fibre glass type is the best as it will not stretch. One with a metal strip attached at one end is useful, especially when taking up hems.

Thread For man-made fibres use a synthetic thread, such as Trylko, Drima or Güterman. Linens and cottons require either cotton or Sylko, 40 or 50. For woollen fabrics use either a silk or synthetic thread as the cloth has a certain amount of elasticity and the thread should have the same quality.

With all types of thread the higher the number given on the label, the finer the thread.

Scissors Small shears, 17.8cm – 20.3cm *(7–8 inches)* long, are best for cutting out most fabrics as they are heavier than scissors and glide through the cloth more easily. Larger shears are advisable when making up heavy fabrics. The handles should comfortably fit the hand (left-handed shears are available).

Small scissors are useful for clipping seams and threads.

Unpicker This is better than scissors for cutting machine-made buttonholes, and for removing buttons and snap fasteners, as well as being useful for unpicking. Various types of unpicker are available at most haberdashers.

Iron It is necessary to have a good medium-weight iron with thermostatic controls. If you use a steam iron you must use distilled water.

Ironing board An essential item for pressing seams flat. It should stand firmly and have a smooth-fitting cover. A sleeve board is useful.

Pressing cloth A piece of finely woven cotton or lawn, 61cm *(2 feet)* square, is essential for steam pressing. Your cloth should not have holes, frayed edges or prominent grains, as these can leave an impression on the fabric being pressed. Nor should the cloth contain any dressing as this will stick to the iron.

Tailor's chalk Have two pieces for marking your fabric, white for dark fabrics and dark for light fabrics.

Tracing Wheel Use this for marking pattern outlines onto fabric. One made from steel with sharp points is best.

Thimble This should fit the middle finger of your sewing hand. Choose a metal one as the needle can penetrate through a plastic one while sewing.

Pinking shears Not essential but useful to give a neater finish to seams, particularly when working with knitted and non-fraying fabrics.

Yardstick Use this for measuring hems. For accurate measuring it should be a firm, straight stick. When the skirt or dress is finished apart from the hem, try it on and measure the distance from the floor with the stick, pinning at the appropriate level all around to get the hem even.

Choosing fabrics

To find out whether a fabric is colourfast wash a small square about 7.5cm *(3 inches)* square. Press while still damp onto some white fabric. The colour will run onto the white fabric if it is not colourfast.

To test for shrinkage measure a similar square of fabric, or draw around it, before washing and measure again when dry and then compare the two measurements.

Needle & thread chart

This chart is to help you select the correct needles and thread for your fabric.

Type of fabric	Synthetic or man made thread	Cotton thread	Machine needle	
Blended fabrics	100		80	12
Cotton and mercerised		50	70–90	11–14
Heavy coating and thick fabrics	30		100–110	16–18
Lace, Cotton		50	70–90	11–14
Lace, Synthetic	100		70–90	11–14
Non-iron cotton	100		70–90	11–14
Light-weight plastics	100		80	12
Medium weight plastics	100		90	14
Poplin blended with synthetics	100		70–90	11–14
Light-weight poplin made from cotton	100	50	70–90	11–14
Silk and most light-weight fabrics	Pure silk or 100		70–90	11–14
Man made fabric, nylon terylene, dacron etc.	100		70	11
Man made fabric, heavy nylon, Trevira etc.	100		70–90	11–14
Taffeta, rayon, blended man-made fibres	100		70–90	11–14
Light-weight draping fabric, tropical light-weight, aerated	100		70–90	11–14
Underwear, cotton, rayon		50	70	11
Light-weight underwear, synthetics and wash-and-wear	100		70–90	11–14
Woollen fabrics	Pure silk or 100		70	11
Medium coating, worsted crimplene	100		90	14
Jersey stretch fabric	100		Ballpoint size suitable for fabric.	
Leather	Pure silk or 100		Leather needle	

Buying a new machine

When buying a new sewing machine, it is advisable to consider the price, which varies according to the type of machine, and to what extent one intends to use the machine. The swing needle machine is quite adequate for general dressmaking, as with it you can neaten edges, work buttonholes and applique. The quality of the machine depends on the price. A most important feature is the after sales service, which varies considerably with the make of machine. Always ask for a demonstration before buying a machine.

The main features to look for are: simplicity in design; a well-made pressure foot; an easily accessible spool race; a strong balance wheel (a plastic one could break off under pressure); a well-positioned light (ensure that new bulbs are readily available for this); metal tension adjuster; easy to thread take-up lever; and drop feed teeth (useful for darning). A free arm is useful (this is where the bed or table slides off to enable sleeves or trousers to slide round the arm when machining). It is advisable to have six metal spools.

Safety precautions to observe when using an electric sewing machine

Do not leave the power switched on when the machine is not being used. Ensure there are no knots or tangles in the leads, no splits in the rubber covering, and that the lead is long enough from the machine to the plug, and socket. Check that the light bulb is screwed in. Do not use a metal screw-driver or any other tool to make adjustments while the power is switched on.

Keep hands well away from the needle, and foot away from the control foot; when not actually machining, and when the power is switched on.

Always plug into the machine and then into the wall socket before switching on the power.

Simple machine techniques

To machine comfortably, make sure that the table and chair are of a suitable height for you. The machine should be in a position to enable you to see exactly where the needle is moving without shadows going across the work.

A high-backed chair is most suitable. Sit well back into it so that your back is supported. This prevents backache.

The ideal shape for a machine table is an L shape (two small tables placed in an L are just as effective). This is an asset when working on long lengths of fabric which can be moved to the side.

The foot should be able to reach the control pedal without excess straining or bending of the leg.

Prepare the machine with the correct needle and thread for the fabric, also the correct foot pressure as advised by the manufacturer. Adjust the stitch length to the required number. Work a row of machining on a test piece of fabric before starting to machine a

garment. Check that the thread when stitching does not pucker the fabric and has no large loops on either side, and that the stitching remains intact when the seam is pulled slightly. The stitch length adjuster is usually positioned on the right-hand side of the machine and is marked 0–4 or gives the number of stitches to the centimetre or inch.

Machine faults and how to rectify them

Top thread breakages can be caused by a bent or blunt needle; poor quality, badly polished needle; the needle too small for thread being used; the needle inserted incorrectly (long groove should be facing the thread as it is being threaded); poor quality thread; top tension too tight; throat plate damaged or requiring repolishing (a mechanic should rectify this); spoolrace not oiled frequently enough; point on spoolrace has become sharp through frequent use and needs repolishing (call the mechanic).

Lower thread breakages This can be the result of the lower tension being too tight; a badly-wound spool (odd threads left hanging out of spoolcase); too much thread on spool; spool damaged or deformed by jamming in the case; or throat plate being damaged and requiring repolishing (a job for the mechanic).

The machine will not stitch either backwards or forwards Usually this means a blocked spoolrace. Open covering of spoolrace and you will probably find that there is a thread visible that is caught round the point of the spoolrace. Remove this as well as the spool case, place one drop of oil in the spoolrace housing and turn balance wheel backwards and forwards a few times. Check that there are no more pieces of thread visible. Replace the spoolcase. This fault is nearly always caused because insufficient length of thread has been left under the machine foot, towards the back, before beginning to stitch.

Faulty stitches Caused by needle not being inserted high enough into the needle holder (it must be placed as high as is possible); a blunt or bent needle; needle not suitable for thread or fabric being used; badly polished, poor quality needle (this often tears the thread and it breaks very easily); or needle too short. When using a zig-zag stitch to neaten an edge it is sometimes necessary to use a larger sized needle than for the straight stitch.

Needle breakages Can be caused by: bent needle; needle too fine in relation to thread and fabric; needle holder not tightened sufficiently; top tension too loose; or pin left in the fabric. When removing work from the machine, be sure that the needle is at the highest point and gently pull work out towards the back of the machine. Cut off thread but leave long threads ready for next row of machining. It is often when work is dragged towards the front that needles break.

Slow operation of machine This is often caused by insufficient oiling of the machine motor. Check with instructions given with machine. Over oiling of motor can cause slowing down because the collector has become oily – a mechanic should be called in this situation. The machine can become blocked because poor quality oil containing resin has been used. This can sometimes be cured by flushing the machine, *not motor,* with petrol, cleaning all accessible parts with a cloth, and then oiling with good quality oil. If the machine has been in a cold atmosphere for some time, this could be a job for the mechanic as the machine may have to be dismantled completely to remove the poor quality oil.

How to adjust the tension of the machine

When the top or bottom thread is too tight or too loose it is usually the top tension that needs adjusting. To tighten, turn tension clockwise; to loosen, turn tension anti-clockwise. Should this not rectify the fault the tension screw should be tightened or loosened on the spoolcase. To tighten, turn clockwise; to loosen, turn anti-clockwise. The thread from the spool should run freely but not so freely that the spool spins round when the thread is pulled.

Precaution The screw on the spoolcase is very small and can easily be lost. It is advisable to adjust this screw whilst holding the spoolcase over a large sheet of white paper so that if it falls out it can be easily seen.

Patching by machine
Straight stitch

Cut a patch larger than the hole. Place it over the hole. Turn in 0.6cm ($\frac{1}{4}$ *inch*) and work a row of straight stitching on the very edge of the fold (figure 1). Turn fabric on to wrong side, trim the hole to 1.3cm ($\frac{1}{2}$ *inch*) from the first row of machining, clip to 0.6cm ($\frac{1}{4}$ *inch*) at the corners, turn under 0.6cm ($\frac{1}{4}$ *inch*) and machine on the very edge of this fold (figure 2).

▲ *Figure 1*

▼*Figure 2*

Correct tension

Bottom tension too tight

Top tension too tight

Zig-zag

Cut a square or oblong larger than the hole and place over it. Work a row of small zig-zag stitches over the raw edge (figure 3). Turn to wrong side. Trim the hole to 0.6cm ($\frac{1}{4}$ *inch*) from first row of stitches and work another row of small zig-zag stitches on this raw edge (figure 4). Turn again on to right side and work a row of larger zig-zag stitches between the two rows of smaller ones (figure 5).

If using an embroidery machine use the curved running-stitch pattern instead of the large zig-zag stitches.

▲ *Figure 3*   ▼ *Figure 4*

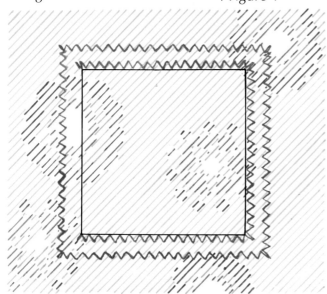

▼ *Figure 5*

Decorative use of patches on children's clothes

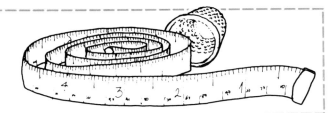

Helpful accessories

Accessories

There are many sewing accessories available which save time and help give clothes a professional finish. Some of the most useful are listed in this chapter.

Tailor's chalk This is available in many colours and comes either as a block or in a plastic tube shaped like a pencil into which the chalk is inserted to give a thin, clear line. Always test on a scrap of fabric as tailor's chalk contains a certain amount of grease and may leave permanent marks (figure 1).

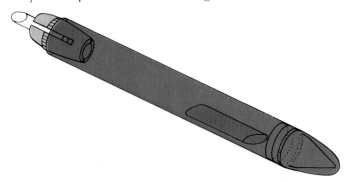

Figure 1

Tailor tacker This is a simple device used to mark dots and darts without sewing. It consists of two plastic cases which hold thin pieces of chalk. A pin protrudes from one piece of chalk and the other piece has a hole in the centre. The pin is inserted through the paper pattern and both thicknesses of fabric. When the pin appears on the back of the work the two halves are pushed together and twisted so that marks are left on both sides (figure 2).

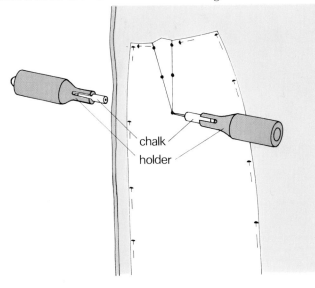

chalk
holder

Figure 2

Adjustable ruler This is a small ruler used for marking pleats and tucks. By following the first pleat or tuck line with the adjustable guide a thin line is left on the fabric by a piece of tailor's chalk held in the end of the ruler (figure 3).

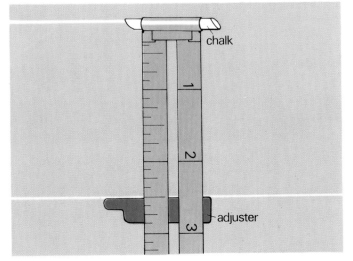

chalk

1

2

adjuster

3

Figure 3

Tracing wheels are used with dressmaker's carbon paper for transferring lines and darts from pattern pieces to fabric through one or two layers of fabric. On fine fabrics they should be used without carbon paper as carbon may mark the fabric permanently. The best types of tracing wheels are those made of steel (figure 4).

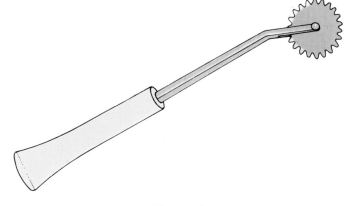

Figure 4

Transparent rulers enable the grain or pattern of the fabric to show through. The most useful type is 38cm (*15 inches*) long and 10cm (*4 inches*) wide marked with centimetres and inches. It has a curved end for pockets and parallel slots through which tailor's chalk can be used.

Magnetic seam guide This is a metal box containing a magnet with a straight metal bar at one end which is used for keeping machine stitching straight on long seams. Place the seam guide on the machine bed to the right of the needle with the straight metal bar the required seam allowance from the needle. This guide will also pick up loose pins (figure 5).

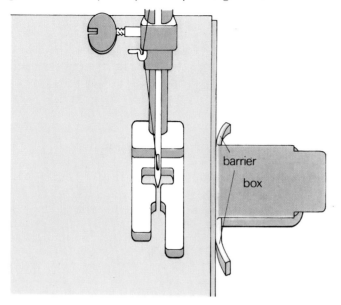

Figure 5

Buttonhole maker This is used for making equal sized piping on either side of a piped buttonhole from 1.3cm ($\frac{1}{2}$ *inch*) to 6.5cm ($2\frac{1}{2}$ *inches*) long. A matching strip can be used for the piping with cording inserted if desired (figure 6).

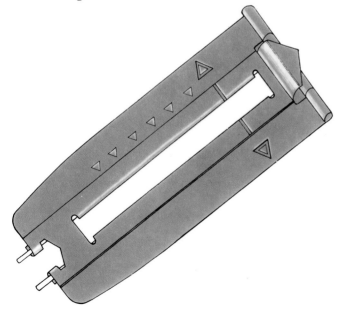

Figure 6

Metallic thread is a twisted cord which is soft and can be used on the spool or through a machine needle with a large eye. The thread is available in gold or silver.

Beeswax holder This is a plastic case enclosing a piece of wax with grooves cut in the top and bottom. The thread is pulled over the wax making it smoother and stronger (figure 7).

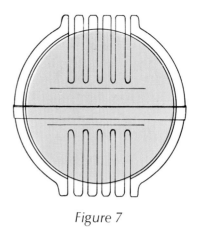

Figure 7

Pressing accessories A double sided sleeve board that folds flat is useful for pressing sleeve seams and areas that are difficult to reach on an ordinary ironing board. They are available with or without heat absorbent covers (figure 8). Rolls and pressing mitts are useful accessories when pressing curved seams.

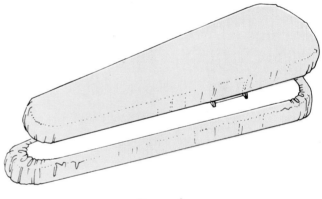

Figure 8

Bodkins measuring 15cm (*6 inches*) long can be used for threading elastic or ribbon through casings, for turning through a rouleau or for pushing out stitched corners. They have a large oblong eye at one end and a ball point at the other end.

Needle threader and magnifier This is a small magnifier with a hollow handle into which a needle threader is placed. It is useful for pulling thick embroidery thread through the eye on the pressure foot of some machines.

Large hooks and eyes which are suitable for heavyweight garments and on fur, can be bought individually or in packs. They are covered in strong ribbon and are usually brown, black, grey or white.

Adjustable hooks and eyes can be used on skirts and trousers and on coats when covered in buttonhole stitch. They adjust to three positions and may be used as a decorative feature on the right side of garments.

The art of pressing

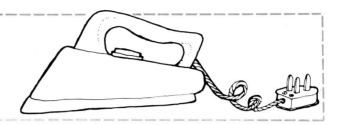

Pressing and pressing equipment

Pressing is a very important part of dressmaking. It improves the appearance of the garment and also helps you to work neatly and accurately. It is essential to press after each line of machining has been worked. It is easier to press on an ironing board, but a table well-padded with a blanket and covered with a cloth is quite adequate for flat seams.

Basic pressing rules

1 Always check that the base of the iron is clean. If not, clean with methylated spirit, a specially-made cleaning agent or you can rub the base gently with a piece of crocus paper, which is similar to emery paper but very much finer. Always polish the base after cleaning by rubbing with a clean soft cloth. Check that vents or holes on the base are not blocked.

2 If using a steam iron it is essential to use distilled water as tap water leaves a deposit in the iron. Distilled water can be bought or water that has defrosted from the refrigerator can be used (not ice as it is not distilled). This should be strained and kept in a clean bottle.
Do not over fill the iron as the water can splash and mark the fabric.

3 Always test on a piece of fabric from which you are making the garment.

4 When using a damp cloth, use a piece of linen if possible. The highest setting on the iron is linen and this therefore prevents scorching.

5 Set the iron to the correct setting.

6 Remove all tacking in the seams before pressing.

7 Press on the wrong side of the garment.

8 Pressing is not ironing. With pressing the iron is placed gently down on to the garment, lifted and placed down again. The iron is not moved backwards and forwards as in ironing.

9 Do not over-press by holding the iron on one part of the garment for too long. This can leave an imprint of the iron permanently showing on the right side.

10 Some fabrics change colour when pressed, permanently if care is not taken. To avoid this use heavy brown paper free from acid and grease over the fabric.

11 Do not press plastic coated fabric with an iron. If open seams are required, they must be glued down.

Pressing for a perfect finish

Seams Press either open or towards the centre-back or centre-front if to be neatened together. Always press a seam before it is neatened, this prevents ridges on the right side of the garment.

Darts Darts are always pressed towards the centre of the body: front towards the centre-front; back towards the centre-back; side bust darts towards the waist; and sleeve elbow darts down. On thick fabric the dart may have to be cut and pressed open. Be careful not to stretch this type of dart.

Facings Have the garment flat on the ironing board or table and, where the facings have been attached, press lightly on the very edge. Remove the tacking stitches and press again to remove any stitch marks. It is advisable to insert a cloth or piece of paper between the facing and the garment when pressing the edge. This prevents ridges on the right side.

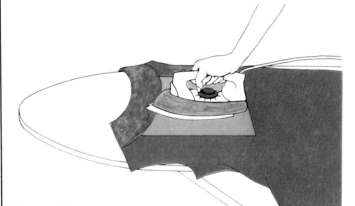

Pleats When pressing pleats, it is essential to have the edge of the pleat fold on the wrong side parallel with the edge of the ironing board. Press on the folds, remove tacking stitches and press again to remove stitch marks. After pressing in pleats with a damp cloth hang up the garment straight away to let the pleats dry completely before doing any more work on the garment.

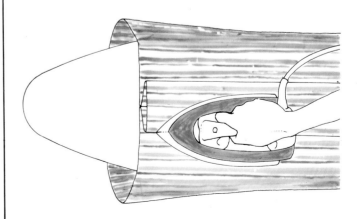

Pressing a shoulder seam Using a pressing mitt, turn your hand upwards and place it under the shoulder join, with the mitt extended about 1.3cm ($\frac{1}{2}$ *inch*) beyond the join into the sleeve. Place the tip of the iron gently on to the seam line with the turnings towards the sleeve and at the same time slightly lift the tips of the fingers in the mitt. This will round the top of the sleeve in the armhole and help to remove any wrinkles. Continue in this way until the top of the sleeve has become smooth and moulded. Do not over-press by holding the hot iron and damp cloth on one spot for too long.

side. Work a gathering thread on the stitching line, pull up to the required length and press with a damp cloth a little at a time. After each press gently pat the fabric, this helps to flatten any bulges. Continue in this way until all the fullness has been eliminated. Remove the gathering thread.

Collars With under collar facing upwards press on the very edge. Remove tacking stitches and press again.

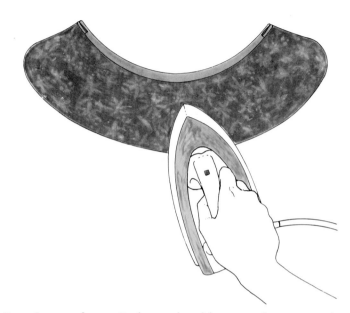

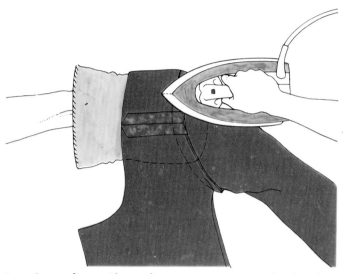

Pressing a hem Place the garment on to the ironing board and gently press. Lift the iron and press again. The nose of the iron should be pointed towards the waistline of the garment. Do not move the iron backwards and forwards, or from side-to-side as this will stretch the fabric.

Pressing gathers Gathers should never be pressed flat. Place the garment on to the ironing board and, with wrong side of fabric upwards, press from the lowest edge, on the straight grain, up towards the gathers. Nose the tip of the iron into the gathers then move the garment around the board and press the next section in the same way. When complete hang up the garment immediately.

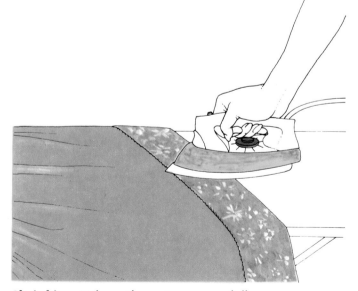

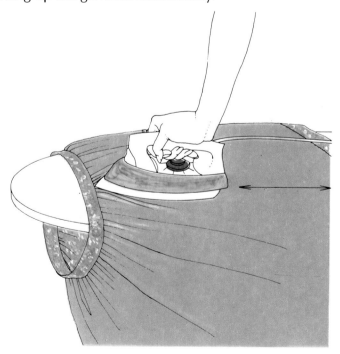

Shrinking When there is excess fullness on a garment such as at the hemline on a flared skirt, or a tight fitting sleeve without elbow darts, the fabric can be shrunk to avoid pleats or creases on the right

Choosing cotton fabrics

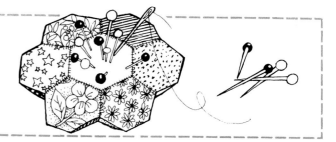

Names and uses

Batiste is made from a fine cotton yarn. It has a plain weave and can be dyed or embroidered. The heavier fabric is suitable for foundation garments and the lighter for dresses.

Calico is a plain woven fabric, medium-weight and usually cream in colour. It can be bleached, dyed and printed and is used for overalls, upholstery and toiles.

Cambric is a plain light-weight fabric which can be treated on one side to strengthen it and give it a smooth finish. It is usually used for handkerchiefs and aprons.

Canvas is available in different weights and strengths. It is closely woven and suitable for coat and jacket interlining, upholstery and accessories.

Cheesecloth is a very loosely woven fabric with an uneven texture. It is obtainable in a variety of colours and prints and is useful for casual summer wear such as long skirts and blouses.

Cloqué has an uneven surface as some of the threads are pulled together tighter than the others, to give a gathered look. It is suitable for dresses, summer coats and jackets.

Corduroy A very hardwearing fabric with a pile and a rib running lengthways. It is available with different width and density of the rib and is suitable for coats, dresses and trousers.

Crepe is a dull surfaced fabric. It hangs well and is suitable for blouses, dresses and evening wear.

Damask has a pattern formed in the weave by use of dull and shiny threads. It is frequently used for napkins and tablecloths.

Denim is a firm, very hardwearing fabric with a diagonal or straight weave. Two threads different in colour or tone are used in the weave which give the fabric a definite main colour on the right side and a pale colour on the wrong side. It is suitable for all outer garments and accessories.

Drill is a hardwearing fabric with a diagonal weave which is suitable for trousers and jackets. It is not advisable for wear in hot climates as it is a heavy fabric and retains heat.

Flannelette is soft with a brushed pile. It has a plain or diagonal weave and is suitable for night-wear. It is highly inflammable and should be bought flame-proofed.

Gabardine is a closely woven fabric with a diagonal weave showing on the right side. It hangs very well and is obtainable in various weights and colours and is especially suitable for outer garments such as trousers, coats and jackets.

Gingham This is a light-weight fabric with a close weave. It is usually woven in a check pattern or contrasting colours and is suitable for children's wear, skirts, dresses and blouses.

Jacquard is woven to give the appearance of tapestry, or knitted to give a multi-coloured design. It is useful for dresses, tunics, blouses and skirts.

Lawn is a light-weight fabric with a plain weave. As well as being suitable for blouses and nightwear, it can be used as interlining and interfacing for fine fabrics. It is slightly transparent and cool to wear.

Lace can be used for dresses, blouses and underwear. It may require mounting on lining as it is semi-transparent. Heavier laces such as Guipure are not comfortable when worn next to the skin.

Muslin is a very fine loosely woven fabric especially suitable for gathered styles and baby clothes.

Needlecord is similar to corduroy but has a much finer rib. It is suitable for dresses, trousers, blouses and children's wear.

Net, although an open mesh fabric, is also fairly crisp and can be used as trimming or interfacing. It is highly inflammable and only flame-resistant net should be bought.

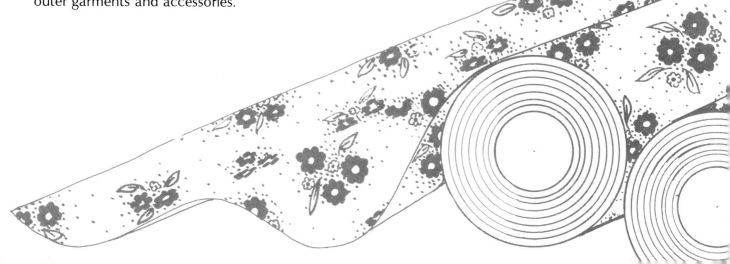

Organdie is a sheer, crisp fabric with a plain weave, made with a fine yarn. It can be dyed or embroidered and is frequently used as interfacing on light-weight fabrics. All organdie is treated when manufactured to retain a crisp appearance. It is suitable for dresses, baby clothes and pram pillowcases.

Panne velvet is a fabric with a silky one way pile, especially effective for evening wear.

Piqué is a firm, medium-weight fabric with a raised surface in the form of dots, ribs or honeycomb stitch. It is strong and hardwearing and is suitable for blouses, sportswear and summer dresses. Pique is often used for detachable collars and cuffs as it retains a crisp appearance.

Plissé has a puckered stripe running either lengthways or across the fabric. It is light-weight and extremely useful for travelling clothes as it needs little ironing.

Poplin is a very adaptable fabric made from mercerized cotton and is suitable for shirts, blouses, dresses and sportswear. It has a fine ribbed weave as the weft (crossways) threads are thicker than the warp (lengthways) threads. It has a soft sheen and is hardwearing.

Repp is a very firm fabric with the weft threads forming a rib. It is suitable for dresses, suits and summer coats.

Sailcloth is a very strong canvas type fabric available in different colours and prints. It can be used for most outer garments depending on the weight of the fabric.

Sateen is a shiny faced fabric used mostly for lining garments and curtains.

Satin also has one shiny side and is available plain, printed or with a woven pattern. It hangs well but is inclined to crease easily unless treated by the manufacturer and is useful for dresses, blouses and nightwear.

Seersucker has puckered stripes or checks. Like cloque, groups of threads are pulled tighter than others to give this puckered effect. It washes well and needs little ironing, so is particulary suitable for holiday garments.

Terry towelling has a looped surface on one or both sides. It is hardwearing and absorbent and therefore ideal for beach clothes, baby clothes and household purposes.

Tobralco is a light-weight fabric with a fine warp rib. It wears and washes well and is pleasant next to the skin. Available in prints or plain colours, it is suitable for dresses, blouses and childrens wear.

Velvet is a piled fabric which has a definite nap. It is closely woven without a rib, and has a deep, rich appearance. It can be used for trousers, dresses, skirts and evening wear but it is not a hardwearing fabric, and is inclined to seat unless lined.

Velveteen is a short piled and closely woven cotton fabric similar to velvet but less luxurious. It can be used for trousers, jackets and dresses but should be lined, especially when making trousers. It is also very suitable for curtains.

Voile has a muslin appearance and is sheer. It can be embroidered, smocked or used for drawn thread work.

Winceyette is a hardwearing fabric with a very soft, brushed pile on one side. It is ideal for nightwear but if used for children's clothes, it must be treated for inflammability.

Caring for cotton

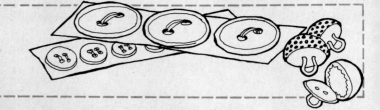

More about cotton
Finishes
Many cotton fabrics are treated in various ways by the manufacturer and indication of chemical treatment or finish is usually printed on the selvedge.

Crease resistance
Resin is often incorporated into the fibres of cotton fabrics to make them more resilient and less likely to crease. Some trade names of these products are: Everglaze; Calpretta Carefree cotton; Quintafix and Tebalized Minimum-iron.

Water repellence
Fabrics used for outer garments are treated by the manufacturers with various silicones and waxes to make them waterproof. With frequent laundering and cleaning the water repellence will eventually disappear and must be replaced. Most dry cleaners will do this but it is also possible to buy sprays to use at home. Some trade names are: Dri-sil; Calpretta stain resister and water repellent and B.D.A. Fondspot.

Flame proofing
Many cotton fabrics likely to be used for making childrens wear are not flame-proofed and could catch fire very easily when in contact with unguarded or electric fires. These fabrics include net, flannelette and winceyette. If a fabric is treated, this will be indicated on the selvedge with the trade name 'Proban'. Proban tends to stiffen the fabric and will only wash out when the fabric is boiled or bleached.

Stain removal
Always test on a spare piece of fabric first, using the mildest form of remover.

Blood, egg and milk stains
Soak in cold water and salt for a few hours. Wash and boil providing the fabric is untreated and colour-fast. Fresh blood stains can often be removed by spreading a paste mixture of starch and water over the affected area, leaving it for a few minutes and then washing.

Grease stains
Soak in hot water and detergent and then wash.

Fruit juice, tea, coffee, grass and wine stains
A fresh stain on white cotton should be placed over a cup or bowl. Pull the fabric taut and put salt on the stain. Pour boiling water over the stain on the fabric and into the bowl. Rinse.
For dried-in stains, place the stain over a cup or bowl and pull the fabric taut. Rub in salts of lemon crystals or oxalic acid with a circular movement. Use a plastic spoon as anything metal will stain. Pour boiling water through the fabric. Then pour a weak solution of ammonia or rub in bicarbonate of soda to neutralize the acid. Wash, boil and rinse.

On coloured cottons, place a pad under the stain and rub in glycerine using a circular movement. Soak in warm water with one teaspoon of borax per pint added. Wash and rinse.

Oil paint
Place a pad of thick blotting paper under the stain and sponge with paraffin or turpentine using a circular movement. Wash with detergent and rinse well.

Nail varnish and cellulose paint
Sponge with acitone, wash and rinse.

Emulsion paint
If the paint is dry, soak the stain in methylated spirits, then wash and rinse. A fresh stain may be soaked in cold water only and then washed and rinsed.

Writing ink
Place a pad underneath the stain. Spread lemon juice and salt over the stain, leave for a few hours and then wash or boil. If this method does not remove the stain use salts of lemon crystals or oxalic acid and neutralize with bicarbonate of soda or a weak ammonia solution.

Ball-point ink
Place a pad underneath the stain and sponge with methylated spirits, benzene, carbon tetrachloride or trichlorethylene. Wash or boil and rinse well. Very obstinate stains can be removed by soaking the garment in a solution of one teaspoon of hyposulphite bleach to one pint of warm water.
Wash and rinse well.

Washing
Cotton fabrics endure a lot of washing and are strongest when wet. They can be scrubbed to remove a very bad mark without fear of stretching or weakening the fabric.

Washing white and colour-fast cotton
These fabrics can be soaked in cold water and detergent overnight or for several hours before actual washing. Always ensure that the soap or detergent is completely dissolved before immersing the garment. Use a water softener or soda crystals to soften hard water. White cotton is not affected by very hot water

but instructions for water temperature and the detergent required should be carefully followed. Cottons are best ironed when slightly damp.

Washing coloured and printed cottons

These should not be soaked if they are not colour-fast and cooler water should be used for washing. It is not advisable to use bleaches on these fabrics. Piled fabrics should be kept moving in the water so that the water passes through the pile. Do not squeeze, wring or spin dry, as this can leave bad crease marks.

Lace and flocked fabric

These should be washed by hand. Rinse well and remove excess water by rolling in a towel. When pressing place over a thick pad and press from the wrong side so that the pattern will be raised on the right side.

Treated fabrics

Crease-resistant and drip dry fabrics should not be bleached, starched or boiled and should be allowed to drip dry.

Pemanent lustre, sheen and glazed fabrics should not be boiled, bleached or starched. Roll in a towel to remove excess water and avoid squeezing or wringing. Iron while the fabric is damp using a very hot iron. Fabrics which are treated for shrink resistance can be washed normally.

Do not boil, bleach or starch stain-resistant, water-repellent and flame-proofed fabrics. Press stain-resistant and water-repellent fabrics using a damp cloth and flame-proofed fabrics when slightly damp.

and can be boiled if necessary. Bleaches can be used providing the garment is rinsed well afterwards, otherwise it will rot the fibres. Starch will also rot the fibres of garments which are stored for a long time, and should be washed out before storing. Starch should not be used on garments which are permanently stiffened, glaze finished or flame-proofed.

Most cottons can be washed in washing machines

New age fabrics

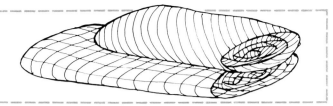

Easy care fabrics
Choosing your fabrics

Synthetic and easy care fabrics are fabrics produced chemically from man-made fibres. With so many weights and types in the stores, it is important for the home dressmaker to know their properties and characteristics in order to choose correctly, both for ease in making up and for wear and care. Because of the enormous variety of different brand names, we are providing a reasonable selection of the synthetic fabrics generally available in Great Britain, but they may be known by different names in other countries.

Acrylic fabrics
Courtelle, Acrilan, Orlon, Sayelle, Dralon, Crylor, Dynel, Teklan

Characteristics

Acrylic fibres have a warm, soft feel which is nearer to that of wool than any other man-made fibre.
Acrylic fabrics are easy to wash, although knitted garments may stretch and crease, and they will drip dry. They shed creases easily, drape well, are moth-proof and mildew resistant and easy to handle. They dye well and are available in a good range of colours. Acrylic fibres are often blended with other synthetic fibres to add warmth or with natural fibres to prevent creasing.

Uses

Acrylic fibres can be knitted to make jersey fabrics or woven to make a firm fabric, and both types are suitable for dresses and suits, although trousers should be lined to prevent bagging at the knees and seat.
Piled acrylic fabrics are often used for fleece linings for coats, dressing gowns and toy-making, and for blankets which are lighter than wool and ideal for people who are allergic to wool.
Most acrylic fibres can be permanently pleated, although with Orlon the pleats may have to be renewed after several washings.
Teklan and Dynel are acrylic fibres which have been modified during manufacture to make them flame-

proof and thus very suitable for children's clothing. Dralon is particularly suitable for upholstery because it is strong and stains can normally be wiped off with a damp cloth. Light-weight Dralon fabrics with an open weave make good sheer curtains.

Acetate fabrics
Dicel, Lansil, Lancola, Tricel

Characteristics
Acetate fibres, often known as a form of rayon, feel and look similar to silk. The fabric made from these fibres can have a rich, lustrous or matt finish, does not stretch or shrink, recovers quickly from creases and is mothproof and mildew resistant. Acetate fabrics wash easily, provided they are not allowed to become too dirty, nor should they be allowed to become too creased while wet as they will be difficult to iron. Woven acetate fabrics tend to fray badly and garments should be cut out with a larger seam allowance than normal.
Tricel is a development of acetate and has the additional qualities of being quicker drying and more crease resistant than other acetates and it can also be set into permanent pleats.

Uses
Acetate fabrics drape softly and are ideal for elegant dresses, long skirts, evening blouses and trousers.

Nylon fabrics
Bri-nylon, Tendrelle, Celon, Enkalon, Banlon, Helanca

Characteristics
Nylon fibres are fine, strong and elastic. The fabrics are cool and smooth to feel, they do not absorb moisture and are light-weight, so can be washed easily and drip dried. They are crease resistant, flameproof, mothproof and mildew resistant although they will rot if exposed to extreme sunlight for long periods. Nylon is inclined to form static electricity when worn with other man-made fibres, although anti-static nylons are now being produced to avoid this.
Nylon can be woven or knitted into fabrics and is often blended with other fibres, such as wool, to add strength and make them washable.

Uses
Pure nylon fabrics tend to be inexpensive and they can be made up into most kinds of garment, although their non-absorbency makes them uncomfortable for many people to wear in warm weather. They are not warm in winter, however, although the brushed versions can make good sheets and nightwear. Knitted nylons drape well and are usually easy to handle. Woven nylons make good overalls and light-weight raincoats.

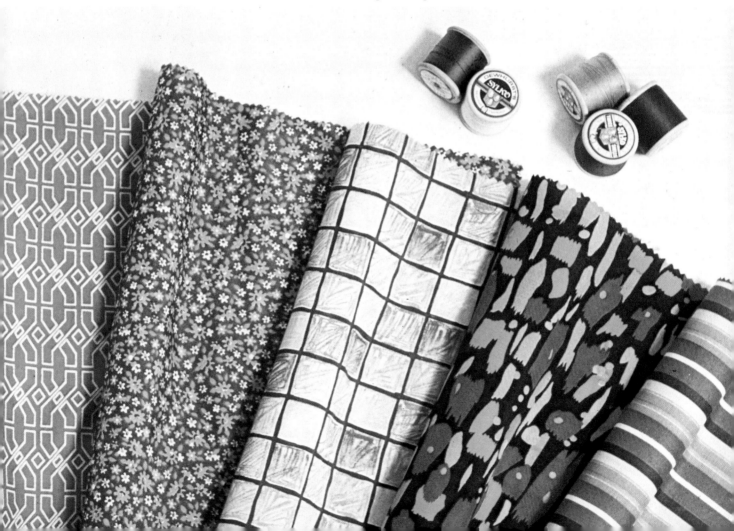

Nylon is not normally suitable for curtains because it is damaged by sunlight, although nylon velvet can be used if it has a bonded backing in a different fibre.

Polyester fabrics
Terylene, Terlanka, Diolen, Trevira, Crimplene, Lirelle, Dacron, Tergal

Characteristics
Polyester fibres are probably the most versatile of the man-made fibres and can be woven or knitted to produce a wide variety of textures and finishes. The fabrics are strong, wear well and are easy to wash and drip dry. They are suitable for permanent pleating, are crease, flame and mildew resistant, are mothproof and not harmed by sunlight. Polyester is often blended with natural fibres to improve their crease resistance and washability, and it usually takes on the feeling of that fibre as with cotton/polyester sheeting which feels like cotton but should be washed (and ironed when necessary) with a cooler temperature.

Polyester fabrics tend to form static electricity and attract dust and dirt, so garments and net curtains should be washed frequently. A fabric conditioning solution added to the rinse often reduces the static electricity.

Uses
Polyester fabrics are suitable for practically every type of garment, depending on the weight and texture. In its bulk form, it can be used as a filling for cushions and quilts and is ideal for people who suffer from allergies.

Viscose fabrics
Fibro, Darelle, Sarille, Durafil, Vincel, Evlan, Tenasco

Characteristics
Viscose fibres, often known as viscose rayon, can be made into fabrics which resemble silk, cotton, linen or wool. The fabrics are soft to handle and drape well, although they are weak when wet and require gentle handling during washing.

They do not shrink or stretch, they are mothproof and mildew resistant, and they absorb moisture which means they are good for spring and summer clothes although they may take longer to dry than other synthetics after washing. Many viscose fabrics fray and should be cut with a larger seam allowance.

Uses
Most viscose fabrics can be made up into almost any type of garment. Tenasco, Durafil and Evlan are modified viscose fibres, however, and are stronger and more resistant to abrasion. This makes them less suitable for clothes as they have a harder feel, but more suitable for upholstery. Durafil is sometimes blended with other fibres to make a strong fabric for trousers and blazers.

Fabrics & you

Fabrics for your figure

We have illustrated here some of the styles which can help to disguise figure problems. But your choice of fabrics is equally important. Before you shop for patterns and fabrics, before you start to sew, take stock of your own figure. Only if you choose the styles and fabrics that flatter *you* most, will you feel you have made a success of sewing for yourself. Use the finger and thumb test to feel if a fabric is right for you. Firm fabrics . . . feel crisp and smooth as you run your finger along them. They will flatter a heavy figure, giving it a smooth line, and will not add extra bulk. The firm fabrics include closely woven cottons, gingham, denim, sailcloth, man-made fibres such as Courtelle, Acrilan and Tricel, close-weave wools,

gabardine, and the finer corduroys. Soft fabrics . . . are those that slide through your fingers or feel extra fine. They can look good on both the heavier and the thin figure as they drape well and have a good hang. Depending on the style of the garment you are making, they can add soft curves, or disguise them. The soft fabrics include silk, crepe, chiffon, silk jersey, voile and the finer cottons such as lawn. Heavy fabrics feel thick and bulky to the touch. Choose them with care if you do not want to add extra inches. They can make you look twice your size, so can be overpowering if you are big, or not very tall. The heavy fabrics include most tweeds, especially those with a slubbed texture, thick pile velvets, heavy corduroy, shaggy fur fabrics, long haired mohair and brushed cotton.

Study your figure before you start sewing. Start with a good long look in the mirror. Know *your* style. It's the secret of sewing success.

1 A short jacket gives an illusion of longer legs. **2** A blouson top is shapely on a skinny figure. **3** A cut-away neckline or revers narrows broad shoulders. **4** A dress with no waist seam is good if you have no waist. **5** A pleated skirt is slimming for big hips. **6** A long line jacket gives a long slim line.

2

Basic skills
& techniques

How to take your measurements

Bust Make sure that you keep the tape measure well up over the shoulder blades at the back, and measure across the fullest part of the bust.

Waist Tie a piece of tape or straight binding round the waist to establish the true waistline. Then run tape measure around your waist over tape so that it is comfortable but not loose. Keep tape on as a guide for other measurements.

Hips This measurement should be taken around the fullest part of the hips, usually between 15 and 20cm (*6 and 8 inches*) below the waistline.

Back neck to waist Measure from the small bone at the back of the neck to the waistline.

Back neck to hem Measure from the same bone to the hemline. Remember to allow extra for a hem.

Sleeve With arm bent, measure from arm top to the wrist around the bent elbow.

Making a pattern from a graph
You will need
☐ Graph paper
☐ Sharp pencil
☐ Ruler

Making the pattern

1 In pencil, number the squares on the graph to cover the total length and breadth of the pattern piece required.

The scale to which the graph has been drafted will be indicated on it. This is usually 1 square = 2.54cm square (*1 inch square*).

Using graph paper with squares of the appropriate size, mark out in pencil the same numbers as on the graph.

2 First mark the basic points, such as centre-front neck, corner of neckline, shoulder, and top of arm-hole, underarm, waistline, and lower edge of centre-front. Letter points A, B, C, D, E, F and G respectively.

3 Using a ruler, join straight lines.

4 To obtain an accurate curved line mark on each square the exact point at which the line crosses it.

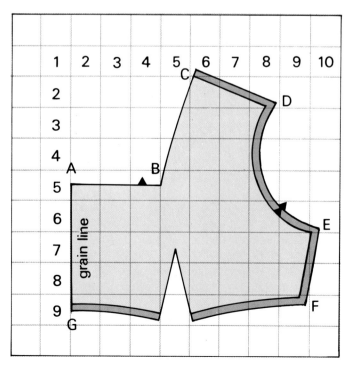

Depth of bust It is important to have the bust dart or fullness in the correct position for a good fit. Measure from centre of one shoulder to bust point.

Inside leg Measure from inside top of leg to length required.

Outside leg Measure from side of waist to length required.

You must take both of these leg measurements wearing shoes with your usual heel height.

Depth of crotch The easiest way to take this measurement is to sit on a chair with your back straight and measure from the side of waist to the chair. Allow 1.3cm to 2.54cm (½ to 1 inch) for ease of movement.

Pattern sizes

If your measurements do not correspond with the body chart it is advisable to select the pattern according to your bust size and adjust the hips and waist as necessary.

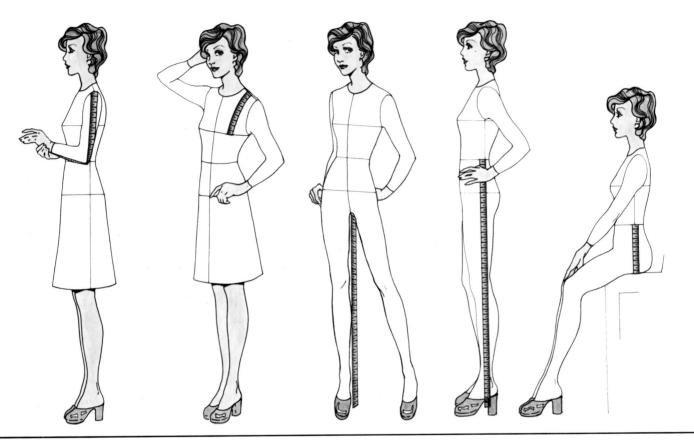

5 The tops of sleeves are usually the most difficult to copy. Mark out in numbers as in step 1 above.
Mark in underarm and shoulder points, A, B and C. Then draw in the straight grain line.

6 Draw three vertical lines to divide sleeve into four equal parts and mark in points D and E. Using ruler draw straight lines from A–D, D–B, B–E and E–C.

7 Plot the curves as in step 4 above. Draw in curves. Having completed the outline check that all notches, all straight grain lines, buttonholes etc. have been marked.

Note To avoid damaging the graph pattern from which you are working place a piece of tracing paper over it, secure with paper clips, and draw the numbers and any markings on this. In the same way, by using tracing paper over your graph paper and drawing on this you will be able to use your graph paper over and over again.

When the pattern is completed the lines may be inked in, but test first that the ink is colourfast to prevent staining hands or fabric.

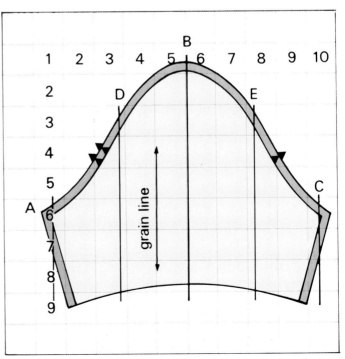

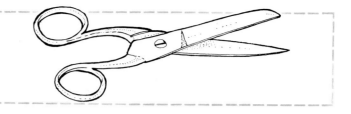

The dressmaker's stand

Preparing a dressmaker's stand

There are various dressmaker stands available in different sizes, fabrics, colours and prices. The most useful stands are adjusted by means of small rotating dials inserted in the centre-front and centre-back, sides and waist, which decrease or increase the width of the stand.

Measurements required

Bust, waist, hips, neck to waist at centre-back and centre-front, across back (half way between shoulder and base of armhole), across front (half way between bust point and base of neck), base of neck to shoulder point, shoulder to waist at centre-front and underarm to waistline (figure 1).

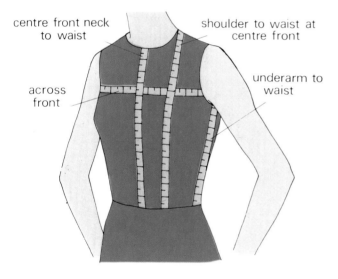

Figure 1

labels: centre front neck to waist; shoulder to waist at centre front; across front; underarm to waist

Adjust the dials on the stand so that the correct measurements are obtained. If the proportions of the stand are incorrect some parts may need padding, for example the bust and hips.

Padding the bust: If the neck to bust point measurement on the stand is too long, set the bust to a smaller size and build up the correct shape with padding. Attach wide straps of non-stretch fabric over the shoulders and on the back of a bra normally worn. Place on the stand and using wadding or cotton wool pad the bust. Bind the stand around the bust with strips of fabric to hold the padding in place and remove the bra.

Padding the hip: If the stand is too long at the waist, it must be adjusted accordingly, so that the correct waist measurement is obtained at the correct depth from the neck. Also check that the hips are positioned correctly and that they are the right width apart,

otherwise padding will be needed in the same way as on the bust (figure 2).

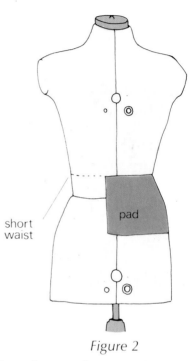

Figure 2

labels: short waist; pad

To lengthen the stand, rotate the waist dials so that the horizontal gap increases, then cover the gap with heavy-weight interfacing or fabric (figure 3).

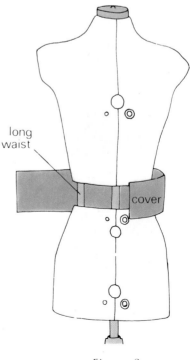

Figure 3

labels: long waist; cover

27

Widening the shoulder: If this is necessary, pin a piece of heavy-weight interfacing on to the stand so that it protrudes the required amount beyond the shoulder.

Ensure that all measurements are correct. If the stand is wire, cover it in a strong, non-stretch fabric to obtain a smooth finish and firm base for pinning.

Marking the stand

Use tape in a contrasting colour to the stand, and approximately 1cm to 1.3cm ($\frac{3}{8}$ *inch to* $\frac{1}{2}$ *inch*) wide. Pin strips down the centre-front, centre-back, underarm to waist and complete length of the stand. Pin strips around the bust, waist, hips and from the base of the neck to the shoulder point (figure 4).

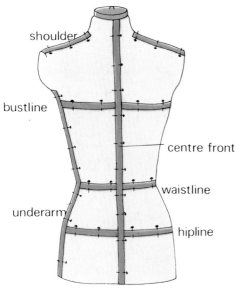

Figure 4

Check all the measurements again. For wide square shoulders cover the shoulder with foam or interfacing until the correct height is obtained. Measure again and note the new length (figure 5). Strips of tape

should now be pinned around the base of the neck and armholes. The edge of the tape nearest the armhole will need pleating to lie flat. Check the base of the neck measurement. If it is too small move the tape slightly away from the neck and move further up the neck if the measurement is too large (figure 6).

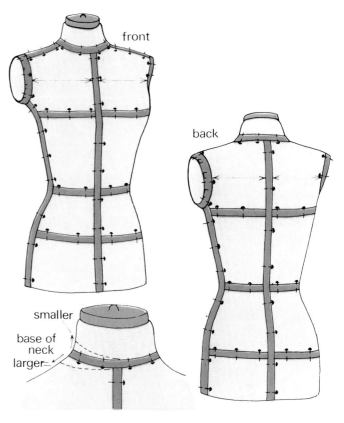

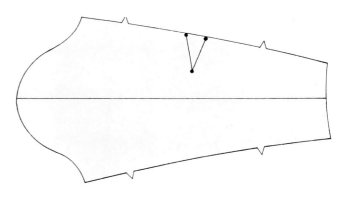

Figure 6

Making a sleeve pad

The first step is to make a paper pattern following the required measurements shown on page 180. Adjust the pattern to a fitted sleeve with an elbow dart. Add turnings on all edges, mark in dots, notches and central line (figure 7). Cut out one sleeve only in

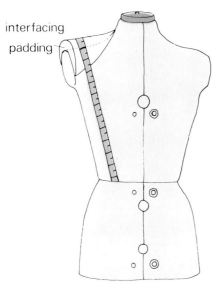

Figure 5

Figure 7

fabric. This is the straight grain line. With right sides together tack and stitch the dart and press towards the wrist. With right sides together tack and stitch the underarm seam (figure 8). Press turnings open

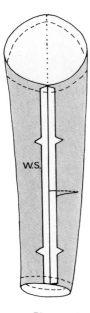

Figure 8

and turn sleeve on to the right side. Pack the sleeve tightly with padding to form a solid even shape (figure 9). Cut two oval shapes from paper, one mea-

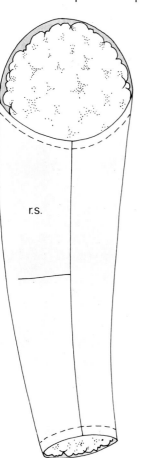

Figure 9

suring 5cm × 5.5cm (*2 inches × 2¼ inches*) and the other 14cm × 11.5cm (*5½ inches × 4½ inches*). Add turnings and mark A, B, C and D on the oval shapes and sleeves (figure 10). Turn the seam allowance on

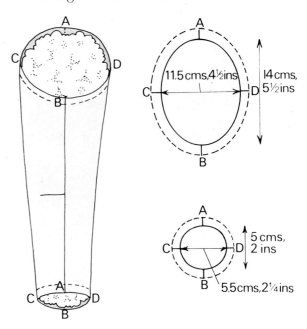

Figure 10

to the wrong side all the way around each oval. Place the larger oval to the armhole, matching letters, and the small one to the wrist. Oversew edges together (figure 11).

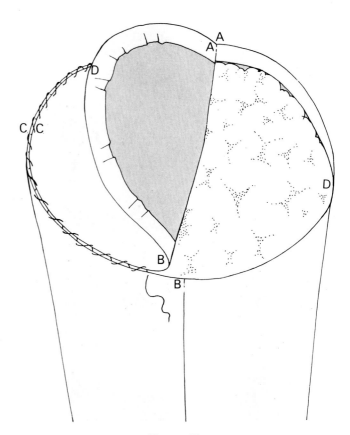

Figure 11

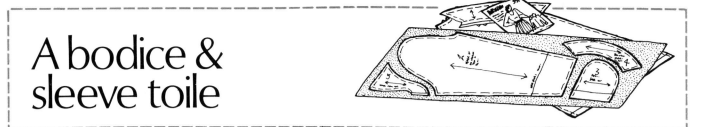

A bodice & sleeve toile

Making a bodice and sleeve toile on a stand

A toile is a prototype of a garment worked in fabric and fitted on a stand, from which the paper pattern is made. It can be made in heavy mull, soft calico, muslin or even old sheeting, depending on the style of the garment. For example a toile for a tailored jacket should be worked in a crisp heavy mull but a toile for a long fine evening dress should be worked in a soft calico or muslin. When the correct design and fit is obtained the toile is taken apart and the shape of each piece transferred on to paper to make a pattern.

The fabric used to make the toile should be pressed well and if there is no selvedge, a thread should be pulled to find the straight grain.

Toile for a waistlength bodice with darts

Back: Take the centre-back neck to waist measurement plus 12.5cm (5 inches) and one quarter of the bust measurement plus 5cm (2 inches). Cut a rectangle of fabric to these measurements. Pin the rectangle to the back of the stand so that one edge lies down the centre-back on the straight grain. The top of the rectangle should be 2.5cm (1 inch) above the base of the neck. Smooth the straight edge down the centre-back to the waistline. Clip 2cm (¾ inch) in from the edge of the fabric at the waistline and fold back excess fabric.

Clip the excess fabric above the neckline between the centre-back and shoulder line. Pin the fabric to the stand on the shoulder line and neck point. Smooth the fabric from the centre-back to shoulder and pin a dart of approximately 2cm (¾ inch). Pin fabric at shoulder point (figure 1).

Smooth across the back towards the base of the armhole and pin down the side seam to waist. Work the surplus fabric at the waist into a dart half way between the centre-back and side seam. Check that the fabric lies smoothly at the armhole. If there is any excess, work this into the shoulder dart. Using a ball point pen or pencil draw along the neckline, shoulder, side seam, waist and centre-back lines and also mark in darts. Draw a line around the armhole corresponding with the tape on the stand. Trim off excess fabric beyond these lines leaving 2cm (¾ inch) all around and fold back (figure 2).

Front: Take the centre-front measurement plus 17.5cm (7 inches) and one quarter of the bust measurement plus 10cm (4 inches). Cut a rectangle of fabric to these measurements. Place one long straight edge of the fabric to the centre-front line allowing approximately 12.5cm (5 inches) excess above the neckline. Smooth fabric towards the neck edge, clipping the excess and trimming to within 2cm (¾ inch) from the neckline. Smooth fabric towards shoulder point and pin into position. Then smooth towards armhole and pin.

From the centre-front smooth fabric towards the bust point and towards the side seam on the waist level, leaving a little surplus in the side seam and

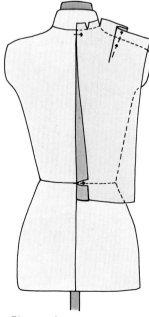

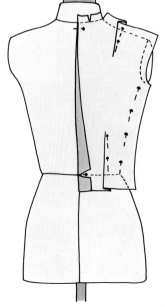

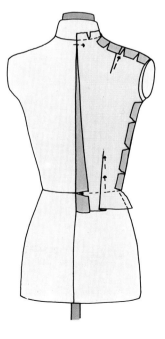

Figure 1

Figure 2

waist seam. Work a dart into the side seam approximately 5cm (2 inches) below underarm point for a small bust, or slightly lower for a larger bust. The dart point should be at least 2cm (¾ inch) to the outside of the bust point (figure 3).

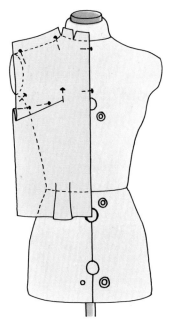

Figure 3

Work a vertical dart half way between the centre-front and side seam finishing approximately 2.5cm–4cm (1–1½ inches) below the bust point.

Using a ball point pen or pencil draw along the neckline, shoulder, underarm and waistline darts and armhole as on the bodice back. Trim excess fabric leaving 2cm (¾ inch) on all edges (figure 4). Remove pins, unfold turnings and pin back and front bodices together at the shoulder seams and side seams. Insert corresponding notches on both these seams.

Adding a hip yoke to the bodice
Back: Take the centre-back waist to hip measurement plus 5cm (2 inches) and one quarter of the hip measurement plus 5cm (2 inches). Cut a rectangle of fabric to these measurements. Place the long straight edge of the rectangle to the centre-back so that the lower edge of the rectangle hangs 2cm (¾ inch) below the hip-line. Pin the fabric to the stand at the centre-back and sideseam on the waistline and clip across centre-back turnings at waist level for 2cm (¾ inch). Smooth and pin the hip yoke at the side seam and work the excess fabric at the waist into a vertical dart corresponding with the bodice dart. (figure 5).

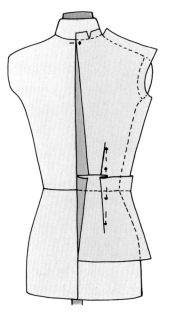

Figure 5

Front: Take the centre-front waist to hip measurement plus 5cm (2 inches) and one quarter of the hip measurement plus 5cm (2 inches). Cut a rectangle of

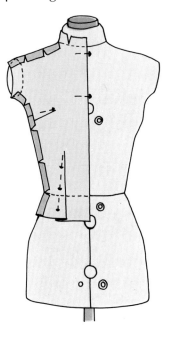

Figure 4

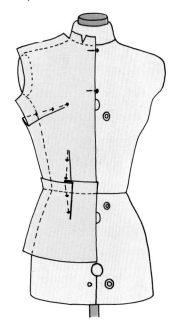

Figure 6

fabric to these measurements. Pin on to waistline at the centre-front and side and on the straight grain. Pin the fabric to the stand at the hip level on the side seam and continue up the side seam to the waistline. Work the excess fabric at the waistline into a dart to correspond with the bodice dart. Using ball point pen or pencil draw along waistline, hipline, side seams and darts both on back and front. Trim excess fabric outside these lines to 2cm ($\frac{3}{4}$ inch) and fold back. Unpin and unfold waistline turnings and pin the bodice to the hip yoke on back and front, and the hip yokes together at the side seams. Mark notches (figure 6).

Sleeve

Use the sleeve pad (see the reference on page 28) as the base from which you make your sleeve toile. Cut a rectangle slightly larger and wider than the sleeve pad. Lay this fabric flat and place the sleeve pad on top so that the straight grain lines on both lie on top of each other (figure 7). Pin the two corners of the rectangle together at the underarm point so that the crosswise grain on the fabric and pad are in line. Continue pinning the edges together to the elbow. Work a dart at the elbow taking enough fabric so that the crosswise grain of the fabric below the elbow lies on top of the crosswise grain on the pad. Then pin the edges together to the wristline. Mark notches at armhole and top of straight grain line. Using pencil draw along all lines and darts. Trim off the excess fabric to within 2cm ($\frac{3}{4}$ inch) of the seam lines (figure 8).

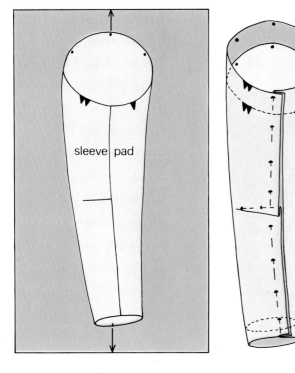

Figure 7   Figure 8

Fitting the sleeve to the armhole

Remove the bodice from the stand and the sleeve from the pad. Tack the front and back bodices to-

gether along the pencil lines. Pin the sleeve pad to the armhole on the stand so that the straight grain line on the sleeve pad is in line with the shoulder line (figure 9).

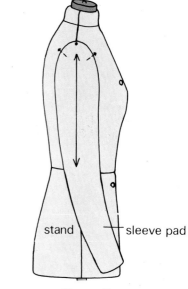

Figure 9

Put bodice toile back on the stand and pin into position. Place sleeve over sleeve pad and pin top of straight grain line to shoulder. Pleat the sleeve head between the dots on the armhole until the crosswise grain is in line with that on the sleeve pad. Pin the rest of the sleeve into the armhole. Mark dots and notches on the bodice to correspond with those on the sleeve (figure 10).

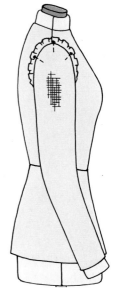

Figure 10

Remove sleeve, sleeve pad and bodice from the stand. Remove all tacking and press the pieces flat. Mark in the straight grain lines on bodice pieces. Place on paper and draw around the edges. Transfer all markings and cut out. Insert 'to fold' mark on centre front and 'cut 1'. Write 'cut 2' on back bodice and sleeve.

A skirt toile

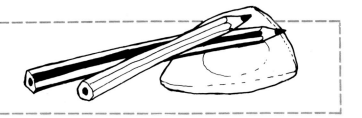

Making a skirt toile on a stand

Straight skirt

A simple straight skirt can be made by working a rectangle of fabric in the same way as the hip toile described on page 30. You should make sure that you cut the fabric to the correct skirt length required.

Flared skirt

Cut a rectangle of fabric the length of the skirt required by half the hip measurement. Pin one long, straight edge to the centre-back of the stand, allowing extra fabric above the waistline. Smooth the fabric towards the side seam at the waist level and down towards the side seam at the hip level so that the weft grain of the fabric drops slightly (*figure 1*). Fold back excess fabric at the side seam, so that it hangs in a vertical line. Adjust the pin at the waist if necessary and work excess fabric into a dart. Clip the excess fabric above the waistline (*figure 2*).

Work the front skirt in the same way. Slant the front dart towards the side seam slightly. Pin the back and front together at the side seam (*figure 3*).

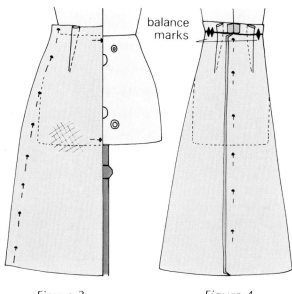

Figure 3   *Figure 4*

Mark the waist seam, side seams and darts with pencil. Using a yardstick, measure from the ground up to the required length on the skirt and mark all around with pins and then with pencil. Mark notches at the side seam and waistline. Trim off all excess fabric leaving 2cm ($\frac{3}{4}$ *inch*) turning all around.

Waistband

Taking just over one quarter of the waist measurement, cut two strips of fabric the width required, on the straight grain. Pin one strip to the centre-back of the stand and the other to the centre-front. Continue pinning along the waist to the side seam and pin the edges together. Mark in notches, centre-back and centre-front (*figure 4*). Remove the waistband from the stand and cut a paper pattern. Mark 'to fold' and 'cut 1' on the centre-front and centre-back. Extend the waistband at one or both ends. Mark the straight grain with a vertical line and add turnings (*figure 5*).

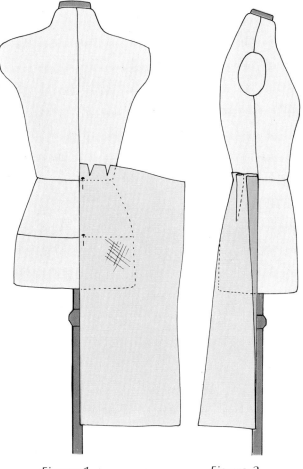

Figure 1   *Figure 2*

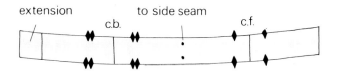

Figure 5

Fuller flared skirt without a waist dart

Cut and attach a wider rectangle of fabric to the back of the stand as for the flared skirt. However, do not work a dart at the waistline. This will mean that the excess fabric at the side seam will not hang in a vertical line but the fabric will fall in folds from the hipline. The more the weft grain is dropped at hip level, the fuller the skirt. Adjust so that the required fullness is obtained and pin at the side seam (figure 6). Repeat for the front and pin the front to the back at the side seam. Draw in all lines with pencil. Work the waistband as above and mark the hem.

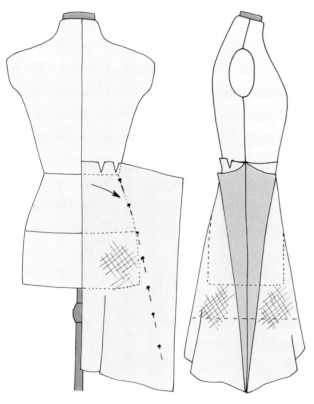

Figure 6

Faced waistband

Remove the skirt toile from the stand and make the paper pattern. Draw a line 5cm (2 inches) below the waistline and trace off. Add extension and mark notches (figure 7).

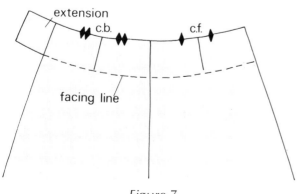

Figure 7

Pleats on a straight or flared skirt

Pleats should always hang parallel to the centre-back and centre-front below the hipline and the waistline darts are worked into the pleats. Cut a rectangle of fabric at least one and a half times the quarter hip measurement. Attach to the stand as for the flared skirt. Decide on the position of the pleats and mark with a row of pins. Insert another row of pins leaving the width of pleat required in between (figure 8). Release the pins at the side seam and move one row of pins under another to form a pleat. When all the pleats have been worked, re-pin the side seams, release the dart and work the fullness into a pleat. If there is more than one pleat, distribute the fullness from the dart evenly between them (figure 9).

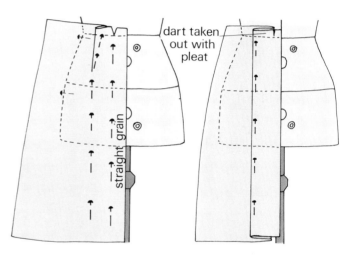

Figure 8   *Figure 9*

For a fuller skirt work the pleats as above, but be sure to keep them the same width apart at the waist and lower edge with one pleat placed centrally between the centre-front and side seam (figure 10).

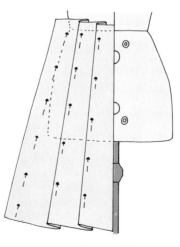

Figure 10

Small straight knife pleats

These are narrower pleats worked closer together. Work in the same way as the larger pleat.

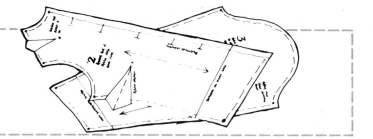

Commercial patterns

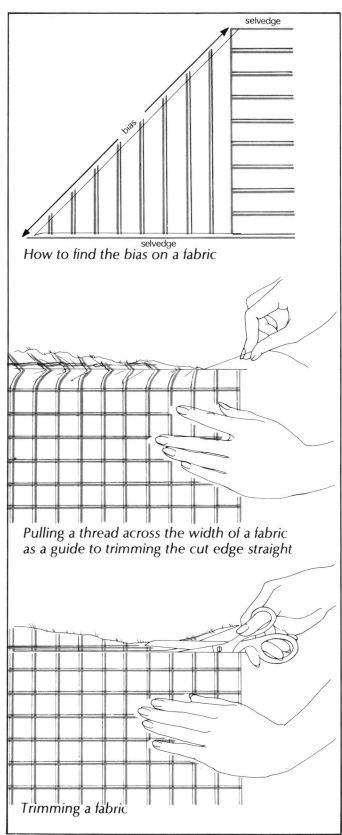

How to find the bias on a fabric

Pulling a thread across the width of a fabric
as a guide to trimming the cut edge straight

Trimming a fabric

Laying out a pattern

Before laying out a pattern make sure that the fabric lies flat when both selvedges are together, as the fabric often becomes slightly warped when wound on to the roll, or can be stretched at the selvedge on knitted fabrics such as jersey or crimplene. If the cloth has a stripe or horizontal pattern trim the cut edge until it is straight: with cotton or heavy linen it is usually possible to pull a thread across the width as a guide.

Place the two selvedges together and providing the warp is even the material should lie flat, if it appears wrinkled pull on the cross at regular intervals down the complete length of the cloth. Then with the material held lengthways gently pull on the selvedge edge and on the fold line. Sometimes the fabric has been folded badly and it is necessary to press it.

Where possible cut out on a large table or the floor as the complete pattern should be placed on the fabric at the same time. When a delicate fabric is being used it is advisable to use a heavy blanket underneath and pin the cloth to it at the edges. It is also necessary to use fine pins or fine needles on this type of fabric as ordinary pins will mark and leave holes.

All alterations such as shortening or lengthening pattern pieces should be made before placing them on the fabric.

Although most commercial patterns have a layout instruction sheet often, because of unusual widths of fabric, difficult stripes, or a big pattern drop, it is necessary to place the paper pattern in a different way from the one suggested.

Always check that the straight grain mark on every pattern piece runs parallel to the selvedges.

If using a napped cloth such as velvet the pile must run the same way on each piece. Test by smoothing the fabric with your hand in one direction.

Patterned fabrics require more attention as stripes and checks must be in line on each piece of the garment, including the sleeves. It is often easiest to place the centre-back body piece on to the fabric, then, matching the bottom edge of the other pieces, work round to the centre-front. The sleeves must match at the underarm point so that the pattern runs in a continuous line round the arm. When a side bust dart is used it is not always possible to match the pattern at the underarm but this usually affects only 5cm–8cm (2–3 inches). It is not always possible to match vertical and horizontal stripes on the shoulder line as there is usually about 1.3cm ($\frac{1}{2}$ inch) of ease on the back. Match at armhole edge as often the neck edge is covered by a collar.

Pockets, tabs and flaps must also line up in the pattern unless intended otherwise. Sometimes these are cut on the cross of a checked fabric as a design feature, or on a cloth striped or ribbed vertically these may be cut with the lines running horizontally.

When pinning the pattern on to the fabric place pins so that the points lie towards the centre. This positioning of pins holds the fabric firmly and there is less risk of scratching hands when smoothing out pattern pieces.

Do not leave facings to be cut out later as these smaller pattern pieces can easily be mislaid.

Count all pattern pieces to ensure that none have been forgotten. Note whether any parts, such as pockets or collars, have to be cut twice.

A garment with checks matching

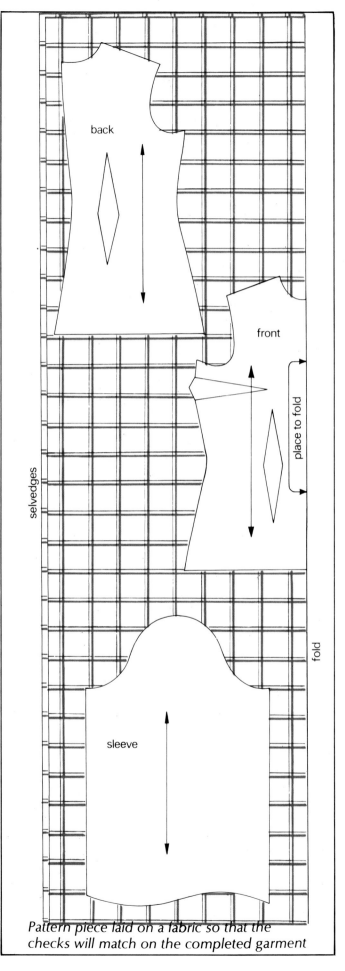

Pattern piece laid on a fabric so that the checks will match on the completed garment

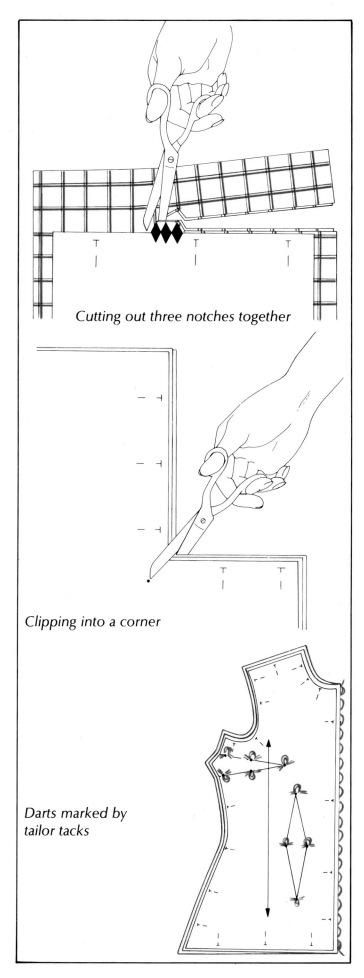

Cutting out three notches together

Clipping into a corner

Darts marked by tailor tacks

Cutting out

Before starting to cut out the fabric make sure you have the necessary tools: a large pair of dressmaking shears for long, straight seams and a smaller well-pointed pair for all the awkward corners and for cutting around notches.

The shears will have a pointed blade and a rounded blade. The pointed blade is used downwards when cutting out patterns to ensure that the two thicknesses of cloth are cut at the same time. The rounded blade is used downwards for such things as trimming large areas and layering (trimming turnings to different widths) so that there is no sharp point to cut the second layer of cloth.

Fabrics made from man-made fibres often blunt shears very quickly. A very light spray from an aerosol silicone polish will help to prevent this. But allow it to dry thoroughly before using the shears.

Notches are marked as diamonds or triangles and are often difficult to cut. Bypass these when using the big shears and go back to them using small pointed scissors. It is not practical to cut into each individual notch when there are two or three together but to cut straight across the top of them.

Often in a corner of a pattern piece there is a large dot and the word clip, do not cut this until you are ready to tack to avoid fraying and stretching.

Using the large shears, with points towards the table, make long clean cuts into the fabric. When using a patterned fabric check that both thicknesses of fabric are matching on all edges. It is sometimes advisable to cut each layer separately as some types of cloth slip very easily. It is essential to cut fur fabric separately as only the backing must be cut, not the pile.

Marking and tacking

It is essential to transfer all markings on the pattern to the fabric before removing pattern.

On cotton and heavy fabrics use tacking cotton which grips the cloth better than most other threads and is less likely to fall out when handling tailor.tacks. With delicate fabrics use light-weight thread such as Güterman 100 or pure silk and a needle no larger than Sharps number 10, otherwise permanent marks or holes may appear in the garment.

Darts should be marked with tailor tacks, which are large looped stitches. With a large needle make a hole in the pattern where the dots of the darts are marked. (With graph patterns make holes at the point of the dart, on the stitching line and halfway between the point and the stitching line.) Using double thread, without a knot, work a small stitch through the pattern and both thicknesses of the fabric, leaving about 2.54cm *(1 inch)* of thread free. Work another stitch in the same place leaving a loop of thread about 3.8cm *(1½ inches)*, cut off the thread about 2.54cm *(1 inch)* from last stitch. Pocket positions and notches (balance marks) are often marked in this way.

Centre-front or centre-back, where placed on a fold of the cloth, is marked out with trace tacking. Using single thread, without a knot, work a row of small tacking stitches through the single fabric on fold. Start and finish with back stitches.

Fold lines for such things as pleats, are marked with thread tacking or trace tacking.

Stitching lines are worked in either thread tacking or trace tacking.

Thread tacking Fold pattern back at stitching line. Using double thread, without a knot, work a continuous line of small tacking stitches through the two thicknesses of fabric, leaving a loop of thread about 3.8cm (1½ inches) between each stitch.

Trace tacking Fold back pattern at stitching line. Using single thread, without a knot, work a row of small tacking stitches through single fabric. Place a row of pins on this line of tacking through both thicknesses of cloth. Turn fabric over and work another row of trace tacking between the pins.

It is essential when marking stitching lines to continue right to the end so that the lines of tacking cross at the corners.

It is advisable when working thread tacking for stitching lines to use a different coloured thread from that used for the notches to avoid confusion.

Do not use a very dark thread on a light coloured fabric as it could leave marks.

A very simple pattern can usually be transferred on to the fabric by working tailor tacks on each corner where the stitching lines cross each other and at about 10cm (4 inch) intervals on the stitching lines.

Tailors' chalk can be used to save time in marking out a pattern but it contains a certain amount of grease and can sometimes leave a permanent mark. On heavy P.V.C. it is often quite safe to mark the complete pattern in pencil. When all markings have been transferred to the fabric remove pattern and cut through tailor tacks and thread tacking. This is done by gently pulling the two pieces of fabric apart and, with small scissors, cutting through the centre of the stitch.

Some patterns do have a great many pieces. To avoid confusion it often helps to pin a small piece of paper at the bottom edge, and write on it the name of the piece of pattern after you have cut it out.

Fitting

The garment is now ready to be put together for fitting. Tack all darts and seam lines with single thread without a knot. Start and finish each line with three back-stitches as knots can cause permanent holes or damage when pulled whilst trying on the garment. It is important that the garment is tacked well to achieve a good fitting. Small stitches produce the best result. Any alteration is made during the fitting. The garment is then re-tacked to the correct line, tried on again, and if it is then satisfactory it is ready to be machined. All tailor tacks are removed at this stage as they could be machined in.

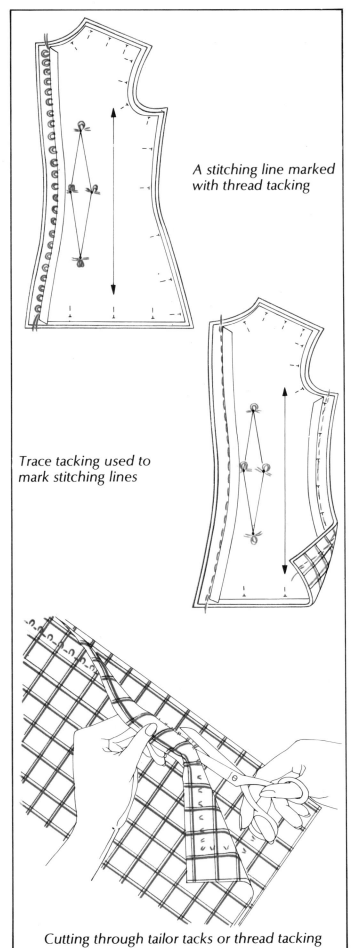

A stitching line marked with thread tacking

Trace tacking used to mark stitching lines

Cutting through tailor tacks or thread tacking

Altering patterns

How to alter a ready-made paper pattern

Even if you are a standard size you may need to alter a pattern at the waist, hips, bust or for length. It saves time and fabric if you know how to alter a pattern correctly.

Enlarging a bodice front

When a pattern fits across the shoulders but gapes at the centre-front neckline, alter it by making a small pleat at the centre-front, tapering it to nothing at the armhole. Place a ruler along the centre-front edge and trim off the excess above the pleat (figure 1). Figures with a large bust often need extra width and length on the front bodice. To add width draw a straight line from the waist dart to the shoulder seam. Cut along this line and place a piece of paper underneath. Spread the two pieces of the pattern so that the space between them provides the extra width required, tapering to the shoulder seam (figure 2). Place a ruler across the bodice front and draw a line so that it runs through the centre of the side dart (figure 3). Cut and insert paper as before. Re-draw the darts (figure 4).

French darts are often used on a tight fitting garment for a large bust and also where there is no waist seam. To enlarge these, draw a straight line from the side seam through the centre of the dart to the centre-front. Cut and insert the paper. Spread out the pattern, tapering off to the original point at the centre-front (figure 5). If the bodice front is also too tight, spread the pattern approximately 2.5cm (1 inch) apart at the centre-front. Re-draw the darts and the centre-front line (figure 6).

Figure 5

Figure 6

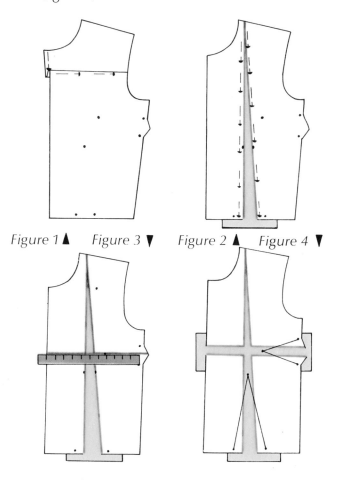

Figure 1 ▲ *Figure 3* ▼ *Figure 2* ▲ *Figure 4* ▼

Enlarging a bodice back

Draw a straight line on the pattern from the centre-back to the armhole approximately halfway between the shoulder seam and underarm point. Cut along the line and insert paper. Spread the pattern pieces to the required width. A dart will now be needed between the neck and shoulder. To do this, place a piece of paper under the centre-back at the neckline. Lay a ruler along the centre-back edge from below the insertion to the neckline. Measure the width at the top edge between the centre-back and ruler. Make a dart of this width between the centre-back and shoulder seam on the neckline (figure 7A). On a very curved back the waist may need shaping at the lower edge of the bodice. To do this, shape the centre-back seam at the lower edge of the bodice. If this makes the waist too small, add the amount taken out at the centre-back to the lower edge of the side seam (figure 7B). On a pattern where the bodice and sleeve are all in one, the shoulder point is usually indicated on the pattern. Measure the distance between the shoulder point and centre-back (figure 8) and if the pattern is too narrow draw a straight line from the waistline to the shoulder point. Cut along the line and spread out to the required width at the shoulder point (figure 9).

If the front neckline gapes above the bust, make a pleat across the bodice halfway between the shoulder seam and underarm point. Re-draw the armhole (figure 11).

A very straight or inverted back will need pleats taken out approximately halfway between the shoulder and underarm point and approximately 5cm (2 inches) above the waistline. Pin at the centre-back and taper to nothing at the armhole and side seam. Draw in the new line at the centre-back (figure 12).

A neckline can be tightened by increasing the waist dart. Draw a straight line from the bust point to the neckline approximately halfway between centre-front and shoulder seam. Cut up the centre of the dart to the bust point. Make a pleat of the required amount between the bust point and neckline on the line drawn. This will automatically open up the waist dart (figure 13). The same applies to a bust dart which runs from the side seam rather than the waist.

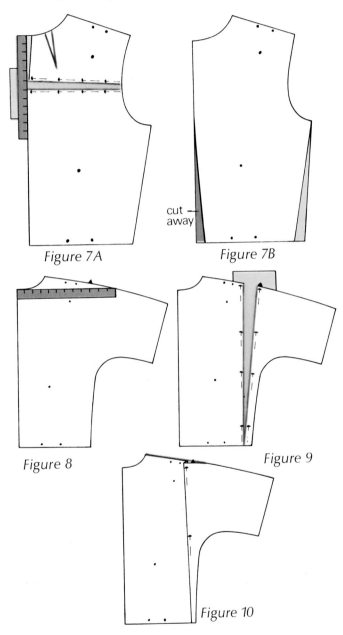

Figure 7A

Figure 7B

cut away

Figure 8

Figure 9

Figure 10

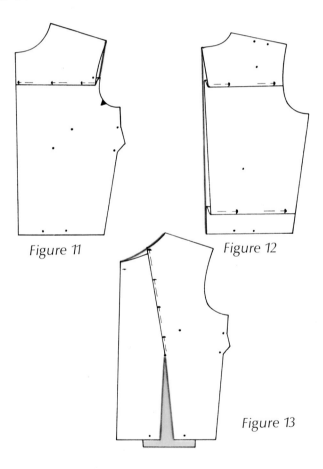

Figure 11

Figure 12

Figure 13

Reducing a bodice

If the pattern is too large on an all-in-one sleeve and bodice pattern, alter as follows: pleat the pattern at the shoulder point, tapering to nothing at the waistline. Place paper under the shoulder seam. Using a ruler with the edge on the neckline and shoulder point, draw in the new line (figure 10).

Enlarging full sleeves

Draw a straight line from the shoulder dot to the centre of the lower sleeve edge. Cut along this and place paper underneath. Spread the pattern to the required amount (figure 14A).

For a thin arm, full sleeves are often too wide on the sleeve head. Draw a line across the sleeve pattern between the underarm points. Then draw a vertical line from the shoulder to the centre of the horizontal line. Cut along all lines. Lap the pattern at the shoulder point approximately 2.5cm (1 inch) and pin together.

This will automatically make the two halves overlap in the centre of the horizontal line. Pin the overlaps to the lower section of the sleeve. Draw a new dot halfway between the overlap on the shoulder point (figure 14B).

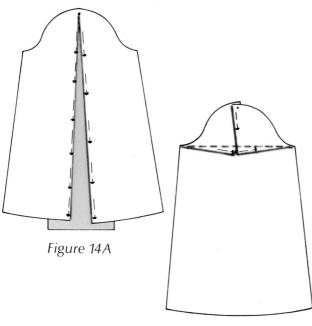

Figure 14A

Figure 14B

Enlarging a tight fitting sleeve
Draw a line down the centre of the sleeve and cut. Spread pattern out at shoulder point approximately 2.5cm (1 inch) on paper. Re-draw dot in the centre of insertion (figure 15).
If the sleeve needs letting out at the elbow, draw a line from the shoulder dot to the elbow point and from the elbow point across to the side seam through the centre of the dart. Cut along both lines. Place paper underneath the elbow dart and spread pattern. This will automatically open the vertical dart. Re-draw

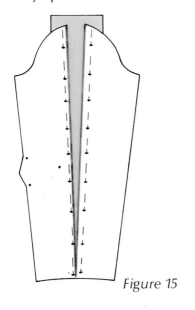

Figure 15

underarm seam (figure 16). To reduce the entire length of a tight fitting sleeve, make a pleat in the centre of the sleeve for the required amount.

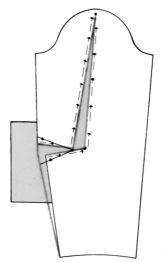

Figure 16

Enlarging a skirt
There are two ways of enlarging a skirt pattern at the hipline. Extra width can be added to the side seams on the front and back at the correct depth below the waistline. Draw a line parallel to the edge of the pattern for the length of the skirt but curve in to the original waistline (figure 17).

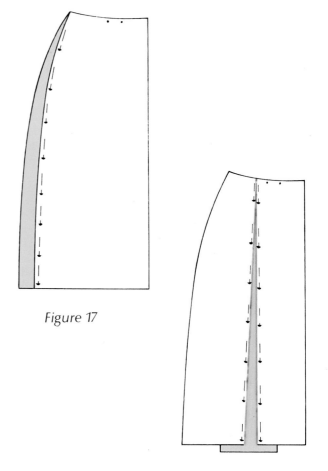

Figure 17

Figure 18

To retain the skirt shape draw a straight line from the waistline to the lower edge of the skirt. Cut and insert paper as before. Spread the lower edge open so that the correct width is obtained at hip level (figure 18).

The two sections of the pattern can be spread out at the waistline to retain the shape, but incorporate the extra fullness into a dart on the waistline between the insertion and side seam.

To enlarge the back skirt only draw a line from the waistline to the lower skirt edge through the centre of the waist dart. Cut along the line, spread out the pattern and insert the paper (figure 19). Re-draw the waistline dart but if it forms an obvious point, work another dart between the side seam and original dart dividing the fullness between the two darts.

Reducing a skirt pattern

Increasing the darts or tapering the side seams between the waist and hip is usually sufficient to reduce a skirt. If the skirt needs reducing considerably the reduction should be worked on the pattern. Draw a straight line from the waistline to the lower edge of the skirt. Cut along the line and overlap the required amount. If the skirt is very tight and tapers at the lower edge, extra width may need to be added on the side seams after doing this (figure 20).

If the pattern is too long between the waist and hips on either back or front, a horizontal pleat should be made halfway between the waistline and hipline. Take in the required measurement at the centre and taper out towards the side seams.

Altering a trouser pattern

It is essential to find the correct crotch depth when altering trousers.

To do this, sit upright on a chair and measure from side of waist to the chair adding approximately 1.3cm–2.5cm ($\frac{1}{2}$ inch–1 inch). Check pattern and alter if necessary. If the measurements differ greatly, tie a band around the waist. Place the end of a tape measure on the tape at the centre-back, take under the crotch and up to the centre-front. The inside leg seam should be approximately 2.5cm (1 inch) towards the front. Check pattern by standing the tape measure on its edge and following the curve of the pattern. To reduce curved seams machine stitch on the turnings side of the seam. To enlarge, machine stitch on the garment side of the seam (figure 21).

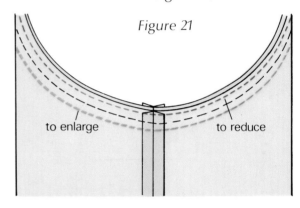

Figure 21

to enlarge   to reduce

To enlarge the back of the trousers, draw a horizontal line from the centre-back seam to the side seam at the required depth. Cut along the line and spread out at the centre-back, tapering towards the side seam. Re-draw the centre-back seam (figure 22). The same method applies to the centre-front.

If making maternity trousers, increase the centre-front by making a horizontal line as before and placing paper underneath. Put a ruler on the centre-front seam and draw a straight line from below the insertion to the waist (figure 23).

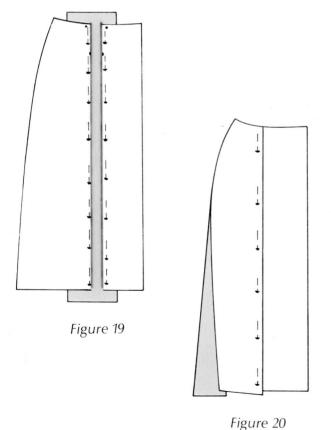

Figure 19

Figure 20

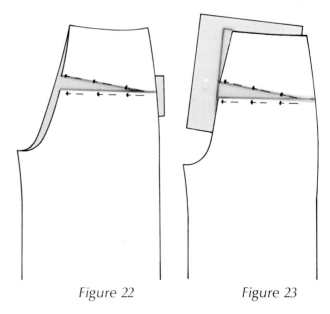

Figure 22   *Figure 23*

Striped & checked fabrics

Stripes and checks

Simple designs should be chosen when making clothes in stripes and checks. Always study a paper pattern before buying as some patterns will advise against the use of striped fabrics for design reasons: for instance details such as tucks and seams will not be as obvious in striped fabric as in plain fabric. Interesting effects can be made by mixing a striped fabric with a plain or contrasting pattern (figure 1) or

Figure 2

Figure 1

by using the same striped fabric but having the stripes running in different directions on different parts of a garment. For example the yoke, cuffs, collar and pockets can be cut with the stripe running horizontally (figure 2). A simple garment in a plain fabric can be livened up by using checks or stripes cut on the cross to bind the edges (figure 3).

Stripes and checks can be used as basic guide lines for gathering. This saves working out grids when smocking and indicates even spaces for shirring and gathering. Vertical lines can be used as a guide for tucks and pleats. Horizontal lines can be used for positioning buttonholes.

Figure 3

Cutting striped and checked fabrics

Always position pattern pieces so that the stripes or checks will meet when the garment is made up. If the fabric has a one way pattern, the pieces must be pinned on so that they face the same way, as with napped fabrics. This could use more fabric but it is necessary to lay the pattern in this way to obtain a good finish. Adjust the pattern first if necessary. When folding the fabric in half, make sure that the stripes or checks lie exactly on top of each other. Use pins vertically along the selvedges to hold the two layers together. Place the centre-back edge of the pattern on the fabric noting where the lower edge of the side seam lies. The lower edge of the front side seam must lie on the same line. The centre-front or back seam should lie exactly in the centre of a stripe or check (figure 4).

When cutting sleeves position the centre of the pattern on a stripe, or in the centre of a check. Also the underarm seam points should lie on the same horizontal stripe, so that when they are joined, one stripe is formed.

Cuffs and collars can be cut on the cross, but a join must be made at the centre-back on the top collar, so that the pattern appears the same on either side of the centre-front (figure 5). Fold the fabric

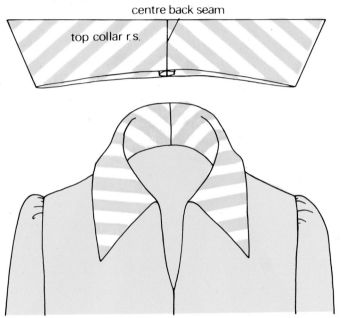

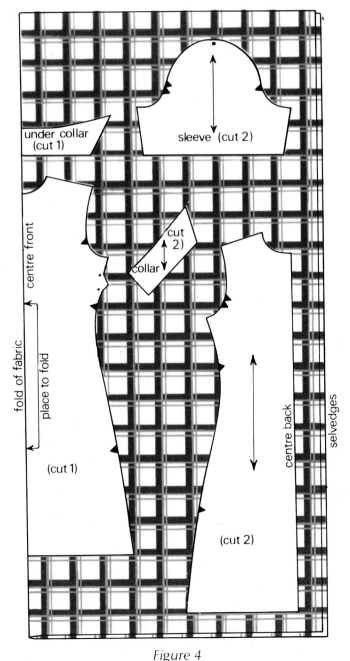

Figure 4

with right sides together and place the centre-back of the collar pattern on the cross grain of the fabric allowing extra for turnings. Pin and cut out (figure 6).

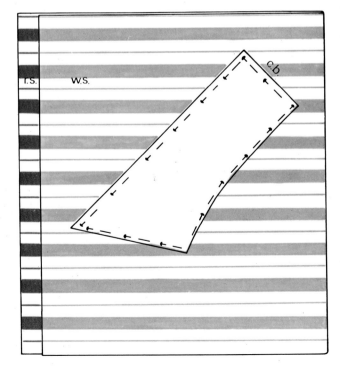

Figure 5

Figure 6

Pockets which are cut on the cross of the fabric must be positioned so that the stripes or checks correspond to those on the garment. To do this, pin the paper pattern on to the garment in the correct position. Draw in the lines on the pattern and then place these lines on top of those on the fabric when cutting (figure 7).

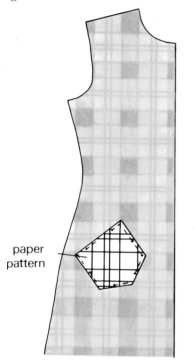

Figure 7

Centre-front openings should be cut so that the seam line is directly in the centre of a stripe or check (figure 8).

Figure 8

Tacking striped and checked fabrics

Slip-tacking is the most accurate way of ensuring that checks and stripes meet exactly at seams on a garment. With right sides together, lay the two pieces to be joined on a flat surface. Fold back the seam allowance on the top piece so that the underneath turnings are visible. Make sure that the seam lines and stripes meet exactly. Using small stitches slip-stitch the two pieces together bringing the needle through the fold of the top fabric and picking up the seam line of the underneath fabric. Continue in this way along the full length of the seam (figure 9).

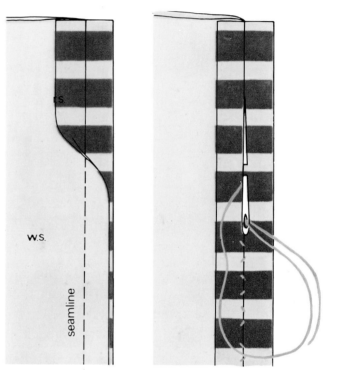

Figure 9

When setting in sleeves the pattern on the fabric will usually meet as far as the dots on either side of the armhole. The sleeve head should be eased into the armhole, matching the stripes or checks on the sleeves as closely as possible with those on the bodice.

If one part of a garment is to be gathered on to another, it will not be possible to match lines except at the centre.

Use the stripes or checks as a guide for positioning buttonholes. This might mean altering the distance between the buttonholes on the pattern, but the finished garment will look much neater.

Basic sewing techniques

Simple stitching

1 Double machine stitch Used to finish cuffs and collars.

Work first row of stitches on edge of fold.

When using a straight stitch machine, place edge of machine foot to first row of stitching and machine a second row of stitching, keeping the outside edge of the machine foot to the first line of stitching.

If using a swing needle machine, swing the needle as far as possible away from the first line of stitching.

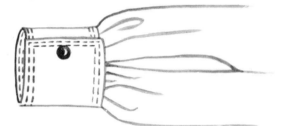

2 Shirring This is an attractive and useful way of dealing with fullness at waistline and at the wrists of full sleeves. Place machine spool on to a knitting needle and place thumb next to it to keep the spool firmly in place close to the knob of the needle. Hold end of shirring elastic down with thumb and wind elastic on to spool from front to back. Do not stretch elastic. When spool is full cut off the end of the thread held down by thumb, as this could get caught in the spool-case. It is always advisable to work a test piece of shirring before starting work on the garment. With most fabrics use the largest straight stitch on the machine, as the longer the stitch the tighter the gathering. If the elastic continually breaks, it usually means that the bottom tension is too tight. If the gathering is not tight enough tightening the top tension should rectify this.

Work required number of rows of stitching, keeping the edge of the machine foot next to the previous row of stitching. It is essential to fasten off all rows of shirring firmly by knotting the elastic and then sewing through it.

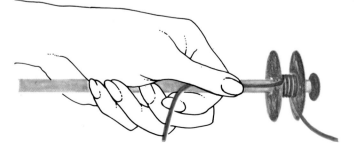

3 Binding Use this for neatening a raw edge, or as a decoration. Cut a bias strip 2.9cm–3.2cm ($1\frac{1}{8}$–$1\frac{1}{4}$ inches) wide. With right sides together, place the bias strip to edge of garment and stitch 0.6cm ($\frac{1}{4}$ inch) from the edge. Turn on to wrong side. Turn under 0.6cm ($\frac{1}{4}$ inch) and hem-stitch on the first line of stitching. Make sure the stitches do not show on the right side.

4 Piping Sometimes used to accentuate a yoke or sleeve edge.

Cut bias strip double the finished width of the piping, usually 0.6cm ($\frac{1}{4}$ inch), plus 3.2cm ($1\frac{1}{4}$ inches) for turnings. Fold strip in half lengthways with wrong sides together and press. Place raw edges of piping to edge of garment. Tack. Place facing edge on to garment and piping edges and tack 1.6cm ($\frac{5}{8}$ inch) from the edge and machine on this line. If piping is used on the edge of a neckline or an armhole, the turnings must be graded or layered before being tacked. When used to decorate a seamline such as a yoke or pocket the piping is usually edge-stitched.

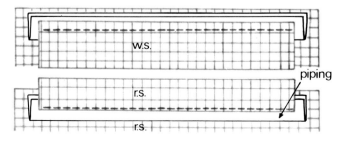

w.s.

r.s.

r.s.

piping

5 Gathering or Ease for skirts and sleeves.

By hand. Use single thread on light-weight fabrics and double thread on heavy-weight fabrics. Start with three back stitches and work small straight stitches. Do not fasten off at the end of the row but leave thread hanging. With right sides together, pin centre of gathering to centre of part of garment to which it is to be attached, and pin together at each end. Pull up gathering thread to fit. Wind thread round a pin in a figure-of-eight. Put in more pins before tacking. Pins should be placed vertically to enable tacking to be done on the gathering line without pins scratching fingers.

When several rows of gathering are required space rows evenly to the given depth. Pull up and fasten off each row with three very small back stitches.

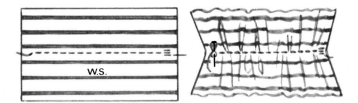

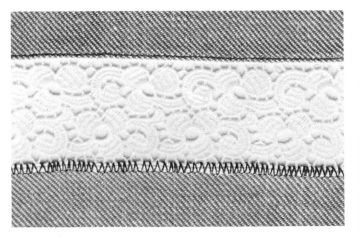

By machine. Loosen top tension on machine slightly, and turn stitch length adapter to the longest' stitch. Working from the right side of the fabric, machine on the fitting line. Pull up gathering from both ends. Wind thread round pins in figures-of-eight. Tighten top tension when you have finished gathering.

6 Attaching lace on lingerie and baby things.

Insertion lace. This has two straight, corded edges and can be attached by hand (whipping), by straight machine stitch, or by zig-zag machine stitch.

Flouncing lace. This has one straight, corded edge. This type of lace usually has a gathering thread woven in at the cord edge which is pulled up slightly before attaching it to a garment. Attach by hand, by straight machine stitch or by zig-zag machine stitch.

Galloon lace. This has one straight, corded edge and a shaped lower edge, such as scallops. There is sometimes a gathering thread with the cord. When this lace is used on underwear, it is not usually gathered before it is attached to the garment as it becomes too bulky.

7 Rouleau This is suitable for lacing, loop buttonholes, belt carriers, shoe-string straps and bows.

Cut a strip, 2.54cm–3.2cm *(1 inch–1¼ inches)* wide, from the true bias of the fabric. With right sides together, fold strip in half lengthways and stitch 0.6cm (¼ inch) in from the edge. Do not trim the turnings to less than the tube width as these turnings make the filling. Sew end of tube on to eye of a large bodkin, or blunt-ended tapestry needle. Push this through the tube until it reaches the other end. Cut thread from tube to needle.

Note It is quite possible to make a wider rouleau for belts by using the same method.

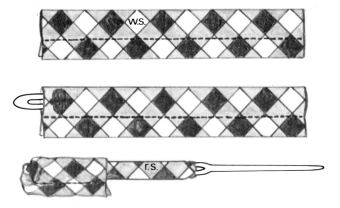

8 Casing This is used to encase tape or elastic.

A hem casing can be used at the hem edge of a garment, such as the bottom of sleeves or waist of trousers. The hem should be about 0.3cm (⅛ inch) wider than the elastic. If a thick elastic is used a little more space may be needed.

When a casing is needed in the body of a garment, such as the waistline of a dress, this must be an applied casing. This is made from a strip of fabric, usually cut on the straight grain, 1.6cm (⅝ inch) wider than the elastic. This allows for an 0.6cm (¼ inch) hem at either edge and 0.3cm (⅛ inch) for the thickness of the elastic.

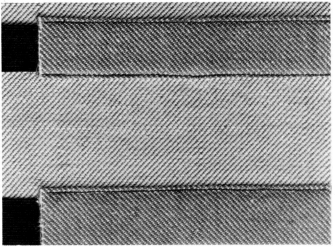

9 Machine edge stitching This is a row of machine stitching worked on the edge of a fold as a decoration. Stitch along one edge as far as the corner. Leaving needle in the fabric, lift pressure foot and turn work. Drop pressure foot and continue along next edge.

10 Buttonhole stitch This stitch is often confused with blanket stitch, but the thread is placed at the back of the needle for buttonhole stitch. This forms a knot on the very edge of the buttonhole which gives strength and longer wear. Horizontal buttonholes have one rounded end and one square end. Vertical buttonholes have two rounded ends.

Always test on a piece of double fabric first.

Measure length of button by placing on fabric. Place a pin at either side. The thickness of the button must also be considered as a thick button needs a larger sized buttonhole.

Work a row of machine stitching around the edge of the cut, or oversew, before buttonholing to prevent fraying. Use a suitable thread for your fabric (see basic equipment). When stitching buttonholes the general rule is that nine oversewing stitches are used at the rounded end and nine buttonhole stitches at the square end. On heavy fabric it is often necessary to punch a hole at the rounded end and work nine buttonhole stitches round this.

To give a really professional finish a very narrow cord known as gimp, or a double thickness of buttonhole twist, can be placed on the edge of the buttonhole and the buttonhole stitch worked over it.

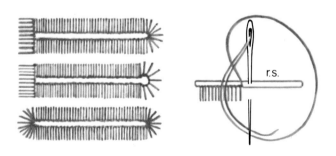

11 Curved seam When there is a curved seam, such as at waistline or on the elbow on a tight fitting sleeve, it is necessary to clip the turning almost to the stitch line so that it lies flat when pressed open. After clipping, and pressing flat, curve the corners of the cut before neatening as corners can be damaged during handling.

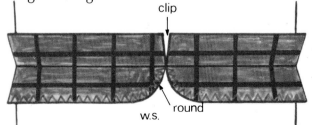

12 Darts A dart is used to deal with fullness on a garment at places such as bust, neck, waist, elbow and shoulder. It is marked on the pattern by a series of dots or a V. Stitch from the widest end of dart to the edge of the fold at its point. Do not stretch the fabric as this will result in an ugly point on the right side. Do not reverse the machine stitching to finish off but, either tie the two threads in a knot, or darn the ends back into the row of machine stitching or just inside it. Always press the dart towards the centre of the garment, i.e. towards centre-back or front on skirt or bodice, side darts towards the waistline.

Sometimes on heavy fabric it is advisable to cut up through the fold of dart and press open and neaten the edges.

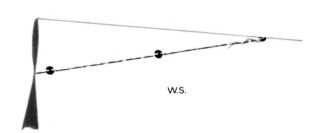

w.s.

13 Neatening an edge

Machining down an edge. Turn under 0.3cm ($\frac{1}{8}$ inch) and stitch as near to the edge as practicable. When using this method of neatening, it is advisable to make a slightly larger seam allowance when cutting out, about 2cm ($\frac{3}{4}$ inch).

Zig-zag stitching. This is a very quick and neat way to neaten most edges using a swing needle machine. It is advisable to work a test piece of fabric first as the depth of the stitch varies according to the weight and fraying qualities of the fabric. The stitch should penetrate deep enough into the fabric to prevent fraying, but not deep enough to make a ridge which may show on the right side when the garment is pressed.

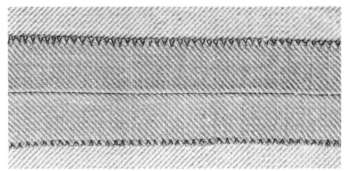

Oversewing. Using a single thread and small stitches work from left to right.

Blanket stitch. This is often used on heavy-weight material. Use a single thread and work from left to right.

Pinking. Pinking shears can be used to neaten non-fraying fabric, but it is not advisable on other types of cloth.

14 Stay stitch This is a row of straight machine stitching worked around a curved edge as soon as the garment is cut out to prevent the edge from stretching. This is most essential on a low neckline, or at the waistline of a bias-cut skirt. After working this line of machine stitching tie off at both ends, or wind round a pin in a figure-of-eight.

15 Back stitch This stitch is used for starting and finishing most hand stitching and is useful for repairing broken machine lines.

Using single thread, and with right side of work facing, insert needle into fabric and make a small stitch on the wrong side. Put needle back into the hole where the thread first entered the fabric. Make another stitch on the wrong side twice the length of the first. Insert the needle back in the hole where it came out for the previous stitch. Continue in this way until the row of stitches is complete.

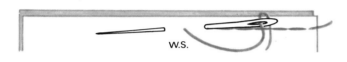

W.S.

16 Basting or tacking
Temporary tacking stitch. Use this for holding two pieces of fabric together before fitting or machining. Start and finish with three small back stitches and work straight even stitches on stitching line.

Slip tacking. This is used for joining a seam on striped or patterned cloth. Fold seam allowance to wrong side on one piece of fabric and pin into place, on right side, along seam line on the other piece of fabric, matching the pattern. Working on the right side, slip needle through edge of fold and then into matching pattern on the other piece of fabric.

Tacking out an edge. This is used for holding an edge in place before pressing or working rows of machining as a decoration. Roll edge with thumb and forefinger of left hand, and work small stitches 0.6cm ($\frac{1}{4}$ inch) in from the edge, keeping the seam line on the edge or slightly towards the facing side.

Permanent tacking. This is worked to hold lining and garment securely together on the seam lines.

Start and finish with three back stitches and work small straight stitches 0.6cm ($\frac{1}{4}$ inch) in from the seam line. When using a non-stretch lining with a stretchable fabric leave a loop every 5cm (2 inches) to prevent pulling on the seams.

Diagonal tacking. This is used for holding two lightweight pieces of fabric securely whilst being joined together. It can also be used to hold an interfacing in place until all the seams have been machined.

17 Slash, cut or clip It is necessary on an inward curved seam, such as a neckline, armhole or shaped stitching line, to cut almost to the machine line to enable the turning to spread out and press flat.

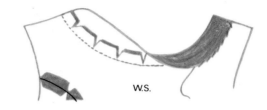

W.S.

18 Pink When working an outward curved seam, it is essential to cut out small V's almost to the machine line. This ensures that the seam lies flat when work is turned to the right side.

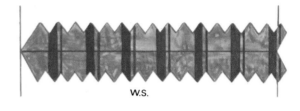

W.S.

19 Layering or grading turnings To avoid a ridge appearing on the right side of a garment it is necessary, especially where an interfacing has been used, to trim the turnings to different widths. These are usually: interfacing 0.2cm ($\frac{1}{16}$ inch); first turning 0.3cm ($\frac{1}{8}$ inch); second turning 0.6cm ($\frac{1}{4}$ inch).

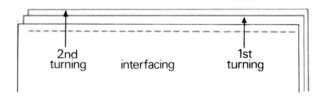

2nd turning   interfacing   1st turning

20 Slip stitch This stitch is used to hold two folds together permanently without any stitches showing on the outside of the garment. Start by running thread through one fold from the inside edge to the outside edge. Insert needle into one fold, work a small stitch, bring needle out and insert into the other fold immediately opposite. Continue working into the alternate folds until the inside edge has been reached. To finish, run the thread through one fold and then the other one. Cut off thread.

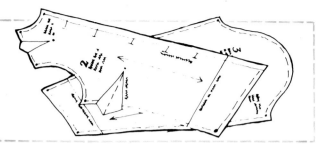

All about seams

Basic seams

There are many types of seams all of which serve the same purpose but have individual advantages. The seam must be chosen to suit the fabric and the design of the garment, which means considering whether or not the fabric will fray and if the seam is to show. Always remember to press seams well after stitching and before neatening.

Flat seam

This is the most commonly used seam in dressmaking as it is suitable for most fabrics.

With right sides together and notches matching, tack and stitch on the seam line (figure 1). Remove the tacking, fasten the ends and press open. The method of neatening depends on the type of fabric, machine and personal choice. For most fabrics, a zig-zag stitch is used or the seam oversewn by hand. Providing the fabric is not too thick, the edges may be turned under 0.3cm ($\frac{1}{8}$ *inch*) on to the wrong side and machined close to the edge (figure 2). On very thick fabrics it is advisable to bind the edges with bias binding. Straight binding may be used on straight seams (figure 3).

Channel seam

This is an ordinary open seam but with the turnings top-stitched down. It is flat and decorative and very flattering when used on dresses, skirts, jackets and coats. With right sides together and notches matching, tack and stitch on the seam line. Press open on the wrong side. If the fabric frays, neaten the turnings before top-stitching (figure 4). Working on the right side, and with the edge of the machine foot on the seam line machine stitch each side of the seam (figure 5). Turn on to the wrong side and trim seam allowance close to the stitch line, providing it is a non-fraying fabric (figure 6).

Figure 1

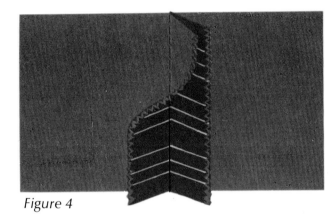

Figure 4

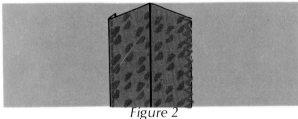

Figure 2

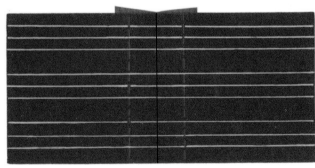

Figure 5

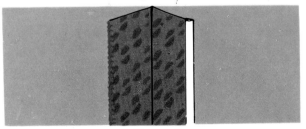

Figure 3

Figure 6

French seam

This is used on sheer fabrics, baby clothes and under-wear.

With wrong sides together and notches matching tack on the seam line 1.6cm ($\frac{5}{8}$ inch) in. Stitch at 0.6cm ($\frac{1}{4}$ inch) outside the seam line (figure 7). Remove the tacking and trim the turning to just under 0.6cm ($\frac{1}{4}$ inch). Press the turnings together to one side. Turn so that the right sides are together. Tack and stitch on the seam line, enclosing the raw edges (figure 8). Press all French seams towards the back of the garment (figure 9).

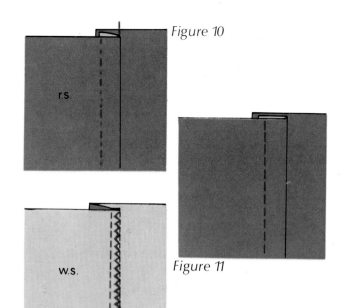

Figure 10

Figure 11

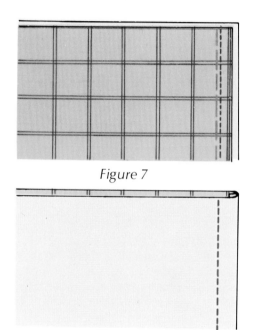

Figure 7

Figure 8

Figure 12

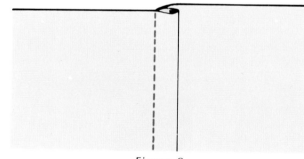

Figure 9

Double tucked seam

A decorative seam to use on dresses and blouses. Turn under 1.6cm ($\frac{5}{8}$ inch) on both seam lines. Tack. Place both folds with edges touching, on to a separate strip of the same material the same length as the seam (figure 13). Tack and stitch the distance of the machine foot from the fold line on either side (figure 14). Remove the tacking, and turn on to the wrong side. Neaten in the same way as for the single tucked seam (figure 15).

Figure 13

Figure 14

Single tucked seam

A seam to use on jackets and coats. Turn under 1.6cm ($\frac{5}{8}$ inch) on one side to create a fold along the seam line. Place this fold on to the corresponding seam line on the right side and tack into place (figure 10). Place the edge of the machine foot on to the fold line and work a row of stitching the width of the foot from the fold (figure 11). Remove the tacking and press on the wrong side. Neaten the edges together (figure 12). If the fabric is non-fraying, it can be trimmed as near to the machine stitches as possible.

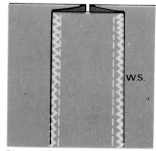

Figure 15

Double machine stitched run and fell seam

This seam is used on shirts and trousers. Turn 1.6cm ($\frac{5}{8}$ *inch*) on to the wrong side of one of the turnings and 1.6cm ($\frac{5}{8}$ *inch*) on to the right side of the other turning (figure 16). Press both folds and trim to 0.6cm ($\frac{1}{4}$ *inch*). Place the first edge with the fold lying on the seam line of the other edge. Tack and stitch very close to the fold (figure 17). Turn on to the wrong side and stitch down the other fold in the same way. This makes a smart finish on both sides and a very flat seam. It is mostly used on shirts and trousers, underwear and baby clothes (figure 18).

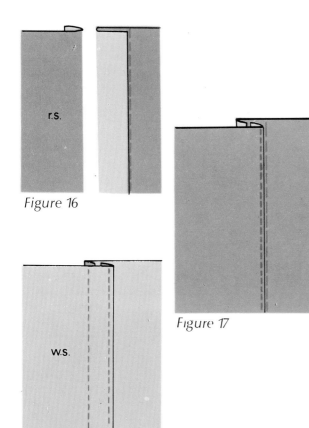

Figure 16

Figure 17

Figure 18

Curved, edge-stitched, lapped seam

This seam is useful for all curved seams, especially on underwear and seams under the bust. Again, it is very flat and should form a smooth curve. Clip the seam allowance on the top overlapping edge. Fold on the seam line and tack. Place the fold line on to the corresponding seam line and pin into place using the pins vertically (figure 19). Tack and stitch very near to the fold (figure 20). Turn on to the wrong side and press. Trim the turning to 0.6cm ($\frac{1}{4}$ *inch*) and neaten the edges by hand or zig-zag (figure 21). It is essential that the seam is not stretched as it is machined. To prevent this, slightly push the material under the foot as it is being machined. When the centre point is reached, leave the needle in the fabric, lift the pressure foot, turn the work, drop the pressure foot and continue stitching.

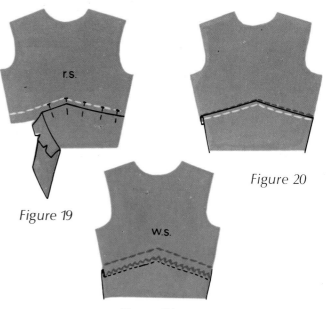

Figure 19

Figure 20

Figure 21

Shaped, faced tucked seam

In the same way as the curved, lapped seam, this method forms a smooth curve and is also used as a decorative feature. With right sides together and notches matching, tack and stitch the facing to the garment. Trim the turnings tapering them very narrowly at centre points and corners (figure 22). Turn the facing on to the wrong side and tack the edge. Press on the wrong side. Place the faced edge on to the corresponding seam line and tack into place. Stitch the distance of the machine foot from the fold. At the angle or centre point, leave the needle in the fabric, lift the pressure foot, turn the work, drop the foot and continue stitching (figure 23). Remove all tacking, turn on to the wrong side and press. Trim the turnings to 0.6cm ($\frac{1}{4}$ *inch*) and neaten the edges together by hand or zig-zag (figure 24). If a non-fraying fabric is being used, trim the turnings as close to the machine stitches as possible.

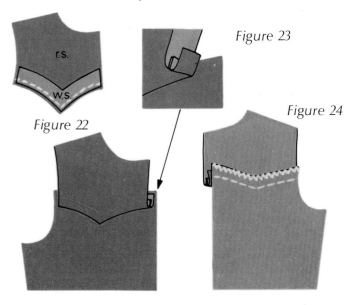

Figure 23

Figure 22

Figure 24

Mantua seam

A very useful seam to use on sheer fabrics when attaching a frill or flounce. With right sides together gather the frill on to the garment. Tack along the seam line (figure 25). Trim the frill to 0.6cm ($\frac{1}{4}$ *inch*) and make a turning of the same amount on the other edge (figure 26). Turn this fold back and place it on the tacking line. Stitch as close to the edge as possible (figure 27). Remove all tacking and gathering threads and press the seam upwards, away from the frill.

Lapped, stitched, single channel seam

This is a flatter version of the machined run and fell, because there is no fold on the under edge. With right sides together, tack and stitch 1.6cm ($\frac{5}{8}$ *inch*) from the edge. Remove the tacking. Trim one turning to 0.6cm ($\frac{1}{4}$ *inch*) (figure 28). If the seam is on a trouser leg, it is usually the turning facing the back that is trimmed.

On the wrong side, press the turnings together to one side with the larger turning on the top (figure 29). Neaten the edge if it is a fraying fabric. From the right side stitch down the seam placing the edge of the foot on the seam line (figure 30). Press from the wrong side. If the fabric is a non-fraying one, the turning on the wrong side can be trimmed as close to the stitch line as possible.

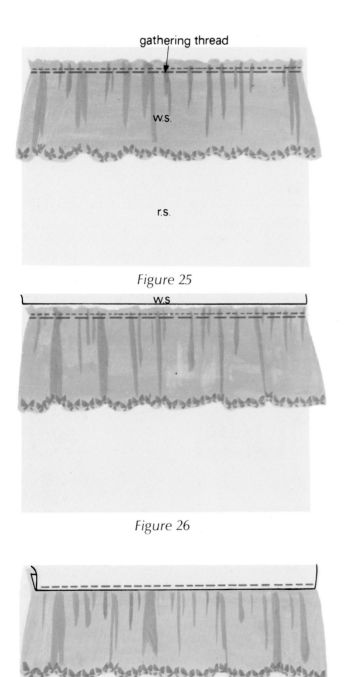

Figure 25

Figure 26

Figure 27

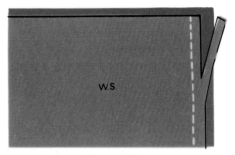

Figure 28

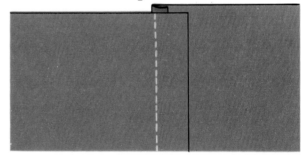

Figure 29

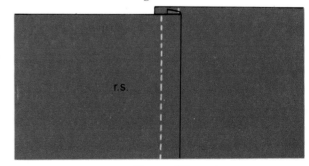

Figure 30

Stitched flat fell seam

This seam is used on shirts, and trousers and is stitched in the same way as the lapped, stitched single channel seam. After pressing the turnings to one side with the larger turnings on top, turn in 0.6cm ($\frac{1}{4}$ *inch*) and machine stitch close to the fold.

3

Advanced techniques

Advanced sewing techniques

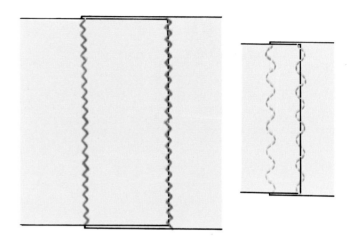

More advanced machine techniques

Once you become experienced, you will want to try some of the more advanced techniques which can save so much time and make a professional finish much easier to obtain. Some of the more useful of these techniques are explained here and can be worked on most modern machines.

Blind hemming

Turn up the hem to the required length and tack 1.3cm ($\frac{1}{2}$ inch) below the top edge. With hem facing down, position the garment on to machine bed. Fold garment back and lower pressure foot on to the top edge of the fold and hem. On most machines there is a metal guide which can be attached to the foot. It should be used for blind hemming against the fold. The stitch length should be altered so that it just picks up the fabric from the fold. This type of hemming is only suitable for thicker fabrics as stitches and indentations tend to show on finer fabrics (figure 1).

Figure 1

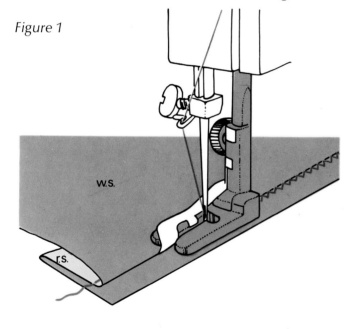

w.s.

r.s.

without pulling it. On garments such as ski pants and baby suits work seams with a small zig-zag stitch. The small stitches can be evenly interspersed with a larger stitch (figure 3).

Figure 2

Seaming stretch fabrics

On most machines, instructions are given for stitching stretch fabrics. The stitching should be tested first on the fabric you intend to use, with suitable stretch thread, for example synthetic thread or pure silk. On very elasticated fabrics the seams are usually stitched lapped seams approximately 1.3–2cm ($\frac{1}{2}$–$\frac{3}{4}$ inch) wide, worked with a zig-zag stitch or a pattern (figure 2). Feed the fabric under the machine foot

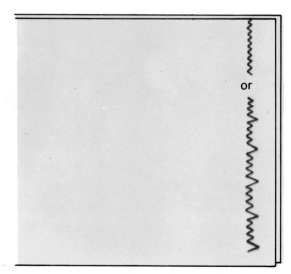

or

Figure 3

Sewing on buttons

Most zig-zag machines will do this quite easily. Often a special foot is supplied and if there is a drop feed, lower this and set the needle at 0. Position the button and carefully lower the needle by hand into the left hand hole. Work a few stitches into this hole. Set the zig-zag to the same width as the distance between the holes. Work a few stitches, reset the dial to 0 and finish off by working a few stitches in the same hole. Take the threads to the wrong side and fasten off by hand.

If a shank is required, work the stitches over a match-stick or pin (figure 4). Remove stick, take threads to the underside of the button and wind these around threads between button and garment. Take threads to wrong side and fasten off.

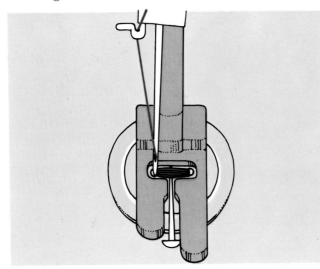

Figure 4

Hooks and eyes and press studs can also be worked in the same way, but ensure that the stitch dial is set to the same width as the distance between the holes. With hooks, take threads to the wrong side and then up under the actual hook. Work three back stitches by hand over the hook to secure (figure 5).

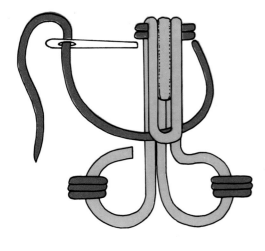

Figure 5

Gathering with a gathering foot
This method is controlled by the length and tension of the stitch rather than the fabric used. The larger the stitch, the fuller the gathering. Test on a spare piece of fabric – measure the width of fabric, work the gathering and measure the width again. If the fabric does not respond to the gathering (some thicker fabrics do not) thread the spool thread through the hole in the spool prong (if there is one) (figure 6). This

will tighten the lower thread. When no gathering foot is supplied, fine fabrics will often gather up sufficiently by tightening the top tension.

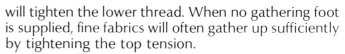
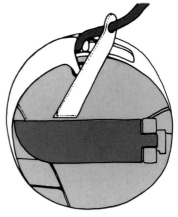

Figure 6

Hemming
A special foot is supplied for this but practice is needed to achieve a good result. Fold under a double hem to the required width and work a few stitches through this. Then, leaving the needle in the fabric, lift the foot and thread the fold of the fabric through the spiral foot. Lower foot and stitch, lifting the fabric and holding it taut when doing so (figure 7A). When working corners on a square trim off the corners to avoid bulk. Then simply fold one hem over the other when stitching and oversew the edges together (figure 7B).

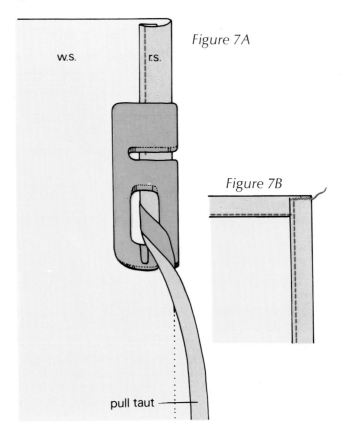

Figure 7A

w.s.   r.s.

Figure 7B

pull taut

Shell hemming

This is ordinary hemming made into a decorative feature by the use of zig-zag stitch. On non-stretch fabrics and fabrics which fray use an ordinary zig-zag with a fairly long stitch. Work it so that the stitches nearest to the fold of the hem go just over the fold.

On stretch fabrics and fabrics which do not fray, use a single hem of approximately 1.3cm ($\frac{1}{2}$ inch) and the broken straight stitch to create the shell shapes (figure 8). Again the stitch should be long and the needle positioned on the fabric so that the longest

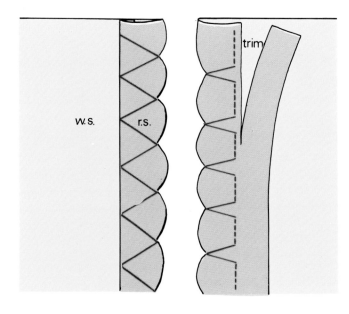

Figure 8

stitch goes just over the edge of the fold and forms a shell. In both methods the excess fabric can be trimmed off close to the stitching or zig-zagged down on the raw edge to form a casing for elastic (figure 9).

Decorative hem stitching on fine fabrics

On most machines a special spear shaped needle is used for hem stitching. This needle pierces a hole in the fabric when stitching for decoration. Ensure that each row of stitching is started the correct distance away from the last so that the needle enters the holes on the left and forms a trellis effect (figure 10). This can be worked on edges, bands or separate fabric and then cut out and appliquéd as a motif. For example an attractive result can be obtained by using lurex on the spool.

Double and treble needles and double hem stitch needles can be bought and used with a transverse c.b. shuttle.

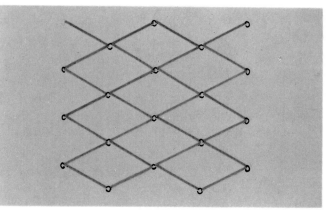

Figure 10

Pin tucking

Some throat plates, as well as the usual needle hole, have an additional hole bored in them. A crochet thread may be inserted from underneath the throat plate and placed under the fabric while stitching. Use a twin needle so that the crochet thread is stitched in from the top as well. This will form a more pronounced pin tuck.

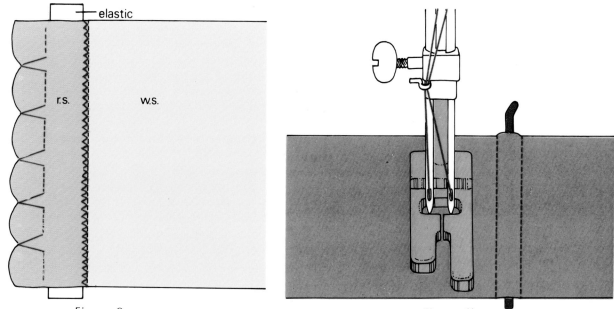

Figure 9

Figure 11

Special grooved pin tucking feet are also available for certain brands of machines. Use a small stitch length and twin needle. Work rows of double stitching an equal distance apart. It is advisable to work rows of pin tucking before cutting out the fabric if a large area of pin tucks is required (figure 11).

Patterns worked with a double/treble needle
Ensure that the length of the stitch is not too great, and can be worked within the hole in the foot. Thread each thread separately around tension disc. Use zig-zag stitch or another patterned stitch.

Drawn threads
On drawn thread work, zig-zag stitching may be used on the edges (figure 12A). For an open trellis effect, draw out threads in small blocks leaving the exact width of the largest zig-zag stitch in between. Work zig-zag stitch along each edge of drawn threads (figure 12B).

Neatened edge
Turn under a single hem. Zig-zag with a small stitch and trim off the excess fabric. A crochet type thread

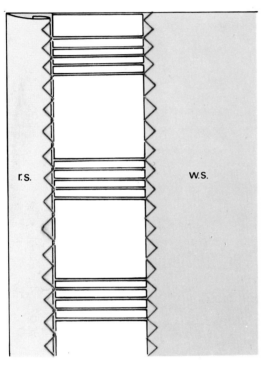

Figure 12A

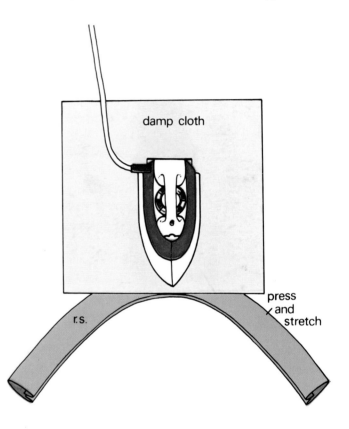

Figure 13

can be inserted through the hole in the front of the pressure foot and zig-zag stitch worked over this thread. If there is no hole, lay the thread on the raw edge and work zig-zag stitch over it. This is a good method for repairing the edges of cuffs.

Attaching bias with the binding foot
Slide the folded binding into the spirals of the binding foot with the raw edge of the garment in between.
If the bias is to be applied as a decorative feature other than an edging, it is advisable to press it into shape before applying. Draw the shape required on a piece of paper. Fold in the raw edges of the bias and then fold the bias in half, so that it will give a raised look when applied. Press and stretch the fold with a damp cloth to obtain the shape required. Tack and stitch on to garment with a straight or decorative stitch (figure 13).

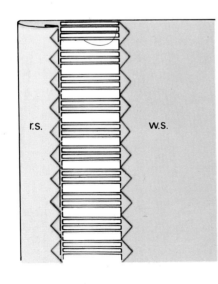

Figure 12B

The art of quilting

Quilting

Quilting is an age old art. It was originally the sewing together of layers of fabric with wadding for warmth. Today it is also one of the most decorative forms of stitching. It can be worked by hand or by machine. There are many interesting decorative designs in quilting, the most basic of which are squares and diamonds. They are easy to work and the simplest for the beginner. Hemlines, collars and cuffs can all be very attractively quilted. You can vary the size of the basic square and diamond shapes and use decorative threads for added interest.

Note It is advisable to work quilting before making up as the fabric will lose some of its length and width through the thickness of the wadding.

Quilting Design

When planning your garment, remember small patterns are preferable when applied to collars and cuffs, and any quilting above the waist. Larger patterns are better for coats, skirts and around a hem. A single flower or motif can also be quilted, and worked individually with attractive results.

Quilting by Hand

This is traditional quilting and should be worked on a frame which is placed on two straight-backed chairs or trestles. The lining fabric is attached first, fairly taut, then the wadding laid on top and the fabric to be quilted on top of the wadding.

Wadding

There are three types of wadding available in most big stores, Terylene and Courtelle, which are man-made and washable, and cotton which has to be dry cleaned. All types are in different weights and approximately 91–96.5cm (*36–38 inches*) wide. The lighter ones are usually used for dressmaking and the thicker ones for bedcovers and sleeping bags. It is essential to use the correct weight of wadding for the fabric you are working with and washable wadding with washable fabric.

Every care must be taken to ensure that there is an even thickness throughout the garment and that the wadding is larger in size than the two pieces of fabric being used as the wadding can be reduced in size when stitched.

The original way of transferring a pattern to the fabric is by tracing round a template (as in figure 1) with a yarn or raffia needle, held almost flat so that it forms a crease line in the fabric.

Note A template is a pattern used as a guide to achieve

uniform size and shape when quilting. It is drawn on card and then cut out.

Figure 1

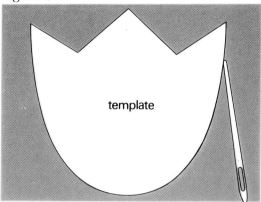

Tailor's chalk can be used, but it is not advisable as it has a certain amount of grease content and it may leave permanent marks.

Tracing paper, tissue paper and graph paper may be used for the design and then needle-marked (figure 2). Remove the paper and needle-mark again.

Figure 2

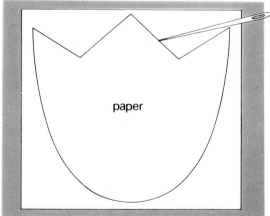

Pencil must not be used as it cannot be erased. Accurate drawing is required for a good finished result. You should start at the centre of a design and work out to the sides.

A pleasing result can be achieved by using a patterned fabric and quilting the outlines of the pattern in a toning thread. When transferring the pattern to the fabric, the fabric should be placed on a blanket and then on to a hard surface. Transfer the pattern then take the top fabric and place it on top of the wadding and lining. Tack all three thicknesses together on one side; the fabric and wadding should not be pulled tightly. Pin the other three sides.

Stitching

Using a No. 9 Between needle and a thread suitable for the fabric, bring the needle up from underneath the fabric through the wadding on the design line, and on to the right side, work a small back stitch, then work a split stitch. This is done by inserting the needle through the thread on the back stitch (figure 3).

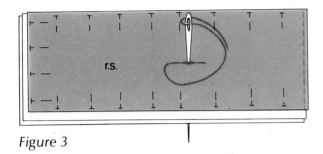

Figure 3

Start with a double back stitch as a knot might pull the fabric. Small running stitches are then worked on the design lines. Work from the right side and work several stitches at a time as this helps to keep them the same size on both sides of the work. Stitches of a regular size are important, as a firm outline of the design is required for a good result. Work only one stitch at a time at corners and curves. Try to keep the stitches as small as the fabric and wadding allow. Work the main central pattern of the design first and then the background. When two lines of stitches cross, it is advisable to have two needles and thread, work a few stitches on one line and then a few stitches on the other. The edges of the work are either bound with matching fabric and all three thicknesses together, or one edge turned in and caught down on to the wadding and the other edge turned in and slip-stitched into place.

Underarm darts and seams on a garment that will open at the back or front should be stitched first if a continuous pattern is desired. If there is no centre-front or back opening the bust darts should still be worked first, and then the pattern applied so that it will match when the seams are joined.

Shadow Quilting

Shadow quilting is decorative quilting on sheer fabric. It is possible to work attractive and original designs with a combination of unusual threads and fabrics. Shadow quilting is suitable for delicate materials used for lingerie and some of the most beautiful evening wear.

For shadow quilting work with the top fabric and wadding only then line the garment afterwards. It is possible to work all three thicknesses but care must be taken to finish off the ends of the quilting wool. Shadow quilting is worked in the same way as traditional quilting but with two lines of stitches around the design 0.3cm ($\frac{1}{8}$ inch) apart. Coloured quilting wool is then threaded through the wadding between the two lines of stitching.

Quilting by Machine

Quilting can be worked on any sewing machine, and as with hand quilting simple designs are often the most effective. Individual flowers or motifs can be worked separately and then appliquéd on to a garment to produce an original result. On zig-zag machines embroidery can be worked first on the fabric and then quilted. A zig-zag machine is needed for intricate designs involving appliqué, and an embroidery machine for more complicated designs and shapes. A straight stitch machine will do simple designs in straight line and gentle curves.

When machine quilting you should first transfer your pattern on to the top fabric by either of the traditional methods. Alternatively draw the design on graph or tracing paper, pin or tack the paper to the fabric, stitch through the paper then tear the paper away.

Twin or triple needles can be used to produce the basis for shadow quilting. These are needles with two or three needles attached to a single bar. They are usually used on zig-zag machines and have a thread through each needle and a single thread on the spool. Quilting wool of a suitable thickness should be used to thread between the stitching lines. Use a crewel needle threaded with the wool and push it through between the stitching lines threading the eye in first as the point of the needle will poke through the fabric. When using some fabrics the quilting will be more pronounced on the underneath fabric, so it is best to work a test sample first and reverse the fabric if necessary. Should this prove the case but teeth or throat plate are causing marks on the fabric, place paper beneath the work and tear it away afterwards. All line designs must be straight and parallel, but to avoid many rows of tacking, a distance piece should be used. Some machines are supplied with these, but if not, clear instructions are supplied on page 62 for making a distance piece for any machine where the pressure foot is held in position by a screw.

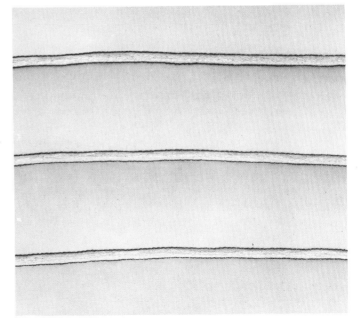

The distance piece is very useful for working lines an equal distance apart, or from the edge of a piece of fabric.

Tack as little as possible when joining the three layers together and tack diagonally. A tacking stitch worked near the outside edge and through the centre both ways will usually be enough to secure the wadding and fabric sufficiently. To tack use a number 9 Between needle and a fine thread. Do not pull the fabric tightly over the wadding when tacking.

When working diamonds or squares machine stitch the lines one way first, then insert a knitting needle carefully between the rows to fluff up the wadding before stitching the crossing lines. You may require a slightly heavier needle when quilting than normally recommended for the fabric due to the thickness of the work. Test first. If using jersey normal ball-point needles may miss stitches so use a 'ball point perfect stitch needle'.

When quilting has been completed remove the tacking and measure the fabric before cutting out the garment. If you have already cut out the garment to work the darts and seams, check the garment pieces with the pattern before taking in the final turnings. Loss of width and length may have occurred during the quilting process. Shake the work to fluff up the wadding and keep in a warm atmosphere as this makes the wadding expand.

Six Quilting Tips

1 If working on a large garment avoid folding the fabric when storing. Roll the pieces you have worked around cardboard if possible.
2 Do not stretch the wadding to cover a larger area.
3 Use fine pins when pinning wadding to fabric.
4 Do not overlap wadding at any part. It must be of an equal thickness throughout the garment.
5 When pressing place quilting wrong side up on a blanket to give a softer base which will not flatten the wadding.
6 When quilting with a machine push the fabric gently through the machine, never drag or pull it as this will flatten the wadding.

Decorative ways of quilting

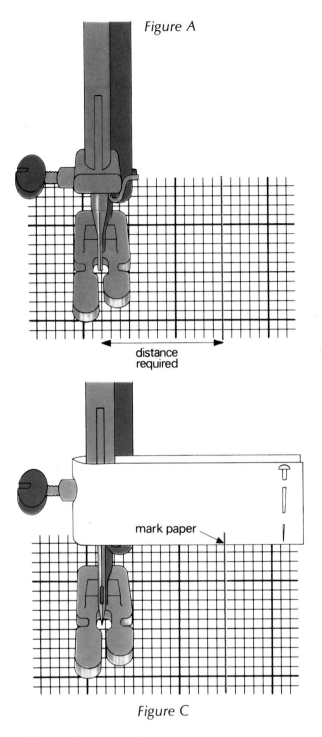

Figure A

Figure C

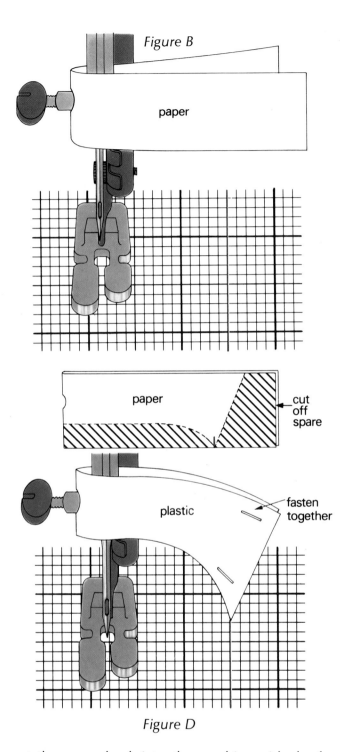

Figure B

Figure D

Making a distance piece

Place a piece of graph paper underneath the machine needle and drop the pressure foot. Mark a line on the paper the distance required between the machine stitching lines (figure A).

Cut a strip of pliable plastic, similar to the plastic used for bottles, 2cm ($\frac{3}{4}$ *inch*) wide by 15cm (*6 inches*) long. Remove the screw holding the foot in place on your machine. Cut a piece of paper the same size as the plastic, fold it in half with the short ends together and make a hole in the centre on the fold large enough for the screw to go through.

Push the screw through the hole in the paper and put the screw back into the machine with the foot in place (figure B). Fasten the two short ends of the paper with a pin. Drop the pressure foot.

Mark the end of the paper where it touches the mark on the graph paper (figure C). Remove the screw and paper, cut off the ends and shape the paper to form a point. Use the paper pattern to cut out the plastic strip making a hole for the screw. Screw the plastic strip lightly on to the machine so that the point rests lightly on the line of the graph paper when the foot is dropped (figure D).

When working parallel lines keep the point of the distance piece on the previous row of stitching.

The art of smocking

Smocking

Smocking is a decorative form of reducing fullness. It can be worked in different colours, stitches and sizes.

Transfers These are grids marked in the form of dots which are used to indicate where lines of gathering should be worked on the garment. Transfers are available in most stores in varying sizes. The size should be chosen to suit the fabric and stitch used. For example large grids are suitable for thicker fabrics and bolder designs, small grids are more suitable for finer fabrics and delicate designs. If the fabric is striped or checked the lines can be used as the grid. On average, smocking reduces the width to one third. Transfers are usually applied to the wrong side of the fabric.

Applying the transfer Select the transfer suitable for the fabric and stitch. Pin the transfer to the wrong side of the fabric ensuring that the lines lie on the straight grain. Using a moderately hot iron, iron over the dots, peeling off the paper immediately behind the iron so the dots are not repeated.

Using a strong thread suitable for the fabric, work the rows of gathering by picking up each dot (figure 1) or

Figure 1

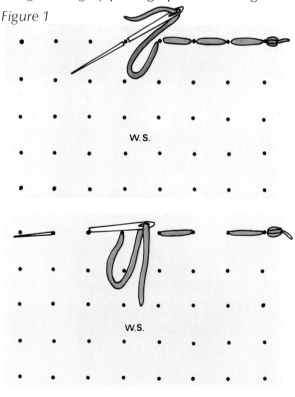

Figure 2

by weaving the needle from dot to dot (figure 2). Fasten the thread at the beginning by working three

back stitches. When all the rows of gathering are inserted, pull up the threads evenly and secure the ends by winding each one in a figure-of-eight around a pin, or tie off in pairs (figure 3). These gathering threads remain in the fabric until the smocking is completed. Before removing them, place the fabric right side down on to a thick blanket. Place a damp cloth over the pleats and press gently for soft, natural looking pleats and heavily for sharp, definite pleats.

Threads These can be used in colours matching or contrasting to the fabric but their thickness should be chosen carefully to suit the fabric: Clarks Anchor coton à broder, fine Sylko perlé and Drima bold stitch are suitable for most fabrics. On heavier fabrics crochet cottons and wools can be used. All stitches are worked on the right side and the ends of the threads secured with back stitches on the wrong side. Here are some basic stitches:

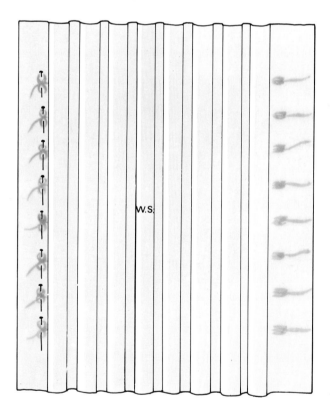

Figure 3

Outline stitch This is a firm, even stitch and is often used as the top and bottom lines of a smocking design to hold the pleats in place. Working from left to right on the first row, bring the needle through on the left hand side of pleat 1. With the thread above the needle, insert through pleat 2 from right to left. Pull up slightly and continue in this way taking one pleat at a time (figures 4 and 5).

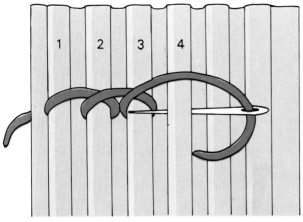

Figure 4

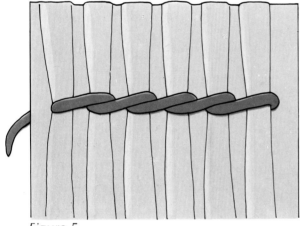

Figure 5

Trellis stitch This is several rows of outline stitch worked diagonally to create an overall diamond shape. Work from left to right starting on the second row. When working upwards to the first row on the left side, insert the needle into each pleat from right to left with the thread above the needle. When working downwards, insert the needle with thread above (figure 6).

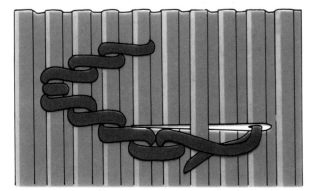

Figure 6

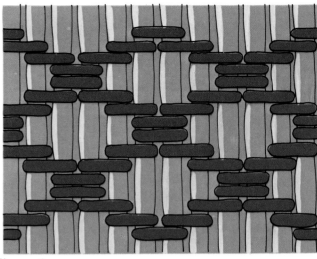

Figure 6

Cable stitch Working from left to right, insert the needle through each pleat from right to left with the thread above and below the needle alternately. Pull up the thread to form a smooth line (figures 7 and 8).

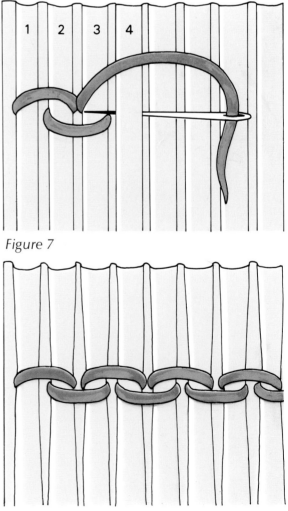

Figure 7

Figure 8

Double cable stitch This is two rows of cable stitch worked close together. The first row starts with the thread above the needle and the second with the thread below (figure 9).

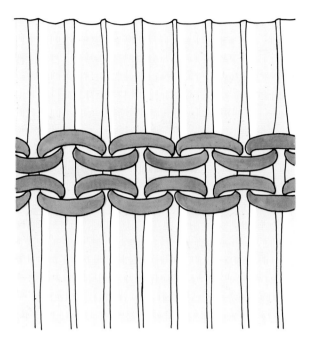

Figure 9

Honeycomb stitch Working from left to right bring the needle to the right side of the fabric through pleat 1. With thread above, pick up pleats 2 and 1 from right to left and pull up together (figure 10). Insert the needle through pleat 2 on to the wrong side and bring out again through pleat 2 on the second row of gathering. With the thread below the needle work pleats 3 and 2 in the same way as pleats 2 and 1 and

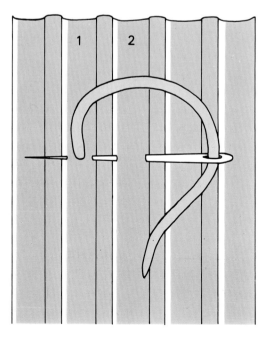

Figure 10

continue to the end of the line taking two pleats at a time on alternate lines (figure 11).

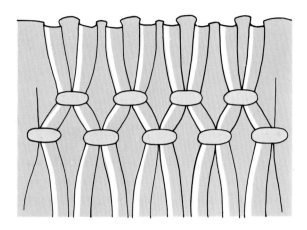

Figure 11

Surface honeycomb stitch This is worked in the same way as the ordinary honeycomb except the diagonal threads lie on the right side of the fabric, and only one stitch is worked over the pleats.

Working from left to right, bring the needle to the right side of the fabric through pleat 1. With thread above the needle make a small stitch on pleat 2 and pull the pleats together. Take the needle to pleat 2 on the second row and from right to left pick up pleat 3 and pull together. Return to the first row with thread below the needle, picking up pleats 3 and 4 and continue likewise (figure 12).

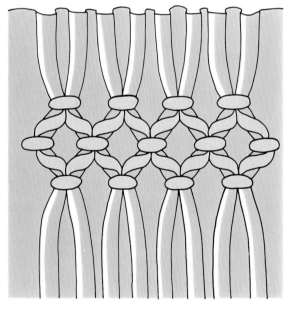

Figure 12

Vandyke stitch This is a simple stitch which is not pulled up very much. Working from right to left bring the needle out at pleat 1 and from right to left work a stitch through pleats 1 and 2. Work another stitch over this. Take thread to the second row and work two stitches, one through and one over pleats 2 and 3.

Return to the first row and stitch pleats 3 and 4. Continue to the end of the line (figure 13A).

Diamond stitch Working from left to right bring the needle out on the left side of pleat 1 on the second row. Work one stitch on this pleat with the thread above the needle and one stitch on pleat 2 with the thread below the needle (figure 14). Take thread to the first row and work one stitch over pleat 3 with thread below the needle and one on pleat 4 with thread above the needle (figure 15). Return to the second row and continue. A second row can be worked in between the first in a contrasting colour to make an attractive design.

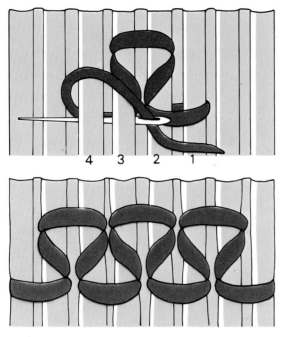

Figure 13A

Double Vandyke stitch This is worked in the same way as the single Vandyke, but using three rows of gathering. Work the loops alternately on the first and third rows of gathering: pleats 2 and 3 on the first row, 4 and 5 on the third, 6 and 7 on the first. Continue like this to the end of the line. Repeat this directly underneath on the fourth, fifth and sixth rows. The loops on rows 3 and 4 will meet and form a double Vandyke (figure 13B).

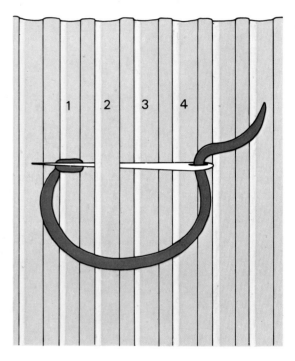

Figure 14

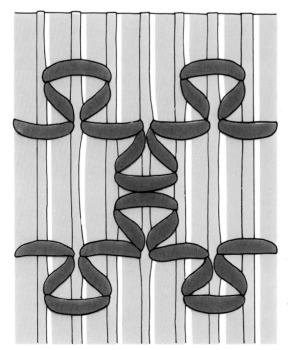

Figure 13B

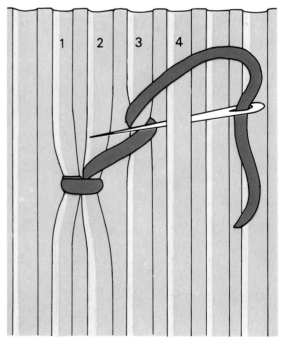

Figure 15

Basic facing techniques

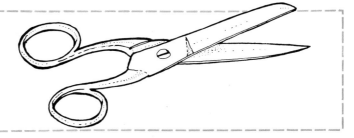

Facings and interfacings
Facings
Facing is a method of neatening and strengthing an edge. It is advisable to fit a garment before stitching on the facing. This is because once the turnings are trimmed, it could be very difficult to alter the facing without the fabric fraying when unpicked. Most patterns are supplied with facings. In some cases however a new facing may be needed due to alteration on the garment. Armholes and necklines often have to be lowered and unless there is sufficient length on the facing to adapt to these alterations, a new facing has to be cut.

Cutting facings
Place the garment so that it is completely flat, on to a piece of graph paper. Match the straight grain of the garment with a line on the paper. Pencil around the edge to be faced and mark in all balance marks and seam lines. If the original balance marks have been cut away, make new ones in corresponding places on the garment and paper. Remove the garment from the paper. Using a ruler, measure 6.5cm ($2\frac{1}{2}$ inches) from the traced line all around the facing at various points. Join these points with a pencil to make a line parallel to the traced line. Work new balance marks 0.3cm ($\frac{1}{8}$ inch) from the edge to be stitched. Trim away the 0.3cm ($\frac{1}{8}$ inch).

Attaching the facing to the garment
With right sides and raw edges together, tack and stitch the facing to the garment on the seam line. Trim and layer the turnings. Clip the turnings on curves and at corners. Use a pair of small scissors for this and clip almost to the stitch line. As 0.3cm ($\frac{1}{8}$ inch) has been trimmed off the facing, the turnings will be only 1.3cm ($\frac{1}{2}$ inch). This allows for roll on the garment, so that the seam line will lie 0.3cm ($\frac{1}{8}$ inch) under the folded edge (figure 1). Turn to the inside, tack

along the folded edge and press. If the raw edge of the facing will show, neaten by hand, by machine or make a small turning and catch-stitch down. If the turning is left loose, catch down on to any seams and darts. Remove all tacking (figure 2). Often through alteration, there is insufficient fabric left to cut new facings. In this case a bias strip may be used.

Figure 2

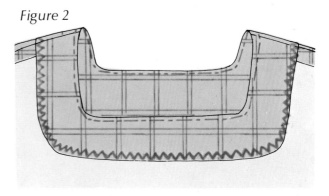

Facing with bias
If using scraps of fabric to make the bias strip, it must be cut on the cross at a 45 degree angle to the straight grain. Cards of bias in various colours can be purchased in heavy cotton, fine lawn, nylon or rayon satin. Choose the type most suitable for the fabric being used, in a matching or toning colour. It is easier to trim the edge to be faced so that the turning is 0.6cm ($\frac{1}{4}$ inch). This is the same width as the turning on the bias. With right sides together place the raw edges of the garment and bias together. Tack on the seam line easing the bias so that it does not stretch. Join the bias at a 45 degree angle and press open. Machine on the tacking line (figure 3). Layer the edges and press on to the bias. Machine stitch the turnings on to the bias and close to the

Figure 1

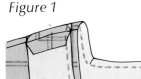

w.s.

r.s.

Figure 3

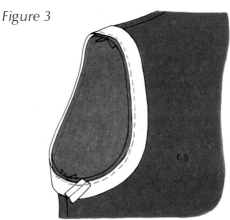

r.s.

seam to hold them flat(figure 4). Press bias to the wrong side and slip-stitch to the garment (figure 5).

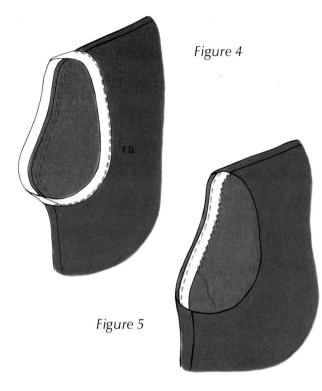

Figure 4

Figure 5

Hemming
The bias should be slip-hemmed, passing the needle through the fold of the bias and picking up individual threads on the garment. If however the garment is to stand up to a lot of hard wear secure the bias with an ordinary hem stitch, which will show slightly on the right side.

Bias is available in a 5cm (*2 inch*) width in most stores and is used for facing hems. Sometimes however this is not sufficient in weight to let the garment hang well. If this is so the facing should be interfaced.

Interfacings
Interfacings strengthen facings and help to hold the shape of collars, cuffs, belts, trouser turnups and coat fronts. Armholes, necklines, pockets, hems and zip openings are all parts of a garment which have to stand up to a lot of wear and therefore require extra strengthening.

Types of interfacing
The choice depends on the weight and quality of the fabric being used. Interfacing is available in many different weights but usually only in white. Organdie is best for extremely fine fabrics, and either organdie or net for sheer fabrics. Lawn or tarlatan is most suitable for light-weight cottons, or another layer of the same fabric can be used. Canvas should be used on coats but make sure that this is pre-shrunk. A woven interfacing cut on the cross must be used on parts of a garment which will still need to stretch. These interfacings are sewn in.

Iron-on interfacing
This is the easiest interfacing to use and is available in various weights. It should be placed with the shiny side to the wrong side of the fabric and ironed with the heat control set at 'wool', or cooler for man-made fibres. The interfacing should be tested on a piece of material beforehand. If the iron accidently touches the shiny side of the interfacing it should be cleaned immediately to prevent marking the fabric.

Attaching interfacing to a garment
Join the interfacing as required and tack on to the wrong side of the garment, matching balance marks and seams. Then attach the facing as before. In this way the bulk of the fold lies under the garment rather than the facing. Clip the turnings almost to the stitch line. Machine stitch the turnings to the facing to help keep them flat and also to keep the facing to the wrong side.

Attaching interfacing to a facing
Interfacing should be tacked on to the facing which is then attached to the garment. If the fabric is sheer however the turnings should be made invisible. To do this, put right sides of facing and interfacing together and stitch 0.3cm ($\frac{1}{8}$ *inch*) from the outside edge. Press open and turn the interfacing on to the wrong side of the facing. The raw edges will then be between the facing and interfacing. Attach the facing to the garment and clip as above.

The pressure of a steam iron is usually sufficient to flatten the facing on the wrong side, although for thicker fabrics a damp cloth is often needed as well.

Interfacing in hems
Cut a strip of interfacing 0.3cm ($\frac{1}{8}$ *inch*) narrower than the depth of the hem. This allows for the roll of the fabric. Place the edge of the interfacing to the edge of the hem and zig-zag (figure 6). Or trim off 0.3cm

Figure 6

($\frac{1}{8}$ *inch*) from the interfacing and turn the edge of the fabric over this. Machine stitch along this edge (figure 7). Turn up the hem and stitch (figure 8).

fabric over this and under the hem on to the wrong side of the garment (figure 10). Hem-stitch and press (figure 11). If necessary catch the turnup to the garment at the seam lines with a small stitch which should not show on the right side.

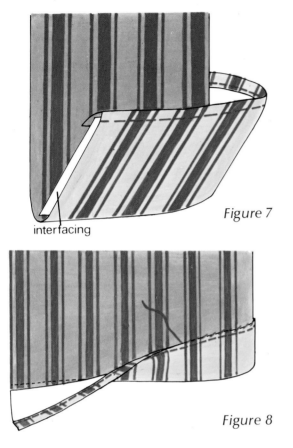

Figure 7

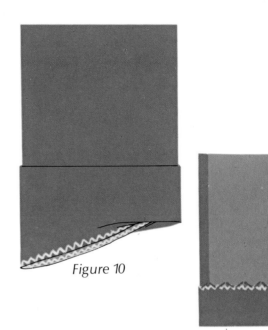

Figure 10

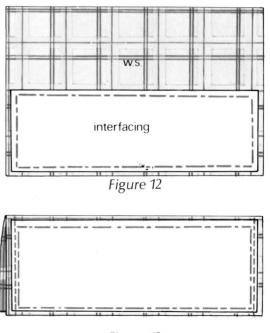

Figure 11

Interfacing in cuffs
Most cuffs are cut in one piece and then folded over. Cut the interfacing half the width of the cuff and iron or tack into place (figure 12). Always place the interfacing on the wrong side of the cuff piece. Fold cuff in half with right sides together, tack and stitch, then trim and turn (figure 13).

Figure 8

Interfacing in turnups
Mark the hem at the required length by pressing the turning on to the right side of the trousers. Cut the interfacing 0.3cm ($\frac{1}{8}$ *inch*) narrower than the required depth of the turnup and stitch the ends together. Iron or tack the interfacing on to the turning placing one edge on the hemline (figure 9). Turn down the

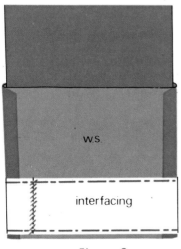

Figure 9

Figure 12

Figure 13

Pockets

There are two ways of using interfacing on pockets. The method used depends on the type of pocket. For flaps, tabs and welts the interfacing should be cut the same size, whereas the lining and interfacing for patch pockets should be cut without turnings (figure 14). The turnings of the pocket enclose the raw edges (figure 15). This avoids bulky edges when the pocket is attached to the garment (figure 16).

Belts

The interfacing should be the width of the finished belt. If the belt has two seams, allow for turnings on the interfacing as well. There are special interfacings for belts, petersham being the most common. This is available in different widths and in black or white.

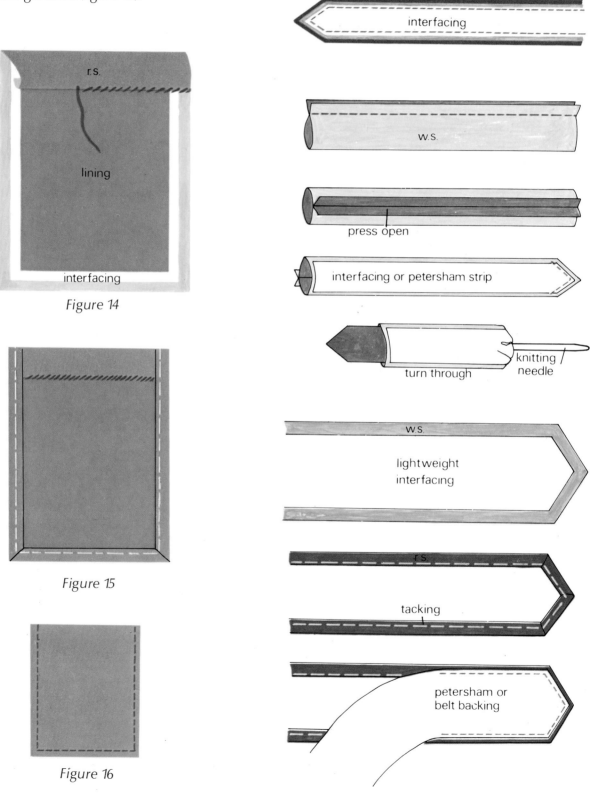

Figure 14

Figure 15

Figure 16

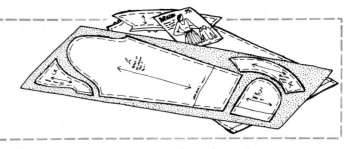

Know-how with collars

Making and attaching basic collars

The method used for making and attaching a collar depends on the style of collar. The method must be decided before cutting out the fabric to ensure that enough fabric is allowed for a facing if one is needed. There are four basic ways of attaching a collar: 1. attached facing method; 2. separate facing method; 3. self-neatening method; 4. the method used for tailored collars on heavy-weight fabrics. The methods for making a collar vary little.

Making a collar

Cut out and ensure that all notches and dots are marked with tailor tacking. Work a tailor tack at sharp corners to mark the point of turning on the machine. There are various types of interfacing to choose from, but all should be attached to the wrong side of the upper collar.

With right sides together and matching notches tack and stitch on the seam line. Trim the turnings and layer to 1cm ($\frac{3}{8}$ inch) and 0.6cm ($\frac{1}{4}$ inch). Trim the turnings very narrowly at corners, almost to the stitch line. When stitching a sharp point work a stitch across instead of making a V as it helps to make the collar lie flat when turned through (figure 1a).

Figure 1a

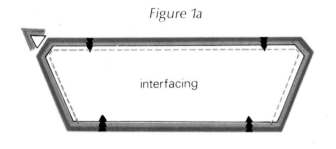

interfacing

On convex curves, the turning must be clipped vertically almost to the stitch line at approximately 1cm ($\frac{3}{8}$ inch) intervals (figure 1b).

Figure 1b

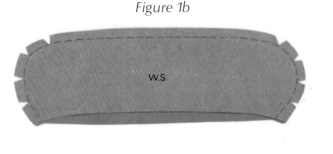

w.s.

On concave curves a small V clipped out at regular intervals helps to avoid bulk when the collar is turned through (figure 1c).

Figure 1c

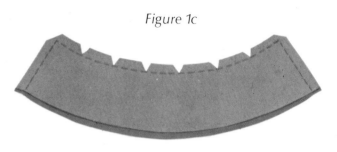

Turn the collar through pushing the corners out carefully with the wrong end of a pencil or the blunt end of a knitting needle. Tack around the outer edge of the collar through all thicknesses to hold the seam in place. Do this from the upper collar to ensure the seam does not show (figure 1d). Press on the wrong

Figure 1d

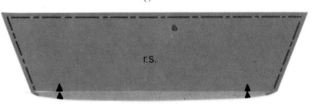

r.s.

side. If the collar is to be top-stitched as a decorative feature this should be done while the collar edge is tacked. Then remove the tacking.

Where only one collar pattern piece is given, trim 0.3cm ($\frac{1}{8}$ inch) off one of the layers. This should be used as the under-collar and will prevent the seam rolling over on to the right side as it is slightly smaller than the upper-collar. Some patterns supply an upper-collar and a slightly smaller under-collar.

Small upright collars and mandarin collars can be cut either on the straight grain of the fabric or on the bias. Cut collar in one piece, then fold in half with right sides together. Stitch short ends, trim and turn through. If collar is to be interfaced, cut a piece of interfacing half the width of the collar. One edge of the interfacing should be placed on the centre fold line of the collar and stitched to the underside with a small herringbone stitch. The other three will be caught in the seams.

Attaching collars

1 Attached facing method This is usually used on garments where the facing will show: coats, shirts, rever collars and lapels. The facing is cut as part of the garment and folded back on to the wrong side. It usually ends at the shoulder seams and therefore encloses part of the collar in between the facing and garment. A separate facing or bias strip can be used to face the back neck or the edge of the collar on the inside of the garment can be turned under and hem-stitched down on to the seam line.

Pin the collar to the garment with right sides together and matching notches. The interfaced side of the collar should be at the top away from the garment. If the interfacing restricts the flexibility of the collar on the curves, clip the turnings at intervals. If a separate facing for the back neck is being used, stitch it to the front facings at the shoulder seams and press seams open (figure 2a).

Figure 2a

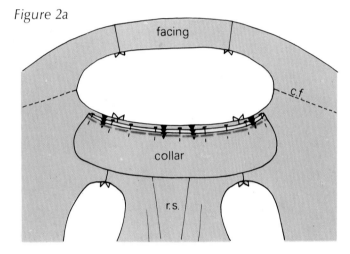

Pin the facing to the garment enclosing the collar in between. Tack and stitch then press the turnings open with the nose of the iron. Trim, and neaten the turnings. Machine stitch the turnings on to the facing to keep them flat. Stitch around the raw edge of the facing with a zig-zag stitch or make a small double turning and stitch down (figure 2b). Turn the facing on

Figure 2b

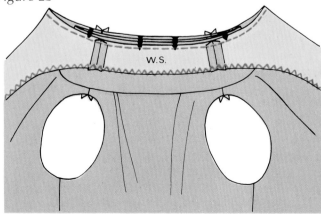

to the wrong side of the garment and catch-stitch on to shoulder seams (figure 2c).

Figure 2c

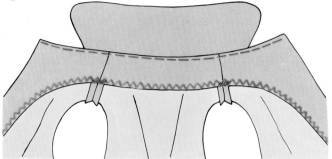

If a bias strip is being used on the back neck, it should be attached after the front facing. Turn the shoulder seams on the facing on to the wrong side and press (figure 3a). Trim and layer the turnings (figure 3b). Turn under the two ends of the facing at the shoulder seams and hem. Hem the bias on to the wrong side of the garment, but without letting the stitches show on the right side (figure 3c).

Figure 3a

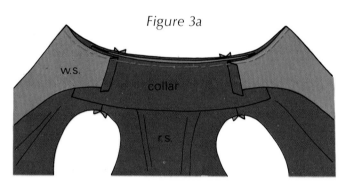

Figure 3b

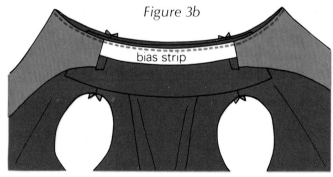

Figure 3c

2 Separate facing method This is usually used when there is no centre-front opening or when there are two collar pieces. Join the facing pieces at the shoulder seams. Neaten and press seams open (figure 4a). Place the collar so that the under side is facing the right side of the garment. Match all notches and shoulder seams and tack (figure 4b). In the same way, tack on the facing. Stitch through all four thicknesses. Layer and clip the turnings and neaten the raw edge of the facing (figure 4c). Stitch the turnings and facing together (figure 4d). On clothes that will be worn and washed often, it is advisable to stitch through the garment as well approximately 0.6cm ($\frac{1}{4}$ *inch*) from the seam line. This will help to keep the facing in place. As the stitching will show on the right side, it can be repeated as a design feature on another part of the garment (figure 4e).

Figure 4d

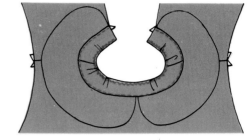

Figure 4e

Figure 4a

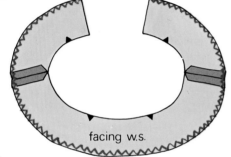

facing w.s.

Figure 4b

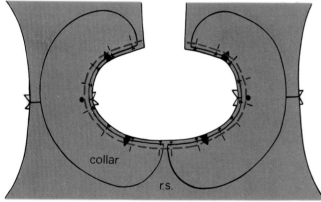

collar

r.s.

Figure 4c

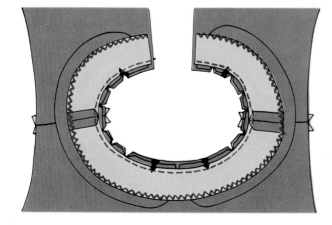

Bias may also be used as a facing worked in the same way as a bias strip on the back neck. If bought bias is used, it is advisable to trim the seam allowance on the neck to the same width as on the bias. This will make it easier to lay the fold line on the bias exactly on the seam line of the garment. Ensure that the bias is eased on so that the lower edge lies flat on the garment.

3 Self-neatening method
A self-neatening collar is attached to a garment without a facing. It is used on upright collars such as mandarin and shirt collars, also bias cut tie collars.
Tack interfacing to half the collar on the inside and with one edge to the fold line, fold the collar in half with right sides together and stitch the short ends. Trim and turn through (figure 5a). With right sides

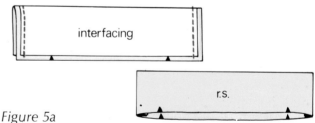

interfacing

r.s.

Figure 5a

together and matching notches tack and stitch one edge only to the garment. Trim and press turnings up on to collar (figure 5b). Turn under the remaining

Figure 5b

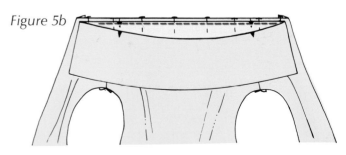

seam allowance on the other edge and slip-stitch to the first stitch line (figure 5c). A shirt collar with a stand can be attached to the garment in reverse with the collar stitched to the wrong side first, then the under-collar stitched to the outside (figure 5d).

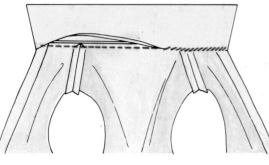

Figure 5c

Figure 5d

Self-neatening method using a zig-zag machine

On thick fabrics or jersey a zig-zag machine can be used to attach a small stand-up collar. The collar is made as in self-neatening collar, then pressed and placed to the garment on the right side with the raw edges together (figure 6a). Tack and stitch through all thicknesses (figure 6b). Trim and neaten the edges with a zig-zag machine and press to the wrong side (figure 6c).

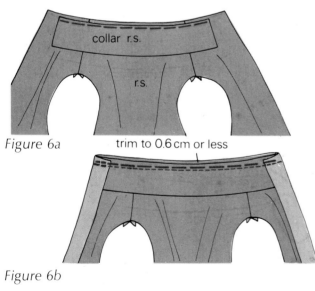

Figure 6a   trim to 0.6 cm or less

Figure 6b

Figure 6c

Tailored collar on heavy-weight fabrics

This method is used on coats and jackets made of very thick fabric. With right sides together and matching notches tack and stitch one collar piece to the facing and on to the garment. Press the seams open and clip (figure 7a). With right sides together and

Figure 7a

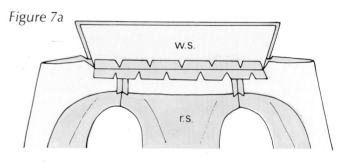

matching notches on the collar and revers and the two seam lines where the collars are attached, tack and stitch from one centre-front fold all around the collar to the other centre-front fold. Trim and layer the turnings, tapering at corners (figure 7b). Turn to

Figure 7b   clip

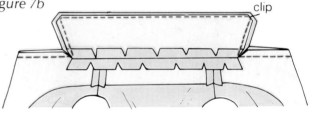

the right side and tack around the edge. Press on the wrong side and work a row of tacking along the seam line where the collars are attached (figure 7c). Turn

Figure 7c

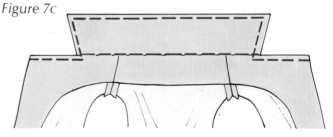

back the facing and tack the two raw edges together underneath. Neaten the raw edge of the facing and catch on to shoulder seams (figure 7d).

Figure 7d

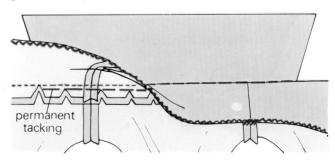

permanent
tacking

Ways with necklines

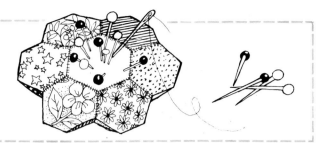

Necklines and detachable collars
Necklines

Whether a neckline is faced or has a collar attached the turnings must be clipped almost to the seam line at regular intervals so the neckline will lie flat. A safety bar worked on the wrong side at any weak point, such as the corner of a 'V' will strengthen the points (figures 1A, B, C, D, E).

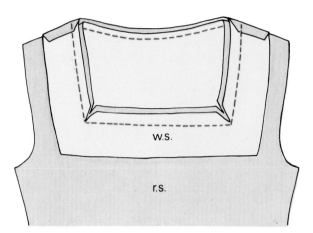

Figure 1C

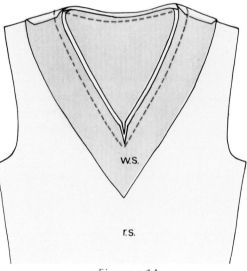

Figures 1A

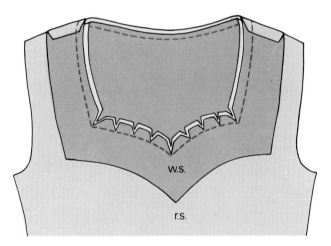

Figure 1D

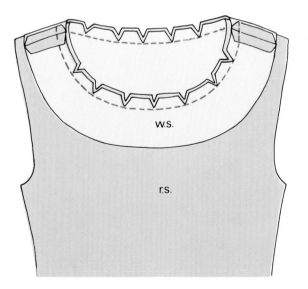

Figure 1B

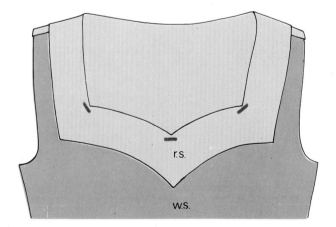

Figure 1E

High necklines are usually straight forward and easy to finish.

Low necklines because they are often cut across the grain of the fabric tend to stretch and gape so it is essential to fit the garment before completing a low neckline.

Before adjusting a low neckline, a row of stay stitching should be worked on the edge of the turning to prevent stretching while handling. It is advisable to use interfacing on some low necklines to strengthen them.

There are three ways in which a low neckline can be altered:

1 If the garment gapes only between the bust points the stay stitching can be pulled up slightly (figure 2). Measure the neck and alter the pattern for the facing accordingly on the fold line (figure 3). Place the new fold line on the fold of the fabric and cut out (figure 4).

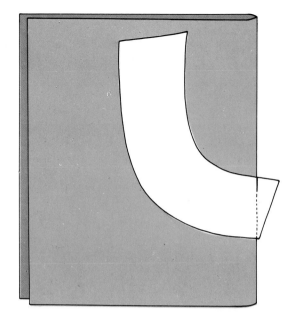

Figure 4

2 When the neckline folds slightly between the shoulder and bust, or if the shoulder seam is too high and loose, it must be altered. To do this work from the wrong side. Lift the seam at the neck edge, taking in equal amounts on the back and front. Taper the lift by meeting the original seam line at the armhole (figure 5).

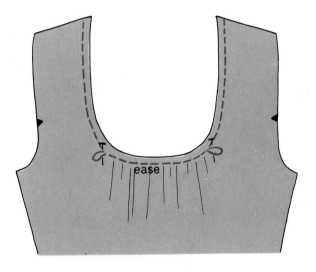

Figure 2

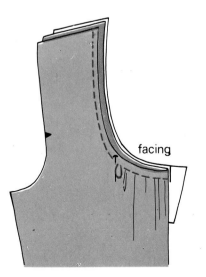

Figure 3

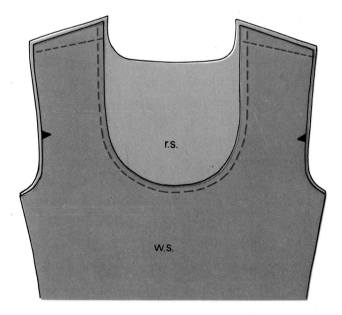

Figure 5

3 The shoulder seam will hang off the shoulder when the neckline is too big at the front. This can be rectified by moving the front shoulder further towards the armhole and cutting the back neckline to match. This will leave some front shoulder protruding at the armhole, which should be cut away between the shoulder seam and notch on the front armhole (figure 6).

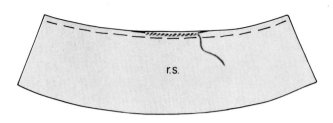

Figure 7B

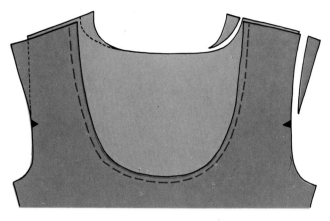

Figure 6

Detachable collars

If a collar is to be made in a fabric which is different from, and needs more frequent washing than, the fabric used for the rest of the garment it should be detachable. Also a detachable collar can be used as an extra design feature with corresponding detachable cuffs. There are two methods of making and attaching them:

1 Extended collar 2.5cm (*1 inch*) extra should be allowed on the neck edge of the collar when cutting. With right sides together and matching notches tack and stitch around the collar leaving approximately a 7.5cm (*3 inch*) gap in the middle of the neck edge. Trim, layer and taper the turnings (figure 7A). Turn the collar through, fold in the neck edge turnings on the seam line and slip-stitch together. Press on the wrong side (figure 7B).

2 Bias binding may be used as an alternative finish for the neck edge of a collar. It is especially good on lace collars as it strengthens the neck edge. Make up the collar in the usual way, leaving the neck edge completely open. Cut a strip of bias the length of the collar. Tack on to the upper collar along the neck edge. Turn in the ends and stitch on the seam line. Turn over on the seam line and hem-stitch the other side of the bias in place (figure 7C).

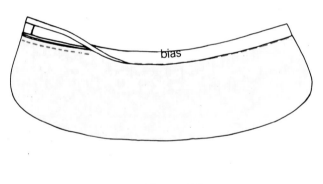

Figure 7C

The finished collar can be attached in several ways: by using press studs; Velcro; hooks and hand-made loops; or by sewing with a loose hemming stitch.

Attached neckline

This is a collar attached to a double layer of fabric about 7.5cm (*3 inches*) wide. The under layer slips inside the garment and can be fastened with a button. This method eliminates the need for studs or hooks.

Cut out and make up the collar leaving the neck edge open. Pin the back and front pattern pieces of the garment together at the shoulder seams. Pin any darts on the neckline before placing the pieces on the graph paper. Place flat on to graph paper. If the fastenings are to be at the centre-back, place the front fold on the straight grain line. Reverse this for a centre-front opening.

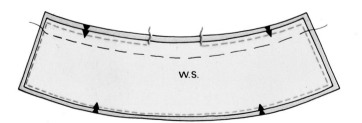

Figure 7A

Draw around the neckline marking all notches and shoulder seams. Extend each end by 3cm ($1\frac{1}{4}$ inches) (figure 8A). Remove the pattern and with the end of a ruler on the neckline, mark 7.5cm (3 inches) all the way round to make an outer edge. Write 'to fold' on the straight grain line edge (figure 8B).

Cut out the pattern and place on the fold of the fabric. Cut out two pieces.
Sandwich the collar in between the right sides of the inner collar. Tack and stitch along the neck edge through all the thicknesses and around the extensions of the inner collar for 7.5cm (3 inches) in from the shoulder seams (figure 8C).

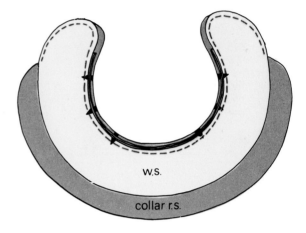

Figure 8C

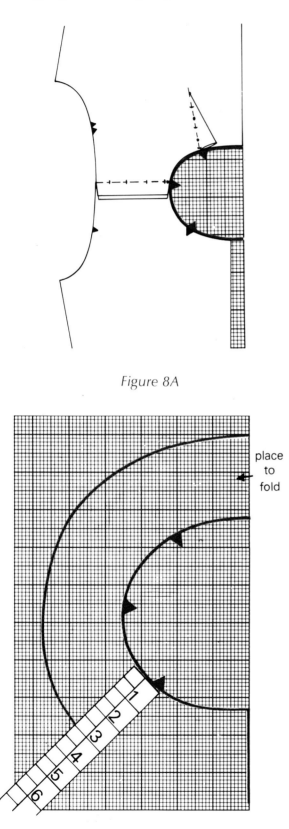

Figure 8A

Trim and clip the turnings and turn through on to the right side. Turn in the remaining edges and slip-stitch together.
Attach the fastenings on the inner collar extension so they face towards the opening and can be fastened before putting on the garment (figure 8D).

place
to
fold

Figure 8B

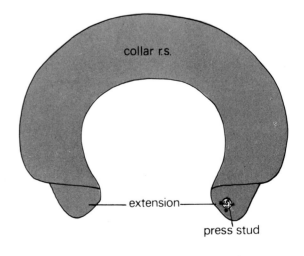

Figure 8D

Fun with flounces

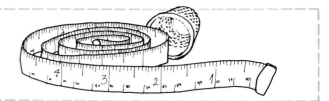

Flounced collars

To make a flounced collar it is first of all essential to choose a fabric that drapes easily and falls into graceful folds when made up. It is worth testing a small piece of fabric first to be sure that it will hang well. To do this, cut a quarter circle approximately 7.5cm (3 inches) in depth, then holding the corners A and B, gently pull out straight. A suitable fabric will fall easily into attractive folds (figure 1).

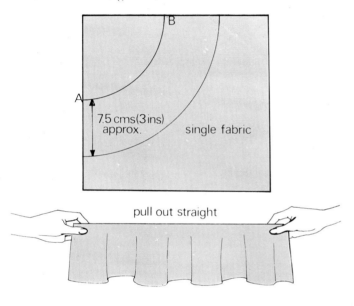

7.5 cms (3 ins) approx.

single fabric

pull out straight

Figure 1

Flat collar with draped front

Place the bodice pattern together at shoulder point B and overlap the shoulder points 2cm ($\frac{3}{4}$ inch). Draw the shape of the collar desired and mark A, B and C.

Draw lines where the folds are required D, E and F, notches and shoulder dot (figure 2). Trace off the collar

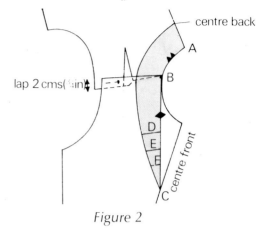

Figure 2

on to another piece of paper. Cut on lines D, E and F from the outside edge almost to the neckline. Open up so that D to D1, E to E1 and F to F1 are of equal measurement, approximately 2.5cm (1inch). Place on to another piece of paper and add turnings and markings (figure 3). If the collar is attached to the garment, front and

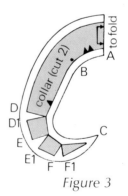

Figure 3

back facings will be required. Trace off the pattern following the shape of the neckline and draw the facings 4cm (1½ inches) wide. Add turnings, shoulder dot and notches (figure 4).

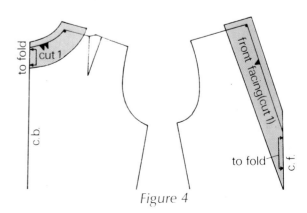

Figure 4

Making up

Fold the fabric in half and place the centre-back to the fold. Cut out the collar twice in the same fabric or the under collar in a very lightweight toning fabric. Using a lightweight, woven interfacing folded in half, cut out from the centre-back to line D. Tack interfacing to the wrong side of the top collar (*figure 5*). Trim off 0.3cm

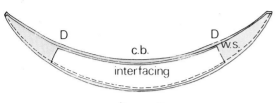

figure 5

($\frac{1}{8}$ *inch*) from the outside edge of the under collar. With right sides facing tack and stitch the collar pieces together round the outer edge. Trim and clip the turnings, turn to the right side, tack the edge and press. With notches and shoulder dots matching, tack the collar into position on the garment. With right sides together tack and stitch the shoulder seams of the facing and press open. With right sides together and matching notches tack and stitch the facing to the neckline. The collar will be sandwiched between (*figure 6*). Trim and clip the turnings and turn the facing

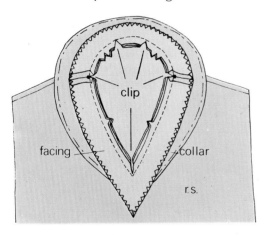

figure 6

to the inside of the garment. With the collar standing up, tack through all thicknesses to hold in position. A row of machine stitching may be worked on the garment close to the seam line to hold the collar permanently in place (*figure 7*). Press on the wrong

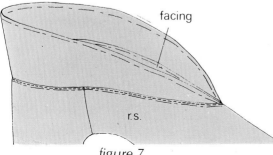

figure 7

side and catch the facing down to the shoulder seams.

Flared collar with stand-up back

Place the shoulders so that they touch at B and D.

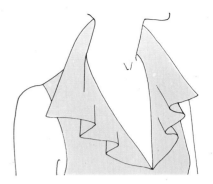

Draw in the shape of the collar and measure the back neckline. Mark in notches and shoulder dot (*figure 8*).

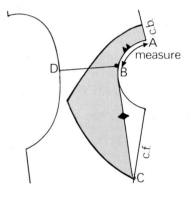

figure 8

Trace off on to another piece of paper and draw in lines E and F, equally spaced between the shoulder dot and centre-back (*figure 9*). Cut from E and F

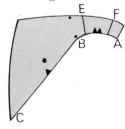

figure 9

almost to the neckline and lap over so that the outside edge measures the same as the neckline A to B (*figure 10*). The collar will then stand up at the back instead of

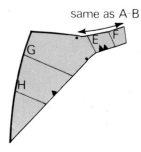

figure 10

laying flat over the garment. Draw in lines G and H and open as before. Add turnings and markings (*figure 11*).

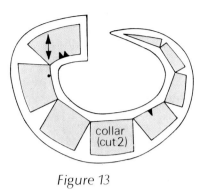

straight grain line running parallel with the centre-back. Add turnings and '(cut 2)' (*figure 13*).

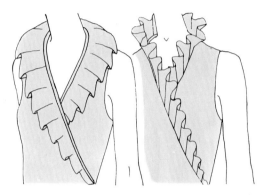

Figure 11

Making up

Work as before, taking interfacing only as far as line G, and attach with a facing.

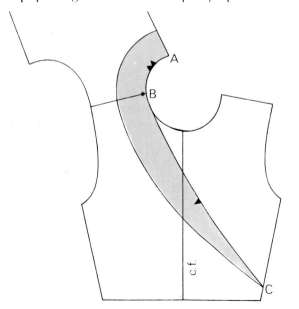

Cross-over flared collar

Draw in the shape of collar required, add shoulder dot and notches and trace off on to another piece of paper (*figure 12*). Draw equally spaced lines from

Figure 13

Making up

With right sides together tack and stitch the centre-back seam. Trim turnings, press to one side and neaten together. On the outer edge turn under a narrow hem to the wrong side and stitch close to the fold. To attach the collar, use one of the following methods.
a) With the wrong side of the collar to the right side of the garment and matching notches tack together at the neckline. Cut a strip of bias fabric the length of the neckline plus a small turning allowance at either end. Turn under and press the ends and with right sides together tack and stitch the strip to the neckline (*figure 14*). Trim the turnings to 0.6cm ($\frac{1}{4}$ *inch*), turn

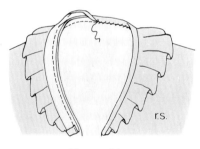

Figure 14

under the remaining raw edge and hem to the stitching line on the wrong side.
b) Join the centre-back of the flounce with a narrow French seam. Tack the collar to the neckline with right sides together. When the bias strip has been stitched on, turn to the wrong side of the garment and press. With the collar standing up tack through all thicknesses on the garment close to the seam line. Turn under the raw edge of the strip and hem to the garment (*figure 15*).

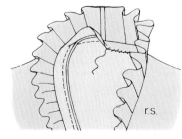

Figure 12

the outer edge to the neckline. Cut on the lines almost to the neckline and open up equally so that the pattern almost forms a circle. Add notches and a

Figure 15

All about sleeves

Setting in sleeves and making shoulder pads

To fit a sleeve perfectly it is essential to start with a good pattern and to cut out with absolute accuracy, making sure that the grain line is on the straight grain of the fabric. If the seam allowance is 1.6cm ($\frac{5}{8}$ *inch*), tack and stitch taking in this amount. You must be aware of all these points if you are to set in any sleeve successfully.

With all types of sleeves, it is essential to mark in dots and notches on both the garment and sleeve before removing the pattern pieces.

The garment should be tried on with the sleeves tacked in before they are stitched.

Check that the sleeves are in the correct position on the shoulder and that they hang straight and are comfortable under the arms.

The angle of the arm varies from person to person, so it is sometimes necessary to alter the pitch. This can be done by moving the underarm seam towards the front of the bodice and altering the notches accordingly. The maximum alteration is 2cm ($\frac{3}{4}$ *inch*). If shoulder pads are used, tack them in before fitting. If one arm is larger than the other, take smaller turnings on the upper sleeve.

Most sleeves have to be eased into the armhole. There are several methods of doing this: easing for a smooth head; gathering; pleating and darting.

Easing Run a gathering thread between dots on the head of the sleeve. Place the sleeve into the armhole with right sides together, tack and stitch easing fullness between the dots (figure 1).

Figure 1

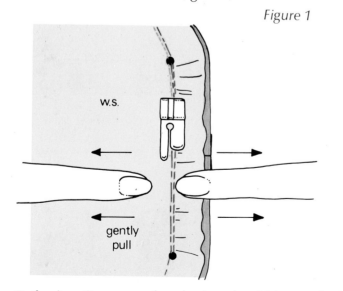

Gathering One row of gathering should be worked between the dots before inserting the sleeve into the armhole. Pull up the gathering thread and distribute the gathers evenly. Tack firmly and stitch with the sleeve and gathers uppermost on the machine (figure 2).

Figure 2

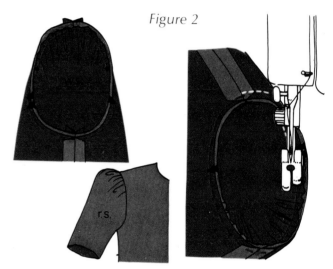

Pleating Pin and tack the sleeve into the armhole from the dot under the arm up to the other dot. Arrange the pleats, pin into place and tack. Machine stitch in the usual way (figure 3).

Darting Tack and stitch darts at the head of the sleeve where indicated on the pattern then tack and stitch into the armhole in the usual way (figure 4).

Figure 3

Figure 4

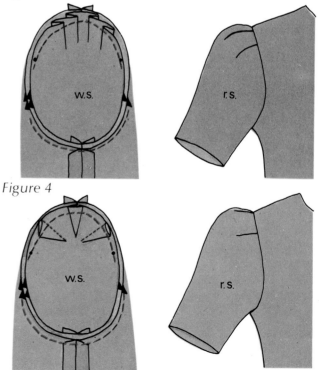

Tailored sleeve Run a single gathering thread around the head of the sleeve between the notches or dots. Place the sleeve to the garment with right sides together matching the notches and dots to the shoulder seam. Place pins vertically and pull up the gathering thread evenly either side of the centre shoulder seam. Wind the thread in a figure-of-eight around a pin to secure. Tack carefully from the sleeve side making sure no pleats or tucks form (figure 5A). Machine stitch into place over stitching under the arm for about 2.5cm (1 inch) either side of the seam to strengthen. Fasten off the ends securely and remove the gathering thread. Work another row of stitches 0.6cm ($\frac{1}{4}$ inch) outside the first row. Press the seam towards the sleeve using a sleeve board or pad, ensuring that no creases are formed at the top of the sleeve (figure 5B).

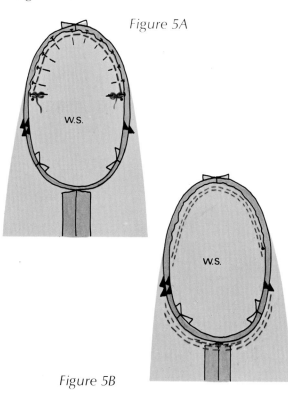

Figure 5A

Figure 5B

Trim the turnings to 1cm ($\frac{3}{8}$ inch) and neaten together with zig-zag stitch or by hand. If possible stretch the turning between the dots and underarm seam by pressing with a damp cloth. Clip and neaten if necessary.

Raglan sleeves A raglan sleeve is attached to the garment at the back and front with the seam running from the neckline to the underarm seam. Decorative seams can be worked before stitching the underarm and side seams.

A dart on the shoulder forms the shape. When fitting check that the dart is the correct length. If the neckline stands away from the neck, take more material into the dart. A dart that is too large will form a point on the shoulder. It must be let out and tapered more finely. Any alterations made at the neckline must be transferred on to the collar and facing.

Having joined the sleeve to the garment tack and stitch, with right sides together, the underarm seam and the sleeve seam. Curves should be clipped and the seams pressed open (figure 6).

Figure 6

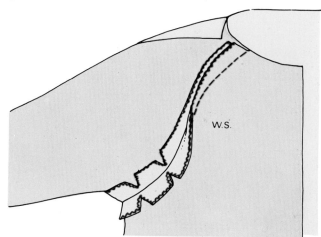

Dolman and Kimono sleeves These are cut in one with the bodice top and have a shoulder seam from neck edge to the bottom of the sleeve and an underarm seam continuing to the side seam. A diamond shaped piece of the same fabric can be inserted at the underarm for greater comfort and a closer fit.

When making a dolman or kimono sleeve without a diamond insert tack and stitch shoulder seam with right sides together matching the notches. Press seam open. The turnings may need to be clipped at the shoulder point to avoid a bump. Neaten around the clips and along the seam. With right sides together tack and stitch the underarm seam. Press open and clip in the same way.

Cut a strip of bias and stitch it loosely to the under-arm seam to strengthen. Neaten the edges together using a zig-zag machine or by hand (figure 7A).

When a diamond piece is required tack and stitch the shoulder seam in the same way as above. With right sides together tack and stitch the underarm seam from either end to within 1·6cm ($\frac{5}{8}$ inch) of the clip mark. Press and neaten the turnings and clip where marked (figure 7B). Working from the wrong

Figure 7A   *Figure 7B*

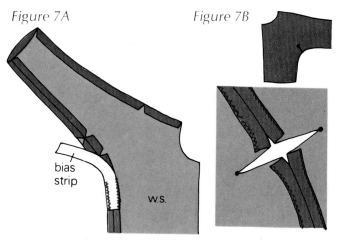

bias strip

side pin the diamond shaped piece into the space, catch at the corners then tack along the seam line on all sides. Stitch with a small stitch and zig-zag or neaten by hand. Should the fabric fray easily, reinforce the corners first with a small piece of fabric or stay-stitch with small stitches at the corners just inside the stitch line (figure 7C). Top-stitch to strengthen (figure 7D).

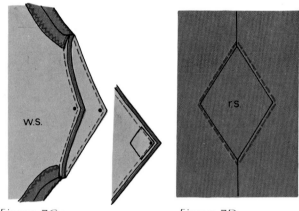

Figure 7C   Figure 7D

Dropped shoulders When the garment has a dropped shoulder line tack and stitch the shoulder seam with right sides together and matching the notches. Press open. With right sides together tack and stitch the side seam and the sleeve seam. Press open. Place the sleeve to the bodice matching the notches and dots. Tack and stitch the top between the dots. Clip to the dots, then tack and stitch around the lower part of the sleeve (figure 8A). Neaten and press the turnings up on to the shoulder and lower turnings on to the sleeve (figure 8B).

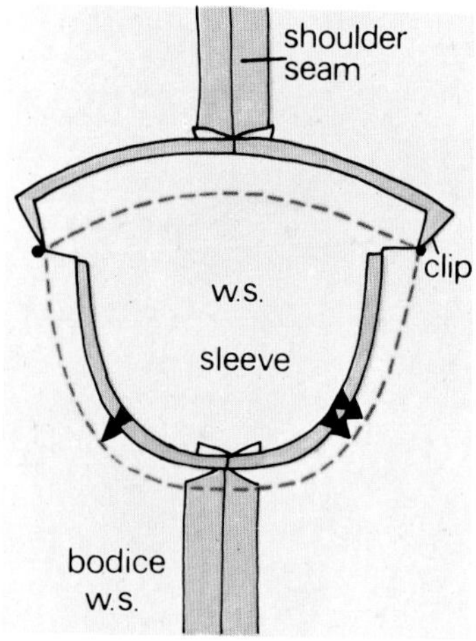

Figure 8A 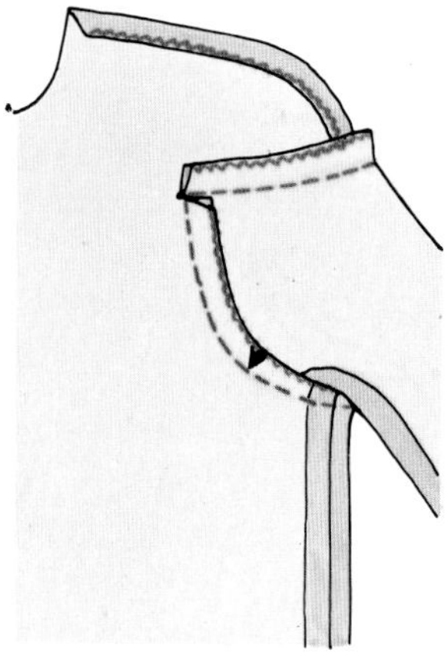   Figure 8B

Shoulder pads
Shoulder pads are very useful for giving extra height and shape to the shoulders. They can be made in different sizes and easily inserted into most types of armhole. They are often used for decorative reasons and can complete the whole shape of a garment such as a squarely cut coat.

Thin foam or wadding is used as padding and is available in most stores. It is advisable to use a synthetic padding on a washable garment as cotton padding is heavy and must be dry cleaned.

Shoulder pad for a tailored sleeve
Cut a diamond shaped piece of iron-on interfacing approximately 14cm–17.5cm (5½ inches–7 inches) across. Cut a piece of the garment fabric the same size and iron the interfacing on to the wrong side of it (figure 9).
Fold the diamond in half to make a triangle. Trim off 0·3cm (⅛ inch) from the edges on one half (figure 10). Cut a piece of thin foam or wadding the size of the triangle. Place this in between the two layers of fabric tapering the bulk of the wadding to nothing at the edges.
Tack and stitch the edges together. The smaller edge will be stretched and therefore make the pad curve slightly (figure 11).
Working from the underside of the pad, machine another row of stitching 0·6cm (¼ inch) in from the edges (figure 12).

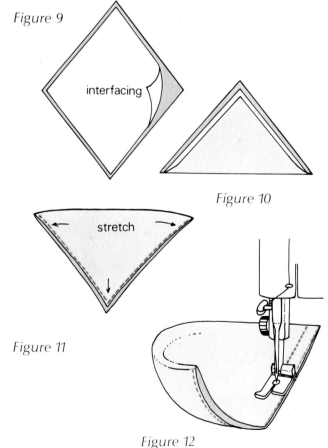

Figure 9

interfacing

Figure 10

stretch

Figure 11

Figure 12

Pad for a high gathered sleeve head
Cut out a piece of paper the length of the gathering on the sleeve head and approximately 4·5cm (1¾ inches) deep. Divide the length into four parts and draw lines at these points. Clip the lines almost to the other edge.

Place the paper on graph paper. Open each clip to approximately 1·3cm ($\frac{1}{2}$ *inch*) and pin to graph paper. Draw around the whole shape, curving at the ends. Cut out (figure 13).

Cut out four pieces of iron-on interfacing, and four pieces of the garment fabric, the same shape as the pads. Iron the interfacing on to the wrong side of the fabric.

With right sides together tack and stitch around the outer curved edge of the pad 0·6cm ($\frac{1}{4}$ *inch*) in from the edges (figure 14). Turn through to the right side and press. Stitch the raw edges together and neaten (figure 15). Fold the pad in half lengthways and mark the line.

With the curved edge facing out and the centre of the pad to the shoulder seams place the pad with the marked line on the edge of the sleeve turnings. Pin into place (figure 16).

Pad for a softer sleeve head

Cut out a piece of oval shaped fabric the length of the gathering and approximately 9cm ($3\frac{1}{2}$ *inches*) at the widest point. It should be cut on the cross.

Fold the fabric in half and pad as with the tailored sleeve pad. Stitch the edges together and neaten (figure 18).

Position the pad in the armhole in the same way as the high sleeve head. Tack and stitch, pushing the padding towards the outside curve so that the pad filling is not on the stitch line and turnings (figure 19).

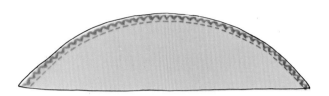

Figure 18

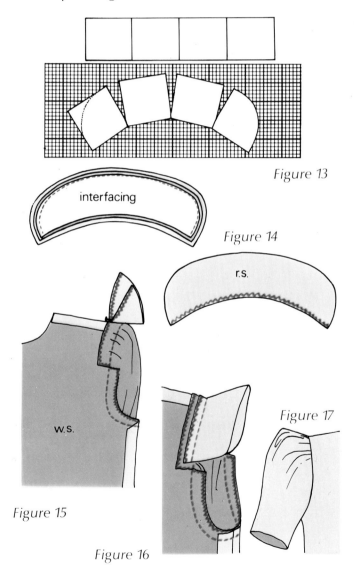

Figure 13

interfacing

Figure 14

r.s.

w.s.

Figure 17

Figure 15

w.s.

Figure 16

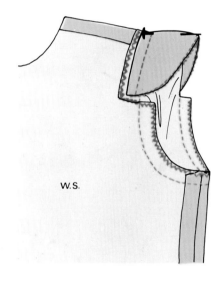

Figure 19

Pin the turnings and the edges of the pad together. Tack and stitch 0·6cm ($\frac{1}{4}$ *inch*) from the edges. The curved outside edge will automatically form an upward curve to hold the gathers away from the shoulder point (figure 17).

Pad for raglan, kimono or dropped shoulder sleeve

This pad consists of two parts. One part is made in the same way as the tailored sleeve pad, but not interfaced. The other part is made as for the softer sleeve head. Also the padding should be slightly thicker at the shoulder point and approximately 2cm ($\frac{3}{4}$ *inch*) deep. Cut an oval shaped piece of fabric on the cross the same length as the pad at the shoulder point and 11·5cm–14cm ($4\frac{1}{2}$ *inches*–$5\frac{1}{2}$ *inches*) wide. Fold in half and pad thinly. Stitch and neaten as with the tailored sleeve pad. Join the pads together on the curved edges with slip stitch making sure the ends meet.

Attaching the pad Try on the garment and mark the shoulder point. Place pad centrally with the join extending beyond the shoulder point by 1.3cm ($\frac{1}{2}$ *inch*). Use French tacks to hold the pad in place.

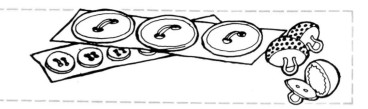

Stylish cuffs

Adjusting, making and attaching cuffs
Pattern pieces given for cuffs usually allow plenty of room for movement and comfort, but the wrist should be measured and alterations made to the pattern if necessary. If the width or shape of the lower sleeve edge is altered, the cuff should also be altered accordingly. Alterations should be made to the pattern before pinning to the fabric.

Adjusting cuff pattern
Plain cuff without wrapover This is usually cut on the straight grain and therefore does not stretch. It can be cut in two pieces, or in one piece with the top edge on the fold. The wrist should be measured at the top and bottom of the cuff (figure 1). As this cuff has no opening, it should be 2cm ($\frac{3}{4}$ inch) longer than the larger wrist measurement.

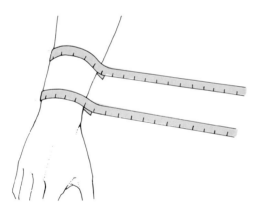

Figure 1

Wrapover cuff This is a cuff with an opening and extended wrapover (figure 2). It is fastened with press studs, buttons or hooks and bars. Usually any adjustment can be made by moving the fasteners, although sometimes it is necessary to alter the pattern.

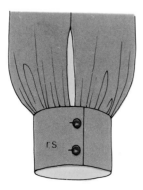

Figure 2

Cuff link style This cuff is also cut on the straight grain. If it is up to 6.5cm ($2\frac{1}{2}$ inches) deep allow 4cm ($1\frac{1}{2}$ inches) extra on the width for movement. A deeper cuff should be shaped and to do this cut a strip of graph paper to the depth and width of the cuff required. Fold the graph paper into four and mark the lines. Cut along lines open to within 0.3cm ($\frac{1}{8}$ inch) from one edge. Place the pattern on paper. Find the difference between the two measurements taken and open or close each slit to a third of this measurement (figures 3 and 4). Draw around the new shape. Remove graph paper and add seam allowances and wrapover to the new shape. Re-mark balance marks and where the wrapover joins the cuff. Cut out.

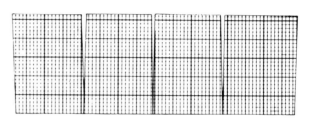

Figure 3

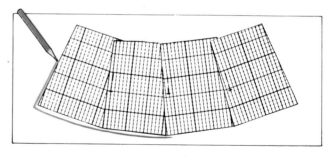

Figure 4

Altering sleeve length
If the depth of any type of cuff is altered the length of the sleeve must be altered accordingly. To measure the length, place a tape measure on the arm from the shoulder point, over the bent elbow, to the wrist (figure 5). Add the measurement of the sleeve and cuff together minus the turnings and compare with length of arm. On a gathered shirt sleeve, allow approximately 2–2.5cm ($\frac{3}{4}$–1 inch) extra. On very full sleeves allow approximately 5–7.5cm (2–3 inches) extra.

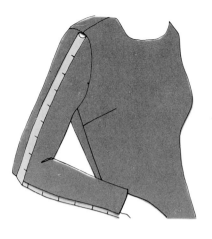

Figure 5

Shirred wristline The sleeve must be cut at least 7.5cm (*3 inches*) longer than the arm measurement to allow for drop in the sleeve and the wrist frill.

Cuff for tight sleeve The pattern for the cuff is usually shaped. Trace the pattern off including notches but excluding turnings. Adjust as with the plain or wrapover cuff. Add turnings and cut out (figure 6).

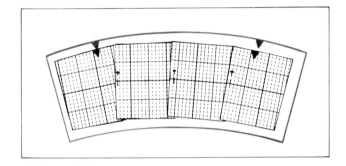

Figure 6

Cuff for short sleeve With the elbow bent measure the fullest part of the upper arm. Most short sleeve cuffs are cut on the straight grain at the lower edge. If the cuff is not wide enough adjust the lower sleeve edge accordingly (figure 7). On well-developed arms,

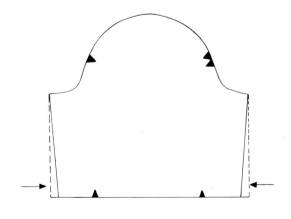

Figure 7

the straight seam line joining the sleeve and cuff can be uncomfortable and should be altered. To do this find the centre of the sleeve pattern widthways and mark a dot on this approximately 2.5cm (*1 inch*) above the lower edge. Draw and cut a curved line from the underarm seam to the dot (figure 8). Mark in balance marks.

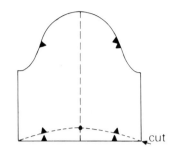

Figure 8

The cuff pattern must also be altered: fold the cuff into four lengthways and cut on the lines as with the cuff link style. With notches matching pin the lower edge of the cuff to the lower edge of the sleeve. The slits will open. Pin pieces of paper under slit, trimming off to the same shape as the cuff (figure 9). Transfer on to a piece of paper and draw around the whole new shape. Cut out.

Figure 9

Circular cuff This is cut in one piece and attached to a tight sleeve. If the lower edge of the sleeve is altered the inside circle must also be altered to the same measurement. Fold the cuff pattern in half.

To reduce – place a piece of paper under the curve. With a tape measure on its side so that it can easily bend, find half the new measurement of the sleeve and draw on the paper at an equal distance from the original edge.

To enlarge – draw a new line on the cuff pattern and check (figure 10).

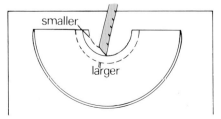

Figure 10

Making and attaching cuffs

One piece cuff Directions are usually given for an interfacing to be attached. One layer should be cut the width of the cuff. Tack or iron on to one half of the cuff on the wrong side. This side will be the upper side of the cuff. With right sides together fold the cuff in half lengthways. Tack and stitch across the ends and as far as the dot on the overwrap. Trim the turnings and taper at corners. Clip to dot (figure 11). Turn the

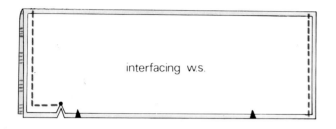

Figure 11

cuff to the right side and press. With right sides together and matching notches pin the interfaced half of the cuff to the sleeve. Pull up the gathering threads on the sleeve and distribute the gathers evenly. Tack and stitch (figure 12). Trim the turnings

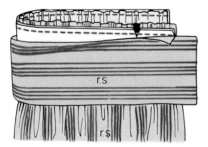

Figure 12

and press on to the cuff. Working from the wrong side make a turning on the raw edge of the cuff and hem-stitch down on to the stitch line (figure 13).
On some tailored sleeves the cuff is attached to the wrong side first and then top-stitched on the edge of the fold on the right side.

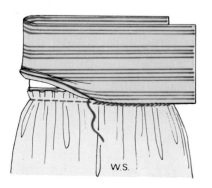

Figure 13

Two-piece cuff This is made in the same way as the one piece cuff except the outer edge has a seam also (figure 14). After stitching, turn the cuff to the right

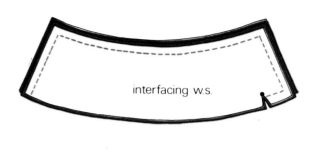

Figure 14

side and tack around the edges before pressing to hold the seam in place. Roll the seam to the inside and hem-stitch the raw edge down.
On some tight-fitting styles the cuff and sleeve are cut all in one, then the cuff is folded back on to the sleeve. Cut the interfacing 0.3cm ($\frac{1}{8}$ inch) narrower than the cuff to allow for the roll of the fabric. Fold back the cuff on the wrist line and press. Attach interfacing (figure 15). Fold the fabric over the interfacing

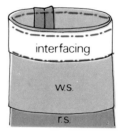

Figure 15

and on to the wrong side. Make a small turning on the raw edge and hem. Sometimes the cuff is worked before the underarm sleeve seam is joined. With right sides together and matching notches tack and stitch the seam ensuring that the cuff ends meet exactly (figure 16). Then turn the cuff back on to the wrong side and hem.

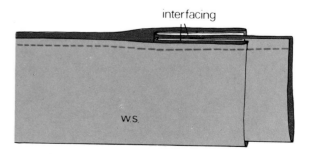

Figure 16

Shirred cuff This is more easily worked before joining the underarm seam. Neaten the wrist edge by making a small hem, zig-zag stitching or attaching trimmings. Work the first row of shirring approximately 1.6cm ($\frac{5}{8}$ inch) from the wrist edge and then work as many rows as required using the machine foot as a guide. With right sides together, matching notches and rows of shirring tack and stitch the underarm sleeve seam (figure 17). A French seam worked on the underarm seam is firmer and conceals the ends of the elastic.

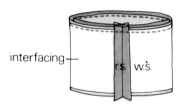

Figure 17

Two-piece and one-piece cuffs attached with bias
Two-piece cuff Join the two pieces of cuff at the side seams with interfacing included. Press the turnings open. With right sides together and seams matching join the two-piece cuff along the top edge (figure 18). Turn through.

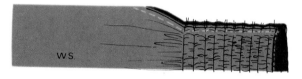

Figure 18

One-piece cuff Tack and stitch the seam. Press seam open. Fold the cuff in half with turnings on the inside and right side outside (figure 19).

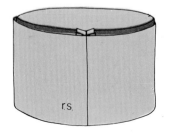

Figure 19

For both types of cuff pin cuff on to the right side of the sleeve with raw edges together and matching seams. Place the facing or bias on top of this with right sides together and stitch into place. Trim and layer the turnings (figure 20). Machine stitch the turnings together on the facing to hold flat (figure 21). Turn the facing to the wrong side by folding on the stitch line. Make a turning on the raw edge of the facing and hem-stitch down.

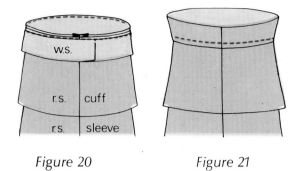

Figure 20   *Figure 21*

Circular cuffs Neaten the lower edge of the cuff with a small hem or with lace. With right sides together and matching notches tack and stitch the cuff on to the lower sleeve edge. The cuff may need stretching on to the sleeve, in which case it should be tacked on before attaching the facing. The facing can be used as a decorative feature worked on the right side (figure 22).

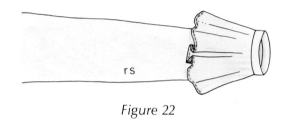

Figure 22

Pointed highwayman's cuff This can be worked in two ways:
A) With right sides together, tack and stitch the interfaced cuff around three edges. Trim and taper the turnings. Turn through and press. With right sides together pin the cuff on to the sleeve so that the two edges meet at the wrist line. Tack and stitch. Neaten the turnings and turn down the cuff. On the wrong side, slip-stitch the edges together as far as the dot. Turn cuff up on to the sleeve.
B) With right sides together tack and stitch the interfaced cuff along the top edge and to the dots on the sides (figure 23). Clip to the dots. Stitch the remaining short edges together on both sides to form a circle. Trim and taper all turnings and press open. Attach the cuff to the sleeve as for method A.
When using either method it is advisable to work a safety bar, i.e. a few back stitches worked over each other, where the cuff parts for extra strength.

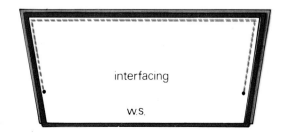

Figure 23

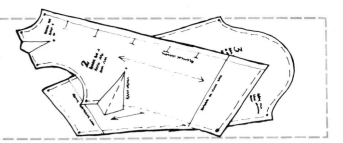

Sleeve openings

Sleeve openings

There are three basic methods of working an opening on a sleeve: slit opening; continuous placket opening and two-piece extension opening.

Slit opening

Cut a piece of matching fabric approximately the length of the opening plus 2cm ($\frac{3}{4}$ inch) by 5cm (2 inches). With right sides together, place the piece of fabric on to the garment over the line marking the opening. Work a line of machine stitching starting 0.6cm ($\frac{1}{4}$ inch) from the line at the lower edge and tapering almost to the point. Make a small U turn around the dot and stitch along the other side of the line, tapering as before (figure 1A). Cut on the line almost to the point of the stitching (figure 1B). Turn to the wrong side and tack the edges. Press the opening on the wrong side. Neaten the edges of the facing. For extra strength a safety bar may be worked at the end of the opening. A row of stitching may be worked on the very edge of the opening if required (figure 1C).

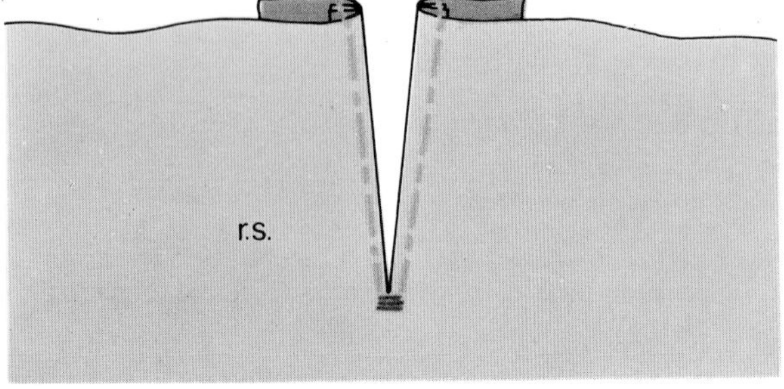

Continuous placket opening

Cut along the line to the dot (figure 2A). Cut a piece of matching fabric double the length of the opening and 3.8cm ($1\frac{1}{2}$ inches) wide. With right sides together, stitch the strip to the opening starting and finishing 0.6cm ($\frac{1}{4}$ inch) from the opening at the lower edge and tapering at the point of the opening (figure 2B). Press the turnings towards the strip. On the other edge of the strip turn in 0.6cm ($\frac{1}{4}$ inch) and hem-stitch to the stitch line (figure 2C). Work a safety bar at the point of the opening (figure 2D).

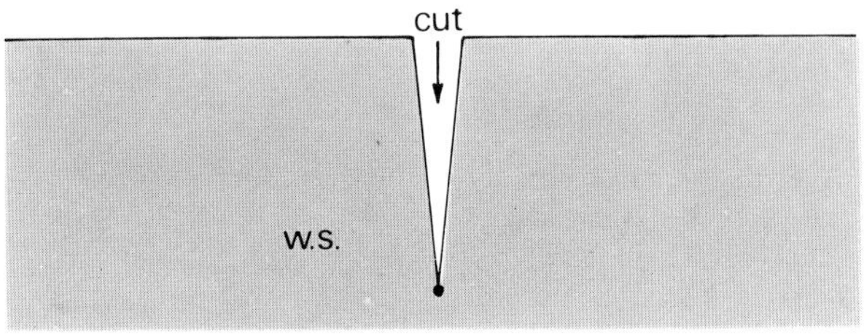

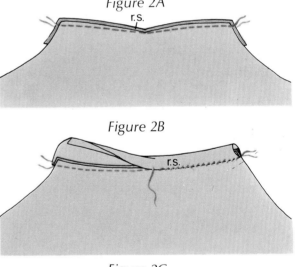

Figure 2A

Figure 2B

Figure 2C

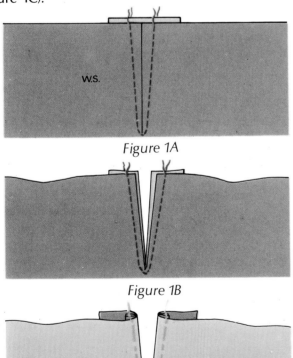

Figure 1A

Figure 1B

Figure 1C

With both of these methods the end of the sleeve is matched to the beginning of the cuff extension (figure 3).

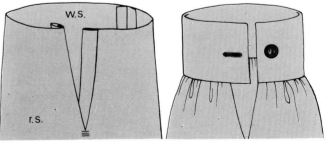

Figure 2D

Figure 3

Two piece extension opening

Cut along the line to within 0.6cm ($\frac{1}{4}$ inch) of the dot. Cut diagonally to 0.6cm ($\frac{1}{4}$ inch) either side of the dot (figure 4A). Press the triangle upwards on the right side (figure 4B).

Cut a strip of matching fabric the length of the opening to the point of the triangle and 3.8cm ($1\frac{1}{2}$ inches) wide. Cut another strip 6.8cm ($2\frac{1}{2}$ inches) wide and 1.3cm ($\frac{1}{2}$ inch) longer than the first piece.

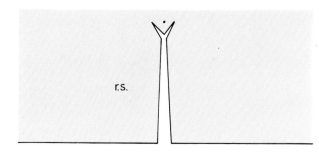

Figure 4A

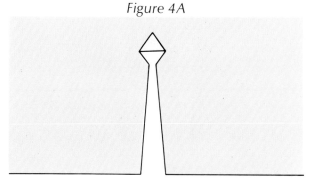

Figure 4B

Place the right side of the narrower strip to the wrong side of back sleeve and stitch 0.6cm ($\frac{1}{4}$ inch) from the edge (figure 4C). Press the turnings on to the strip. Fold in 0.6cm ($\frac{1}{4}$ inch) on the other edge of strip and stitch on the right side so that the fold just covers the first row of stitching (figure 4D).

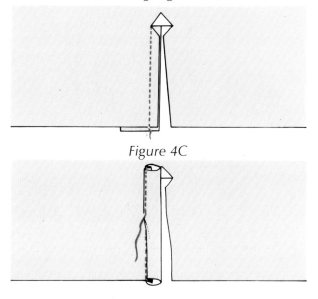

Figure 4C

Figure 4D

With right sides together stitch across one short end of the larger strip (figure 5A). With right side of strip to wrong side of front sleeve stitch 0.6cm ($\frac{1}{4}$ inch) from the edge. Press turnings towards strip (figure 5B).

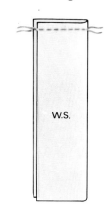

Figure 5A

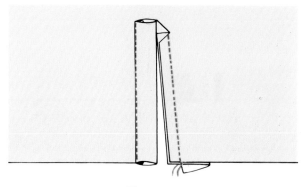

Figure 5B

Fold in 0.6cm ($\frac{1}{4}$ inch) on the other edge of the strip and stitch on the right side so that the fold covers the first row of stitching (figure 5C). The extra piece extending above the opening is stitched down on to the sleeve and a line of stitching worked across the strip to hold the triangle and extension in place (figure 5D). The top strip can be extended even further should a point be required. This is stitched on the wrong side first, then attached in the same way.

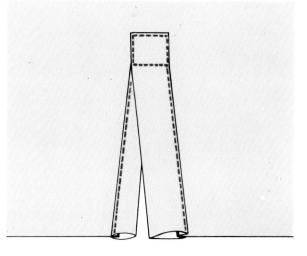

Figure 5C

The opening extension should match the end of the extension on the cuff.

Should a point be required on the cuff, this is drawn beyond the extension.

mark buttonholes in the centre of the folded cuff and 1cm–1.3cm ($\frac{3}{8}$ *inch*–$\frac{1}{2}$ *inch*) from the edge (figure 6C). On more than one button fastening, divide the width of the cuff into equal parts (figure 6D). With large buttons a longer extension will be required and the buttonholes must be further from the edge.

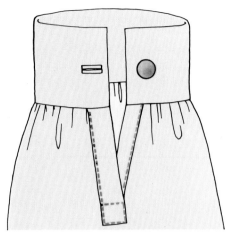

Figure 5D

French cuff

This cuff is cut in two pieces and is double the width required and the length of the wrist measurement plus 2.5cm (*1 inch*) at each end for extensions, plus turnings (figure 6A). When completed the cuff is folded back on itself and four buttonholes worked in corresponding positions so that the cuff link type of fastening may be used (figure 6B). Mark in all buttonholes on the cuff pattern. For one button fastening

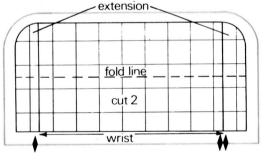

Figure 6A

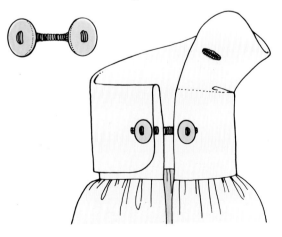

Figure 6B

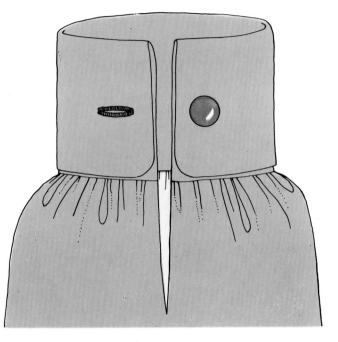

Figure 6C

Figure 6D

There will be further chapters on sleeve adaptations, including the shirt type sleeve with a gathered sleeve head.

Ways with waists

Waistbands

Waistbands are inserted into dresses and used at the top of skirts and trousers to give a finished look. As well as being very practical they can be a decorative feature when made in a contrasting fabric. The width of the band can correspond with the width of the cuffs or trouser turn-ups. Different fastenings can be used on waistbands depending on the type of opening on the garment.

Interfacing

Most waistbands have some form of interfacing. Where the waistband is in one piece with a fold, the interfacing is usually half the width and is tacked to the upper side of the waistband, on the wrong side. One edge is caught in the waist seam and the other is herring-boned on to the fold of the waistband. The stitches must not show on the right side. Iron-on interfacing can be used for light fabrics.

Straight waistband

This is the most common type of waistband, cut either on the straight or cross. It conceals all turnings and, like all waistbands, can be made longer than the waist to form an overlap at the opening. With right sides together and notches matching, tack and stitch the waistband to the waist edge (figure 1). Trim and layer

the turnings, press up on to the waistband. Fold the band with right sides together. Tack and stitch the ends together. Trim and layer the turnings, tapering them narrowly at the corners (figure 2). Turn to the

Figure 2

right side and push out the corners gently with the blunt end of a pencil. Make a 1.6cm ($\frac{5}{8}$ *inch*) turning on the raw edge of the band and slip-stitch this down on to the seam line on the inside of the garment (figure 3). The short ends of the waistband can be stitched together before it is attached to the garment in which case the exact length of the band must be decided on beforehand. The turnings on the overlap of the band should be slip-stitched together.

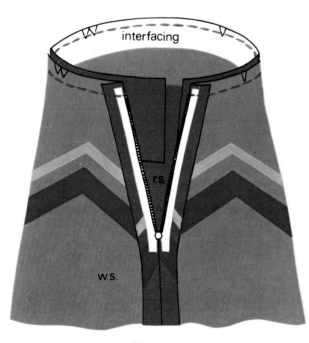

Figure 1

Figure 3

Waistband with visible turning

The method for making this waistband is almost the same as for the straight band. It is however very much more appropriate for thick fabrics as it avoids bulk. In the same way as above, tack and stitch the band to the waist (figure 4). Press the seams open. Clip the

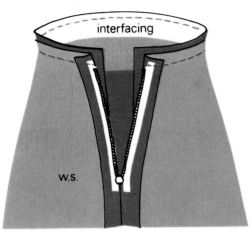

Figure 4

turnings as close as possible to the seam line on either side of the zip tape and at an angle away from it. With the right sides together tack and stitch the ends (figure 5). Trim ends and turn the band to the

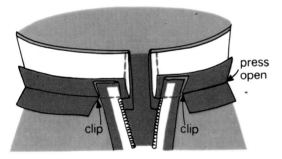

Figure 5

right side. Push out the corners gently. Turn in 1.6cm ($\frac{5}{8}$ *inch*) on the raw edge to just cover the zip tape. Clip to release the rest of the turning. With the skirt uppermost, and the band lying back on to the right side of the skirt, and using a zipper foot, stitch the raw edges together close to the first stitch line. Neaten with a zig-zag stitch or neaten by hand. Press on the wrong side with turnings down on to the garment (figure 6).

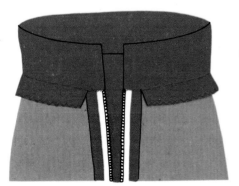

Figure 6

Shaped and curved waistbands

These waistbands are made with a seam on the top edge of the band. This seam should be stitched and pressed, then trimmed and clipped on curves. It is easier to stitch the ends together at this stage so that the corners can be successfully tapered (figure 7). Then turn to the right side and tack to hold in position (figure 8). Attach to the waist as before (figure 9).

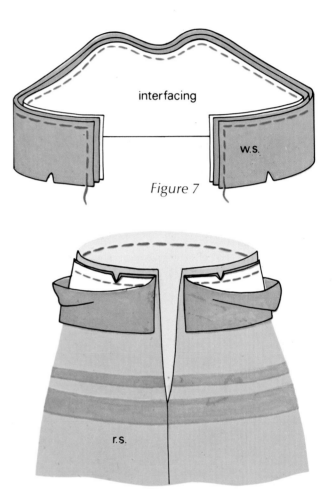

Figure 7

Figure 8

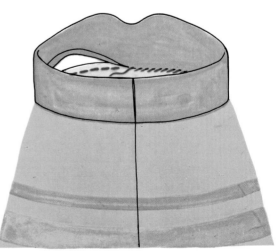

Figure 9

Faced waistband

This is a waistband that does not show on the right side, but is used as a facing to strengthen the waist area. With right sides together tack and stitch the side seam of the facing on the garment. Turn in 1.6cm ($\frac{5}{8}$ *inch*) at the top of the zip tape in the lapped side and slip-stitch together (figure 10). To release the rest of the

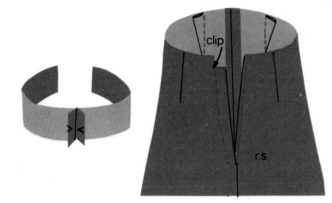

Figure 10

turning, it will be necessary to clip almost to the seam line on the outside of the zip tape. With right sides together and notches matching, tack and stitch the facing to the waist edge. Fold back the extension so that the right sides are facing and stitch across this as well (figure 11). Press and layer turnings. Taper the

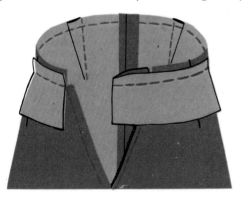

Figure 11

corner on the extension. Machine stitch the facing and turnings together close to the seam line (figure 12).

Figure 12

Turn the facing on to the wrong side and slip-stitch down at the lapped seam. Tack along the top of the waistband extension. Clip the raw edge of the facing if it is pulling and then neaten. Catch the facing on to the seams and attach fastenings on to the under side of the lapped seam, and the top of the extension (figure 13).

Figure 13

Elastic casing

For comfort and simplicity, elastic casings are very useful, especially on stretch and jersey fabrics. Decide on the width of the casing before cutting out the fabric and alter the pattern accordingly. Make a turning of 1.6cm ($\frac{5}{8}$ *inch*) on the raw edge and fold down on to the wrong side of the garment. Machine stitch close to the edge of the turning and on the folded edge. Open the seam on the wrong side of the casing, or cut a slit between the fold and turning (figure 14). If the opening is not on a seam, it should be

Figure 14

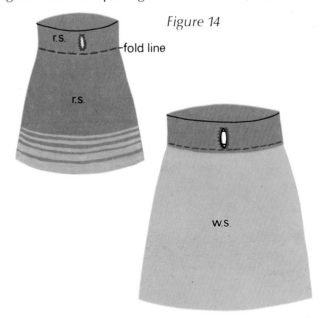

Figure 15

neatened with buttonhole stitch. Insert the elastic and oversew the ends together. Leave the slit open as elastic stretches and wears with washing and is then more accessible for alteration (figure 15).

Visible elastic

Join the two ends of the elastic and zig-zag the turnings. Divide the waistline of the garment into four equal parts and mark with pins. Work a gathering thread around the top on the seam line (figure 16).

Figure 16

Divide elastic into four equal parts. Place the edge of the elastic on the seam line on the right side of the garment. Pull the gathering up so that the waist fits on to the elastic. Zig-zag on the edge of the elastic on the right side. Work another row of zig-zag stitches 0.6cm ($\frac{1}{4}$ *inch*) above this to secure the turning to the elastic on the wrong side. Trim off the excess turning to the zig-zag line (figure 17).

Figure 17

Invisible elastic without a casing

Dart the elastic to fit the garment and attach to the waist as above. Turn in the elastic when completed and catch down on to any seam lines or darts in the garment (figure 18).

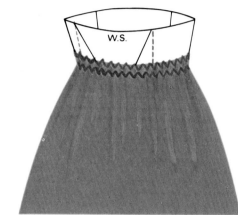

Figure 18

Petersham

Curved petersham is available at most big stores, usually in black and white. Place the concave curved edge on to the seam line. Tack and straight stitch very close to the edge. If the fabric is very thick, and the addition of petersham is going to make a bulky fold, a strip of bias in a thinner fabric may be used. Stitch the bias on to the petersham 0.6cm ($\frac{1}{4}$ *inch*) from the edge and stitch the other edge on to the seam line. Then turn the petersham to the wrong side and catch down on to seams and darts (figure 19).

Figure 19

Straight petersham If curved petersham is not available, it is possible to slightly curve a straight piece of petersham using a hot iron and damp cloth. Pull one edge of the petersham as it is pressed hard under a damp cloth. Do this down the entire length of the petersham and gradually, as it stretches it should form a smooth curve. Straight petersham is always available, often in different colours. It can be darted in the same way as elastic if it is necessary.

Ways with zips & plackets

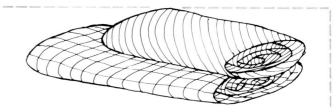

Zips and Plackets

Zips come in many sizes and types. The teeth of the zip can be made from metal, nylon or polyester and can be fixed to a cotton tape or a tape made from cotton/rayon, cotton/nylon or polyester. The type of zip you use depends on the garment for which it is to be used, and it is important to choose the correct zip for the garment, i.e. a zip on polyester or cotton/nylon tape for a garment in nylon or other synthetic, and a metal teeth zip for cotton – a nylon zip could be damaged if brought into contact with a hot iron as it could melt or fuse.

There are different weights of zips for different weight fabrics and the correct choice of weight is important, as a zip should last as long as the garment into which it is sewn. The table below indicates the weight of zip to use for different garments and fabrics, and you will usually find a guide on the zip packet.

Zip table

This table gives an indication of the weight of zip to use. In general the heavier your fabric, the heavier the zip you will need.

Type of zip	Used for	Fabric
Extra Light-weight	Lingerie, evening wear, blouses, light dresses.	Nylon, chiffon, silk, lawn, voile, satin, crepe de chine.
Light-weight	Skirts, trousers, dresses.	Woven and knitted cotton, woven and knitted fine wool, crepe, light-weight velvet.
Medium strength	Heavier trousers, children's wear.	Denim, jersey, light-weight cord, gaberdine, fine leather and suede, brocade, heavy velvet.
Heavy-weight	Jackets, coats, overalls, bags.	Heavy wools (velour), heavy cord, canvas, leather and suede.

Inserting a zip

The method of inserting a zip will vary, according to the type of garment for which it is being used. These are the main ways of attaching a zip:

Tucked seam zip

This is the simplest way of inserting a zip in a dress. Tack the garment on the seam line where zip is to be inserted and press seam open on wrong side. Tack zip on to turning so that the centre of the zip is on the seam line on the wrong side. Turn to right side and machine with zipper or cording foot attached 0.6cm ($\frac{1}{4}$ inch) from the seam line (figures 1 and 2). Remove tacking and press on the wrong side.

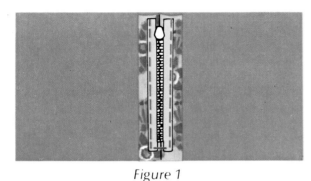

Figure 1

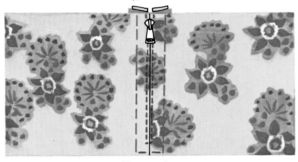

Figure 2

Lapped seam zip

For a more invisible zip tack the garment on seam line and press seam open on wrong side. Remove tacking, extend the back seam by 0.3cm ($\frac{1}{8}$ inch) from the fold line, tack this close to the teeth of the zip and machine as close to the edge of the teeth as possible but still leaving enough space for the zip to move freely (figure 3). Tack the lapped fold on to the other half of the zip with the fold touching the opposite fold. Machine with zipper foot about 0.6cm ($\frac{1}{4}$ inch) from fold (figure 4). Take threads through to the wrong side and fasten off securely. It is always advisable to work a safety bar in matching thread at the bottom when inserting zips. Make three back stitches where the two folds meet and work either blanket stitch or whipping stitch over these. Fasten off on the wrong side (figure 5). It is advisable, especially in a close fitting garment, to place a zip guard at the back of the zip to prevent damage to the zip and underclothes.

Note a zip guard is a piece of fabric the length of the zip tape plus 1.3cm ($\frac{1}{2}$ inch), and 5cm (2 inches) wide. Fold fabric in half lengthways with right sides facing and machine 0.6cm ($\frac{1}{4}$ inch) from each end. Turn to right side and press. This piece is machined on to the tape of the zip on the underneath half, right-hand side and zig-zagged or oversewn on the edges of the tape.

Stitch the bottom end of the guard to the seams of the garment, without the stitches coming through on to the right side (figure 6).

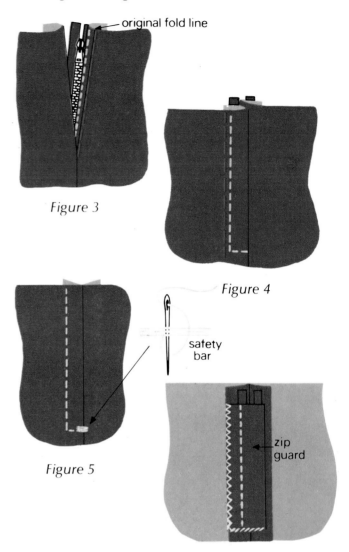

Figure 3

Figure 4

Figure 5

Figure 6

Curved seam zip

When a zip is being inserted on to a very curved seam you will need to clip the turning underneath before tacking close to the teeth. The top half of the opening is then faced with a bias strip to allow it to curve with the garment, then placed to the corresponding fold line on the underneath (figure 7).

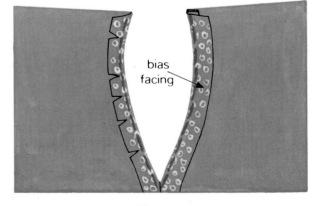

Figure 7

Decorative zip

If the zip is meant to be a fashion feature and intended to show, you should first mark the position of the zip, as you would mark out buttonholes (figure 8A). Carefully cut on the line to 1.3cm ($\frac{1}{2}$ inch) from each end (figure 8B). Measure the width of the teeth of the zip whilst it is closed. Mark this measurement at both ends of the line and equally either side, cut into each corner carefully (figure 8C). Turn in the same amount as this measurement on either side of the line. Tack and stitch close to the edge of the teeth with zipper foot. Edge stitching, braid or embroidery is usually worked just outside this row of machining (figure 8).

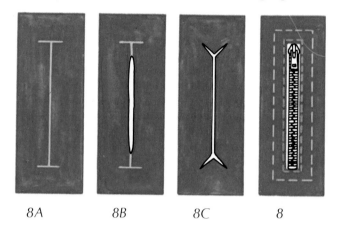

| 8A | 8B | 8C | 8 |

Invisible zip

These are tacked in a similar way to the tucked seam method, but with the teeth of the zip standing up and through single fabric only. Special plastic machine feet for machining this type of zip are usually available at stores and shops, or can be obtained from the manufacturer. It is however also quite easy to insert an invisible zip by hand.

Open end zip

This type of zip is used for jackets and coats. The zip is usually inserted in a tucked seam, but the turning is pressed down on the wrong side without tacking the seam together first. The folds are then placed to the edge of the teeth whilst the zip is open. The zip is fastened up to check that the folds meet exactly, unfastened and machined, usually 1cm–1.3cm ($\frac{3}{8}$ inch– $\frac{1}{2}$ inch) from the fold, depending on the size of the teeth. There is usually a heavy ring at the end of these zips and this must be moved away as the needle passes. It is safer for an inexperienced machinist inserting a zip to work the rows of stitching from the wrong side on the tucked seam both sides and on the lapped side of the lap seam. The teeth can then be seen clearly and this prevents broken needles.

Plackets

A placket is a concealed opening usually placed at the side of a garment. It can be fastened with buttons, studs or hooks. It is usual to face the opening with a continuous bias strip. Cut the bias strip twice as long as the slit opening, and about 2.5cm (1 inch) wide.

With right sides facing, place bias strip on to garment with edges together. Tack. Stitch 0.6cm ($\frac{1}{4}$ inch) from the edge, so that the stitches cover the dip in the centre (figure 9). Turn in 0.6cm ($\frac{1}{4}$ inch) on the other edge of bias and hem over the machine line (figure 10). If using a zig-zag machine, the bias strip may be folded in half wrong sides facing and pressed. The strip is then attached in the same way as before but 0.3cm ($\frac{1}{8}$ inch) from the edge, and then the edges neatly zig-zagged with a small stitch (figure 11).

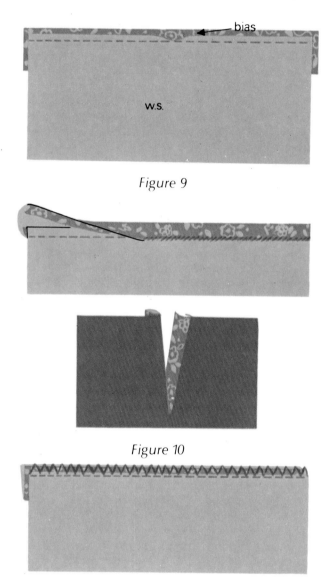

Figure 9

Figure 10

Figure 11

Faced opening

Take a piece of fabric the length of the slit opening plus 2.5cm (1 inch) by 5cm (2 inches) wide. Place the right side of this facing piece to the right side of the garment and work a line of stitches, starting 0.6cm ($\frac{1}{4}$ inch) from the slit at the raw edges, tapering to a point then working back to the raw edges 0.6cm ($\frac{1}{4}$ inch) from the other side of slit. It is advisable to make a small U turn rather than a V at the bottom point. This helps prevent fraying when the slit is cut (figure

12). Cut on line as near to the stitches as possible without cutting them, smooth out flat and press. A row of stitching may be worked on the very edge to add strength, if required. Trim the facing to 2cm ($\frac{3}{4}$ *inch*) from the opening, round off the corners and neaten edge of facing (figure 13). A safety bar can be worked at the bottom for extra strength.

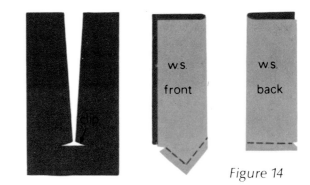

Figure 14

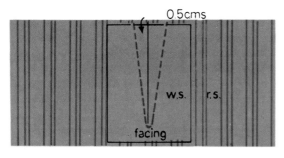

Figure 12

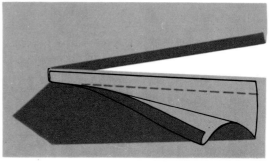

Figure 15

Extended decorative placket

This is the type of opening used on shirts and dress fronts, often worked in a contrasting fabric as a design feature. On shirts and blouses where there is no seam line, the garment is slashed or cut to the required length, then clipped to 0.6cm ($\frac{1}{4}$ *inch*). Stitch the two points on the additional placket together first (figure 14), trim and turn through then stitch one edge of placket to the wrong side of the garment to clip mark. Stitch 0.6cm ($\frac{1}{4}$ *inch*) from the edge (figure 15). Turn the placket extension on to the right side of garment and turn under a 0.6cm ($\frac{1}{4}$ *inch*) single hem and stitch on top of first machine stitched line. The under-placket is worked the same way and sewn down on the wrong side. A row of machining is then worked along the edge and around the point. For additional strength, especially on boy's shirts, a line of stitches is worked crosswise on the point. Sometimes on a dress front the placket is worked at the top of a seam (figure 16). The garment is slashed or cut to indicated dot, the placket prepared as before, stitched on (figure 17) then the seam line is joined and the point stitched down (figure 18). It is essential to strengthen the fabric at the end of all clip marks, usually by a safety bar worked on the wrong side.

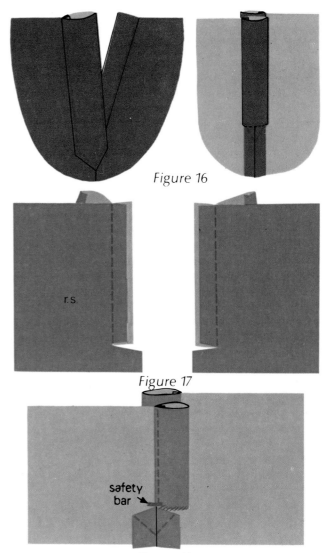

Figure 16

Figure 17

Figure 18

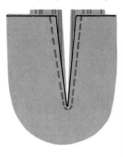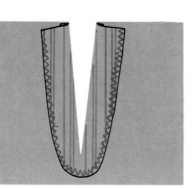

Figure 13

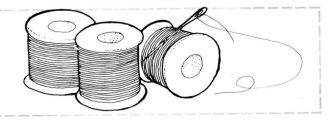

The useful bias

Working with bias strips
Cutting on the bias

When fabric is cut on the bias, it means that the cut edge is at an angle of 45 degrees from the selvedge. The easiest way to ensure that the fabric is cut on the true bias is to use a corner of the cloth formed by two straight grain edges; the selvedge may be used for one side, but if this has been cut off, a thread can be pulled out in each direction. Lay the fabric on to a flat surface, place one straight edge on to the other and pin together. The fold line formed will be the true bias of the fabric. Press to form a crease line (figure 1).

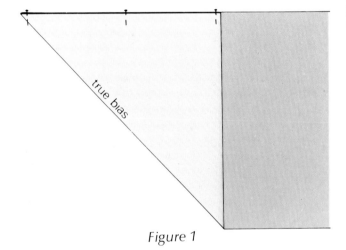

Figure 1

Binding and Piping

Binding is usually cut in strips approximately 2.5cm–3cm (*1 inch*–*1¼ inches*) wide. Mark out strips from crease line and cut on the lines (figure 2).

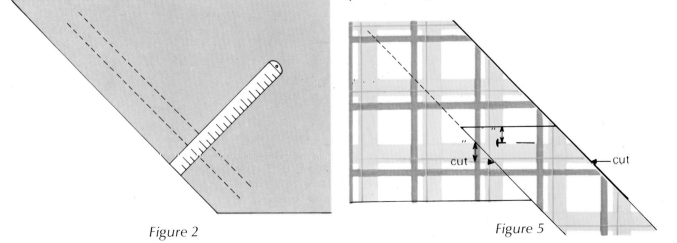

Figure 2

To join the bias strips pull a thread at each end and cut on the straight grain. Place strips on a flat surface with right sides up and angles matching (figure 3).

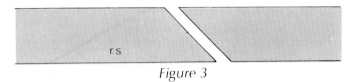

Figure 3

Place one strip on to the other with right sides facing and the edges cut on the straight grain together so that bias cut edges cross each other 0.6cm (¼ *inch*) from the pointed ends. Tack and stitch strips together 0.6cm (¼ *inch*) in from the edge (figure 4).

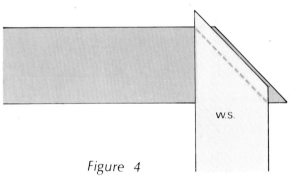

Figure 4

Press seam open and trim off points.
When joining stripes or checks the join must be made so that the pattern is not broken. Cut one strip first, straighten the end and note the pattern line 0.6cm (¼ *inch*) in from the edge. Place this on the uncut bias to check that stripes, etc., are running the same way and are on exactly the same pattern position as the piece already cut (figure 5). Pin on the line and cut the

Figure 5

101

other piece of bias 0.6cm (¼ inch) beyond this (figure 6).

Join so that when the seam line is stitched no break appears in the pattern or line (figure 7).

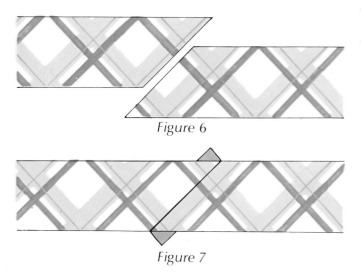
Figure 6

Figure 7

Collars

Roll collars are cut on the bias so that the folded edge, when turned back, will stretch out slightly over the neckline of the garment. If interfacing is required, a woven one must be used, and it must be cut on the same grain as the collar.

On most roll collars the fabric is cut the same length as the neckline plus turnings and 9cm–10cm (3½ inches–4 inches) wide plus turnings. It is advisable to cut a wider roll collar 2.5cm (1 inch) longer than the neckline. The collar is then eased on to the neckline and this prevents the fold from being too tight on the outer edge (figure 8).

Figure 8

Tie Belts

Cut fabric on the bias twice the finished width required plus turnings by the length required, again

plus turnings. For the tie or bow allow 23cm–68cm (9 inches–27 inches) extra, depending on the width of belt. The wider the belt, the longer the length of fabric required.

With right sides together fold the belt in half lengthways. Tack and stitch the short ends and the long edge leaving an opening to turn through. Trim, turn through, slip-stitch the opening and press (figure 9).

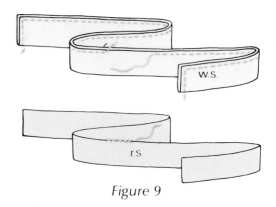
Figure 9

Bows

The wider the bow the longer the length required for tying. Normally the centre of the bow is slightly narrower than the ends. Cut the bias fabric double the widest finished width required plus turnings. Fold in half lengthways and pin edges together. Fold in half the other way and shape so that it is slightly narrower at the fold line (figure 10).

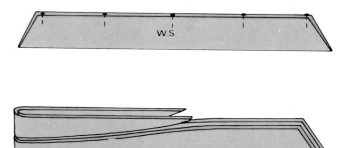
Figure 10

With right sides together stitch ends and long side leaving 5cm (2 inches) unstitched in the centre (figure 11). Trim turnings to 0.6cm (¼ inch) and cut off

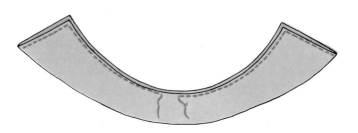
Figure 11

corners. Turn through to right side. Press seam line first, then towards the fold, pressing with the straight grain. Slip-stitch opening.

To tie bow, fold in half and mark centre with a pin. Make a loop either side of this (figure 12). Take right

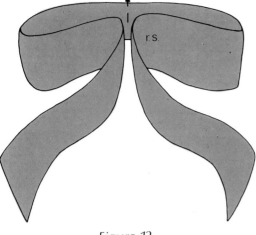

Figure 12

hand loop in right hand and left hand loop in left hand and bend loops forward. Take right hand loop over left hand loop and bring it out between loop and the pin marking central position (figure 13). Pull tightly until both loops are equal in size (figure 14).

This type of bow will lie flat without any unnecessary knots. It can be attached to the garment with three back stitches taken through the garment and the back of the bow.

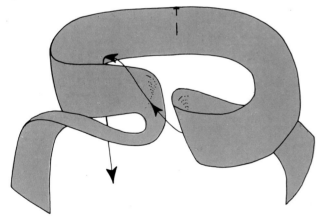

Figure 13

Figure 14

Frills

On some of the finer fabrics where a neatened edge does not look attractive a double frill cut on the bias may be used. This is cut double the finished width required plus turnings and about one and a half times the length of the fabric to which it is to be attached. With some fabrics this type of frill does not look attractive if made too full so it is advisable to test first for the best effect (figure 15).

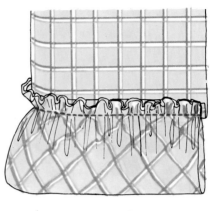

Figure 15

Ties

With most widths of fabric a man's styled tie will have to be cut in two pieces and joined. The wider piece should be cut on the bias for the full width to the length allowed by the fabric. Fold in half lengthways and taper one end. Matching the pattern at the narrow end, cut the other piece on the bias to this width (figure 16). Cut a facing for each pointed end of the tie.

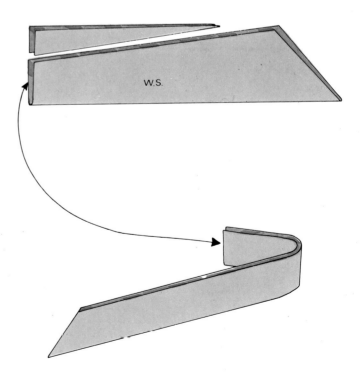

Figure 16

With right sides together stitch facings to each end. Trim turnings and cut off corners. Turn facings to wrong side and press on facing side. Do not put the iron on to the right side of the tie.

With right sides together fold tie in half lengthways and stitch on seam line (figure 17). Press seam open

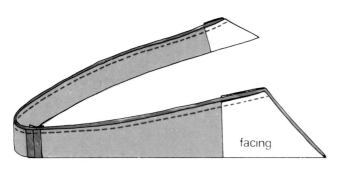

Figure 17

with seam line central. Cut interfacing the same shape as the wider end of the tie from the V at the end of the seam line to where the tie is to be tied. Tack interfacing either side of the seam line with permanent stitches (figure 18).

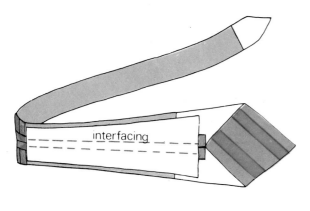

Figure 18

Turn tie out to right side. Working from the wrong side press so that the seam line is central. Do not press beyond the V at either end as marks may show through on the right side (figure 19).

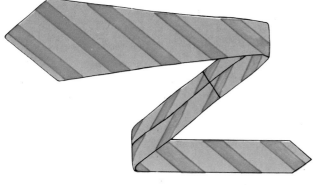

Figure 19

Cravat

This is cut from two pieces of bias fabric approximately 12.5cm–15cm (*5 inches–6 inches*) wide and 1.37 metres (*54 inches*) long. The ends of the cravat must be shaped so that the points are central.

With right sides together tack and stitch 0.6cm (*¼ inch*) from the edge leaving an opening in the centre of one long side (figure 20). Trim turnings and cut off corners. Turn cravat to right side and press. Slip-stitch the opening.

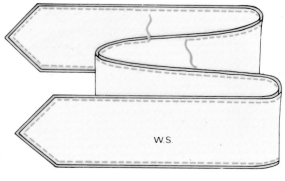

Figure 20

Fold cravat in half and mark centre with a pin. Measure 18cm (*7 inches*) from the fold and mark with pins either side. Open out flat and tack in two or three tucks between the pins until the width of the cravat is reduced by half. Press into place (figure 21).

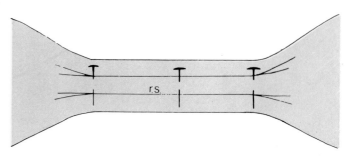

Figure 21

Work straight lines of machine stitching across the tucks at the pin marks, in the centre and half way between these lines of stitching at either side (figure 22).

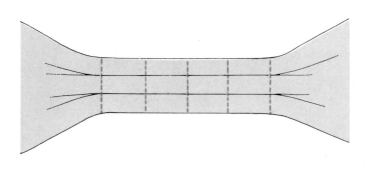

Figure 22

High fashion belts

Shaped belts and half belts

There are many interesting ways of varying the shape of a belt; the front and back can be shaped and fitted, or the front only can be shaped and ties taken to the back.

Using the bodice block adjusted to personal measurements, (details for making one are given on page 180), trace the area where the belt will be worn on the garment. Trace the front and back for a fully shaped belt or the front only for a partly shaped belt. Draw the belt to the shape required (*figure 1*). Cut out and

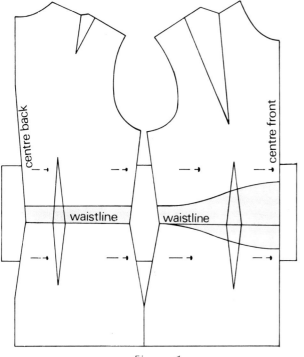

Figure 1

pin together at the side seam. Mark the pattern as shown (*figure 2*). Cut on the waistline from A almost to B and pin the back and front darts. Place on to another piece of paper with A1 touching the waistline.

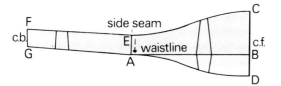

Figure 2

Draw a straight line through B and cut off the shaded parts. Draw in lines from A to G and from E to F and add extension beyond the centre-back. Redraw the front shape to give a smooth line (*figure 3*). Add turnings, mark 'Place to fold' on the centre-front, (Cut 2) plus 1 interfacing, the buttonhole and notches (*figure 4*).

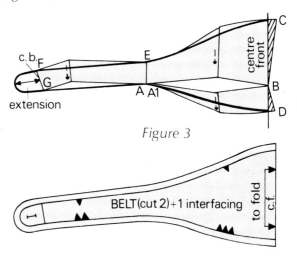

Figure 3

BELT (cut 2) + 1 interfacing

Figure 4

For a partly shaped belt make the pattern for the front only. For the back cut two crosswise strips of fabric the length required by twice A – E plus turnings (*figure 5*).

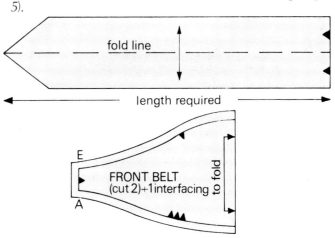

fold line

length required

FRONT BELT (cut 2) + 1 interfacing

Figure 5

Making up the fully shaped belt

Cut out and transfer notches. Attach interfacing to the wrong side of one piece. With right sides facing tack and stitch the two belt pieces together, leaving a small opening on one edge.
Trim turnings to 0.6cm ($\frac{1}{4}$ *inch*), clip almost to the stitching on all concave curves, pink on the convex curves and turn through to the right side.

Tack out the edge, slip-stitch the opening together and press on the wrong side. If desired the edge may be top-stitched, or embroidery or other decoration added. Work a buttonhole on one end of the belt and attach a button to the other end to correspond (figure 6).

With right sides and raw edges together tack and stitch the ties to the top belt. Turn under the seam allowance on the under-belt and hem into place. Press (figure 7).

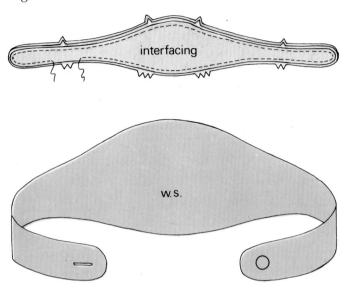

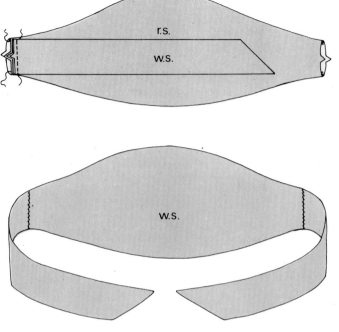

Figure 6

Partly shaped belt

Attach interfacing to the wrong side of one belt piece. With right sides facing tack and stitch the two front pieces together along the top and lower edges. Trim and clip the turnings, turn to the right side, tack the edges and press. With right sides together fold the crosswise strips in half lengthways. Tack and stitch the long edges and the shaped ends. Trim the turnings to 0.6cm ($\frac{1}{4}$ inch), turn to the right side, tack and press.

Figure 7

Wide corselet belt

Make the pattern as before (figure 8), then cut away 2.5cm (1 inch) on the centre-front and add turnings on

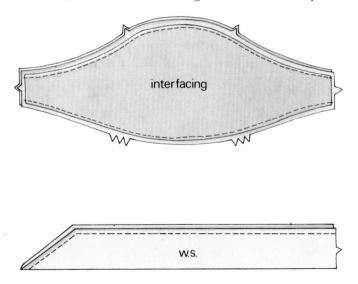

Figure 8

all edges. Mark in notches, (Cut 4) plus 2 interfacing and the straight grain line parallel with the centre-front (figure 9).

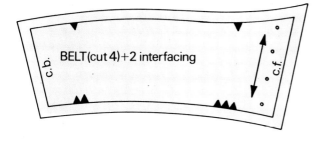

Figure 9

Making up

Tack or iron interfacing to the wrong sides of the top belt pieces. With the right sides together tack and stitch the belt to the facings, but leaving an opening to turn through. Trim and clip turnings and corners, turn to the right side, tack the edges and press. Attach eyelets approximately 1.3cm (½ inch) from the centre-front, spacing them evenly. On the wrong side sew hooks and eyes to the centre-back. Thread cord or ribbon through the eyelets (figure 10).

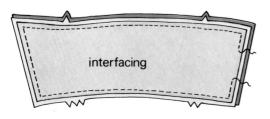

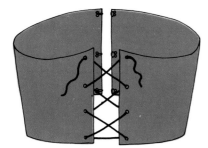

Figure 10

Hip or waist belt

Make the pattern as before. After pinning the darts re-draw to give a smooth line. When a buckle is required the extension must be at least 7.5cm (3 inches) long. Sew a buckle to the centre-front and trim off the excess fabric. On the shaped end place the first eyelet on the centre-front, spacing the others approximately 2cm (¾ inch) apart (figure 11).

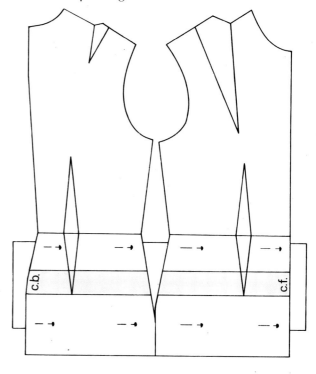

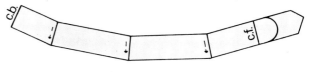

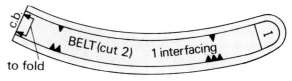

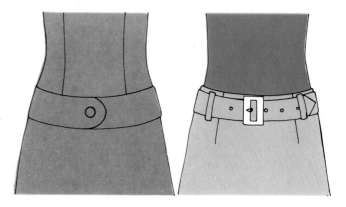

Figure 11

Half belts

These can be varied in shape and placed on the front or back of the garment. Draw the shape and position of the belt on the pattern (*figure 12*). Trace off and add turnings. For a loose belt held in position with buttons, cut out two pieces and one piece of interfacing.

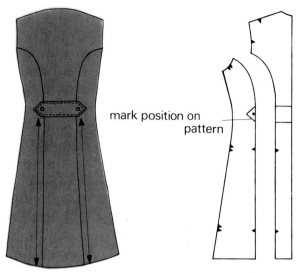

Figure 12

Attach interfacing to the wrong side of one piece. With right sides facing tack and stitch the two belt pieces together, leaving an opening for turning through. Turn to the right side, tack out the edge and press. Slip-stitch the opening together. Top-stitch the edge if desired. Position the belt on the garment and sew the buttons through all thicknesses (*figure 13*).

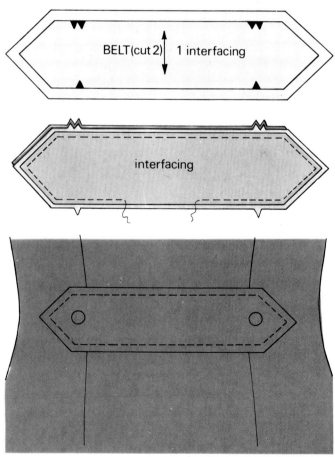

Figure 13

Attached single belt

On thick, bulky fabrics it is often advisable to stitch the belt on to the garment to avoid weight and strain on the buttons. Cut out one piece of fabric with turnings for the belt and one piece of interfacing without turnings. Tack or iron the interfacing to the wrong side of the belt. Fold the turnings of the belt to the wrong side and slip-hem to the interfacing.
Fold over the point of the belt so that it touches the interfacing and trim off 0.6cm ($\frac{1}{4}$ *inch*) from the fold. Fold the turnings over the interfacing and slip-stitch the two edges together at the point. Press (*figure 14*).

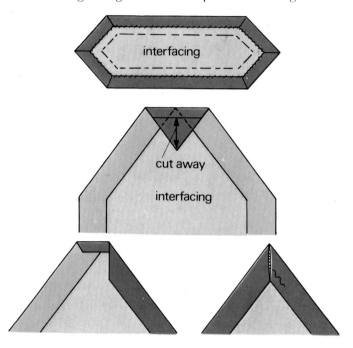

Figure 14

Position the belt on the garment and work a row of top stitching 0.6cm ($\frac{1}{4}$ *inch*) from the edges, taking the stitching through the belt and garment. Press on the wrong side. Sew on the buttons through all thicknesses. If the belt has curved ends work a row of oversewing on the edge of the curve and pull up to shape. On very thick fabrics, pink the edges before oversewing (*figure 15*).

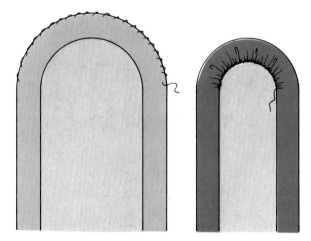

Figure 15

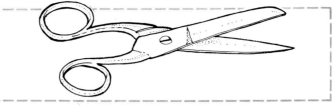

Loops, tabs & cummerbunds

Belt carriers
Straight belt carrier
Cut a strip of straight grain fabric approximately 3cms ($1\frac{1}{4}$ inches) wide by the width of the belt plus approximately 4cms ($1\frac{1}{2}$ inches). On the long edges fold 0.6cm ($\frac{1}{4}$ inch) to the wrong side and press. Place the folds together and stitch close to the edge through all thicknesses. Work another row of stitching close to the other edge. Fold under 0.6cm ($\frac{1}{4}$ inch) at each end of the carrier and place in position on the garment. Work a row of stitching close to the fold at each end and another row 0.6cm ($\frac{1}{4}$ inch) inside (figure 1).

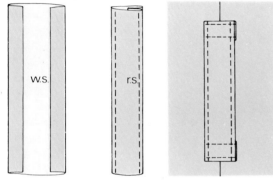

figure 1

Tab buttoned belt carrier
Place the belt on to a piece of paper and draw either side of it. Draw the shape of the tab required, add turnings and mark (Cut 2) and one interfacing for each carrier required.

Making up
Place interfacing to the wrong side of a tab piece. With right sides together tack and stitch the tab to the tab facing on the side and shaped edges. Trim and clip the turnings and corners, turn to the right side, tack the edges and press. Work a row of top stitching 0.6cm ($\frac{1}{4}$ inch) from the edge. Turn under the raw edges 0.6cm ($\frac{1}{4}$ inch) and press. Position the belt carrier on the garment and stitch the top twice through all thicknesses. Sew on the button through tab and garment, making sure that there is sufficient space for the belt to move freely (figure 2).

Rouleau loop
Cut a strip of bias fabric approximately 3cms ($1\frac{1}{4}$ inches) wide. Fold in half lengthways with right sides together and stitch 0.6cm ($\frac{1}{4}$ inch) from the raw edges. Turn through to the right side and press. Measure round the belt and cut two pieces of rouleau this length plus twice the seam allowance on the garment. Fold the loops in half and place to the right side of the garment at the waistline and with the raw edges together sandwich the loop between the back and front. Place the other piece of garment on top, with right sides together, and stitch through all thicknesses (figure 3).

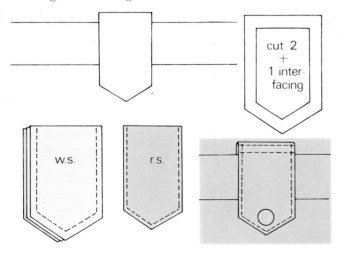

figure 2

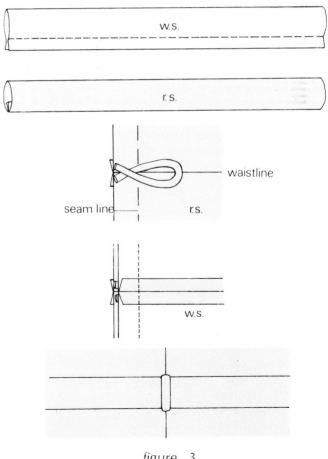

figure 3

Pleated cummerbund

A cummerbund is usually made between 7.5 – 10cms (3 – 4 inches) wide. Woven interfacing should be used and the fabric and interfacing cut on the cross. With lightweight interfacing two thicknesses may be required.

Cut a crosswise strip of fabric the width of the cummerbund required plus turnings, and either 2.5 or 5cms (1 or 2 inches) for every pleat, by the waist measurement plus approximately 10cms (4 inches). Make three pleats for a 10cm (4 inch) or two pleats for a 7.5cm (3 inch) cummerbund. On a heavy fabric 2.5cm (1 inch) pleats are sufficient (figure 4).

Making up

Mark out the pleats with rows of tacking or tailors tacks. Fold into position and tack close to the folds through all thicknesses (figure 5). Press on the wrong

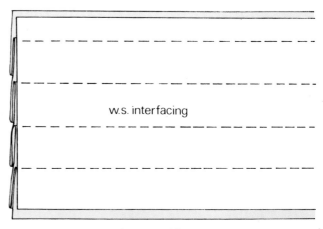

figure 5

side. Place the wrong side of the cummerbund to the right side of the interfacing. Starting at the lower edge stitch the underneath fold of each pleat to the interfacing to hold in position (figure 6A and 6B). Turn under

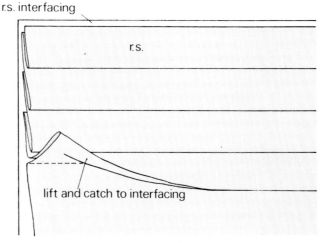

r.s. interfacing

r.s.

lift and catch to interfacing

figure 6A

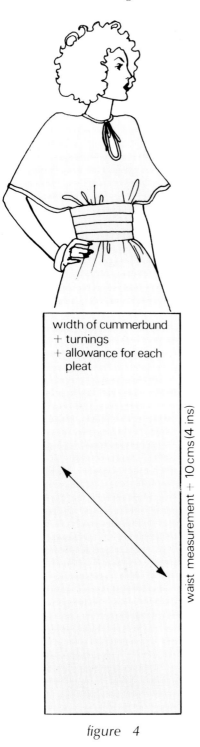

width of cummerbund
+ turnings
+ allowance for each
  pleat

waist measurement + 10 cms (4 ins)

figure 4

w.s. interfacing

figure 6B

the seam allowance at the top and lower edges and hem into position on the wrong side, taking the stitches through the interfacing only (*figure 7*). With the pleats laying downwards try on the cummerbund. By gently pulling the top edge the band can be curved slightly

figure 7

for a neater fit. Mark the centre-back opening, and press lightly on the wrong side keeping the curved shape. Fold the centre-back turnings to the wrong side and hem into position on the interfacing, mitring the corners. Sew on hooks and eyes (*figure 8*). With the

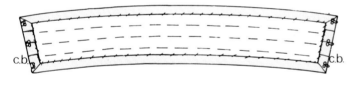

figure 8

straight grain to the centre-front cut a strip of toning or matching fabric to the shape of the cummerbund plus turnings. With wrong sides together turn under the seam allowance of the facing and slip-hem into place (*figure 9*).

figure 9

Gathered cummerbund

Cut a crosswise strip at least one and a half times the width required (on lightweight fabrics it can be twice the width), plus seam allowance by the waist measurement plus approximately 10cms (4 inches). Work rows of gathering stitches each side of the centre-back and centre-front. Additional rows of gathering may be worked at the side.

With wrong sides together place the gathered strip on to a piece of interfacing cut to the required width of the cummerbund. Pin both ends of the gathering rows, with the turnings laying beyond the interfacing. Pull up the gathers until the strip is the same size as the interfacing and work a row of stitching between each pair of gathered lines through both thicknesses. Remove the gathering threads and complete as for the pleated cummerbund (*figure 10*).

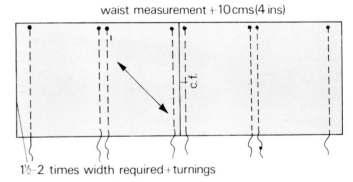

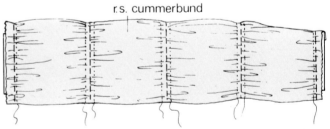

figure 10

How to make fastenings

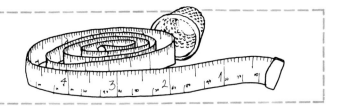

Fastenings

Metal Press studs These are usually silver or black, in various sizes, and are used at the top of an opening. The studs are in two parts, convex and concave. The convex part is always attached to the top fold of the opening on the wrong side, as near to the edge as possible and invisible from the right side. The stud is sewn on with buttonhole stitch, about four stitches to each hole, and the thread taken just beneath the fabric into the next hole. The stitches must not show on the right side. Fasten off with three back stitches worked round a group of buttonhole stitches. The convex part is attached first, then the concave part of the stud placed in the correct position by either of two methods: a) by pushing a pin through both parts of the stud to obtain the correct position on the other edge of the garment, then marking, b) by pressing the two parts of the stud together and rubbing the concave half with tailor's chalk and pressing on to the garment in the correct position. Sew on with buttonhole stitch in the same way as for convex part, this time letting the stitches go through the fabric, fasten off on the wrong side with three back stitches.

Nylon press studs are in one size only and are used for baby clothes or fine fabrics. They are attached in the same way as metal press studs.

Hooks and eyes These are in silver and black. They are usually sewn a short distance from the actual opening, and are mostly used for extra strength on waistbands. They are sewn on with buttonhole stitch, four stitches to each hole, the hook pointing towards the opening with the flat side to the fabric. After working the buttonhole stitches, the needle is then slipped just beneath the fabric and three back stitches worked under the tip of the hook.

The eye should also be facing the opening and after buttonhole stitches have been worked in the holes, three back stitches should be worked just above the hole on each side to help keep the eye flat.

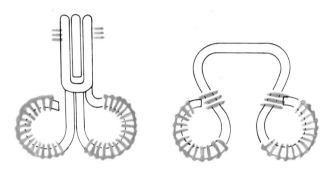

Hooks and bars These are usually attached very near the edge of the fabric using buttonhole stitch in the holes. Sometimes the bar is also covered in a thread which matches the fabric in buttonhole stitch, so that it is practically invisible.

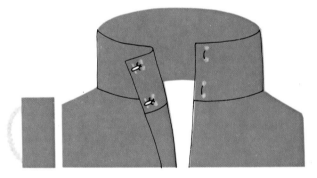

Velcro This is a strip either 1.6cm ($\frac{5}{8}$ inch) or 2.25cm ($\frac{7}{8}$ inch) wide, and is available in various colours. It consists of a strip of small nylon hooks and another strip of soft piled nylon. The hooked side is always placed on the underwrap with the hooks facing outwards. The piled side is placed on the overlap with the pile facing inwards.

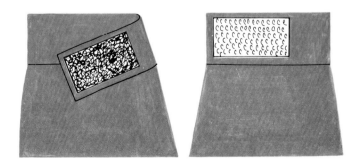

Buttons These should be selected with care as they can add an individual look to a very simple garment. The size and the thickness of the buttons must be suitable for the garment. For example, heavy rough-faced ones should not be attached to a fine fabric as they will pull holes in the fabric and tear threads. Most cards of buttons have instructions stating whether or not it is safe to use an iron near them, as they may have a synthetic content like nylon. Most large stores have various types and sizes of button moulds, to which you can attach your own fabrics. Some stores have a button covering service where two coloured fabrics can be used together. However if the garment is a light coloured one, it is advisable to wash the two fabrics first to test for colour permanency. It is advisable to buy one or two extra buttons in case of loss or breakage. When sewing on the buttons, use a suitable thread for the fabric and work at least four stitches through the same place on the fabric. If using a button without a shank insert a pin or match-stick between the button and the fabric and work the stitches over it. Then wind the thread several times around the stitches between the button and fabric. Take the thread to the wrong side and work about four blanket stitches over the original stitches and fasten off with three very small back stitches.

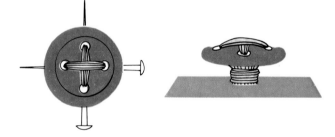

Button fasteners These are becoming available in most large stores and can be attached in the same way as press studs. This avoids making buttonholes.

Gripper snap fasteners These consist of a stud, socket and two sets of prongs and can be attached to most garments very quickly with the aid of a hammer and cotton reel or a special gun that can be purchased separately. The hammer and reel method is often easier to manipulate.

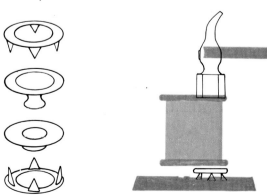

Buckles There is an enormous variety of shapes, sizes, colours and styles of buckles in most shops. It is best to use the prong type on belts, provided the fabric is not too delicate. Kits are available to cover buckles with the same fabric as the garment. The instructions on the packet are quite clear and very easy to follow.

Eyelets This is a form of fastening that can be very decorative when used for lacing the front of a bodice or shirt. Ribbon, cord or rouleau in the same or contrasting colour can be threaded through the eyelets to complete the fastening. Eyelets can be purchased in different colours and sizes and inserted with a gun or punch which is supplied in the package. They can also be worked by hand. Make a hole with a stiletto or knitting needle and buttonhole-stitch around the hole. For extra strength, place an eyelet over the top of the hole and buttonhole-stitch together disguising the metal.

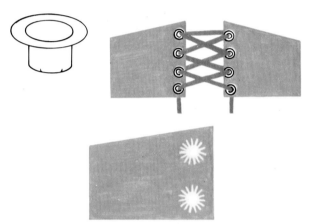

Loose belt fastening For this, a woggle made of matching fabric, or two D rings or curtain rings covered in rouleau of matching fabric can be used. Curtain rings are attractive when disguised by buttonhole stitch or crochet in a matching thread. The woggle is made like a tube, with interfacing inserted, and then stitched together at the ends and turned to the right side.

Frogs and toggles These are made of cord or rouleau stitched into an attractive shape, forming two or more loops. The toggles are rather elongated and are sewn on vertically.

Sideway adjustment zip They are extremely useful for maternity garments, and are attached to the waist-band horizontally. They are easily adjustable.

Button or buckle and chain This is another decorative way of making a fastening. There is a variety of shapes and sizes to choose from in most stores and they always give a finished look to the garment.

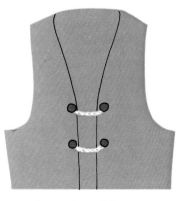

Suspender type fastenings These are used mostly on garments with straps, for example dungarees, skirts and trousers. If the straps or loops are elasticated, they allow for extra movement and are therefore very useful on children's clothes.

Decorative metal fastenings These fastenings can be adapted for many uses. Most consist of a hook and a D ring, with a small piece of fabric stitched on the right side to cover any unsightly ends, or buttonhole stitch worked along the straight side of the D ring in a heavy matching thread.

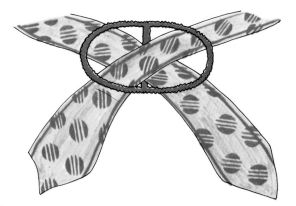

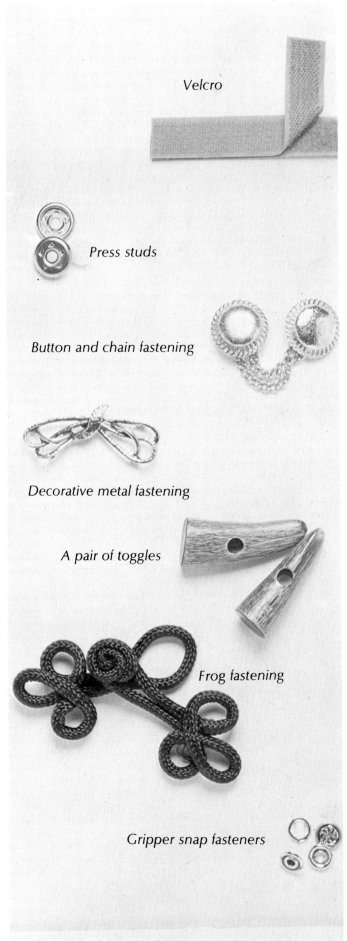

Velcro

Press studs

Button and chain fastening

Decorative metal fastening

A pair of toggles

Frog fastening

Gripper snap fasteners

A variety of buttonholes

Buttonholes

Choose your buttons before making buttonholes, as the depth and the width of buttons varies. All types of buttonholes should be practised first on a spare piece of double fabric with a layer of interfacing between the fabric. All buttons should be tested through the buttonholes to ensure that the buttonholes are the correct size. Work covered buttons before trying them through the buttonholes. An extra 0·6cm ($\frac{1}{4}$ inch) is needed on the length of some buttonholes to allow for the depth of the button.

Machine-made buttonholes

If you have a swing-needle machine, these are the most simple buttonholes to make. Mark out the positions of the buttonholes. Set stitch dial on machine to a small stitch. Swing the needle to the left and place the centre of the machine foot to the buttonhole line. Work stitches down one side of the buttonhole to make the bead. Finish at the end of this line with the needle in the fabric at the right hand side of the bead. Leave the needle in the fabric, lift pressure foot, turn the work towards the right and drop pressure foot. Hold the fabric to prevent it moving and alter the stitch length to a larger size. Work a few stitches in the same place at the end of the buttonhole. Finish with the needle in the left hand side of these stitches. Turn stitch dial to small stitch setting and work another bead down the other side. Repeat larger stitches at the other end (figure 1). Remove garment from the machine and pull the top threads through to the wrong side. Cut between the beads. Work a few stitches over the ends of the buttonhole with the loose threads. Finish off on the wrong side (figure 2).

To prevent stretching some machines are supplied with a special foot to hold cord in place and the stitching is worked over this. To rectify a stretched buttonhole thread a needle with one or two thicknesses of matching thread. Insert underneath the stitches on the wrong side of the buttonhole and around the ends. Pull up the threads and these will hold the buttonhole in shape (figure 3).

Hand worked buttonholes

When worked horizontally on a garment buttonholes have one round end and one square end. The round end should be nearest the edge of the garment. Vertical buttonholes as on shirts and blouses have two square ends.

Mark out the buttonhole positions before removing the pattern. Work a row of machine stitches down the line indicated. Cut along the line and oversew the edges (figure 4). To give a neater finish the stitches can be worked over a thin cord or a few strands of matching thread. With right side up, insert the needle from wrong side to right side at the end of one line approximately 0.3cm ($\frac{1}{8}$ inch) from the cut. Work buttonhole stitch along the line (figure 5). Work seven or nine whipping stitches around the round end. Buttonhole-stitch down the other side and work the same amount of whipping stitches on the square end (figure 6). Finish off on the wrong side.

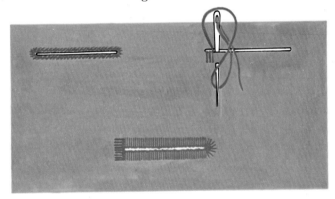

Figure 4 *Figure 5* *Figure 6*

For a button with a large shank make the round end larger and buttonhole-stitch around it (figure 7).

Figure 7

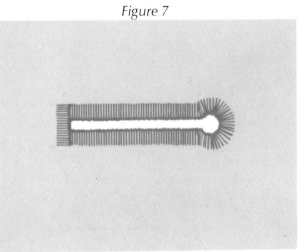

Figure 1 *Figure 2* *Figure 3*

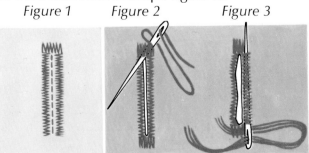

Bound buttonholes

Each buttonhole requires a piece of fabric cut on the straight grain, 2.5cm (*1 inch*) longer than the opening and approximately 5cm (*2 inches*) wide. When working a continuous line of buttonholes cut one strip the length of the line of buttonholes plus 5cm (*2 inches*) (figure 8). Mark the lines on the garment. Tack a rect-

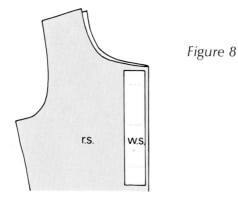

Figure 8

angle around the buttonhole line at the required distance. Place the square of fabric on the right side of the garment with the straight grain parallel to the tacking line. From the wrong side, machine stitch on the tacking line. Do not start at a corner (figure 9).

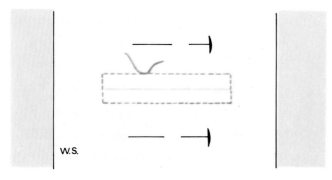

Figure 9

Cut down the centre through both thicknesses to within 0.6cm ($\frac{1}{4}$ *inch*) of either end. With small pointed scissors cut diagonally into each corner (figure 10).

Figure 10

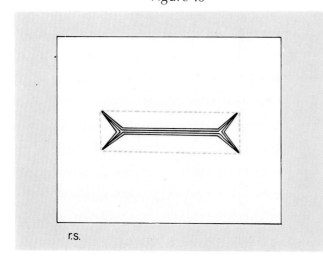

Turn strip through to the wrong side and fold the sides of the facing to meet in the middle. Work two or three stab stitches close to each end to hold in place, and two or three stitches at either end beyond the opening. Temporarily stitch the folds together in the middle (figure 11). Press on the wrong side. Fold back the

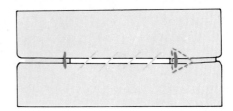

Figure 11

centre-front facing and cut along the marked buttonhole lines. Fold under the edges and slip-stitch on to the wrong side of the buttonhole (figure 12).

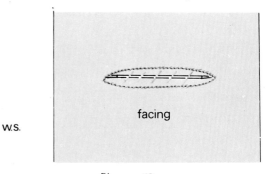

Figure 12

Loop buttonholes

Cut a strip of fabric on the cross approximately 3cm (*1$\frac{1}{4}$ inches*) wide by the length required plus 3cm (*1$\frac{1}{4}$ inches*) extra for each loop. With right sides together, fold the strip lengthways and stitch 0.6cm ($\frac{1}{4}$ *inch*) from the fold. Trim the turnings to 0.6cm ($\frac{1}{4}$ *inch*) and turn the rouleau through (figure 13). Place the end of the rouleau to the edge of the garment on the right side. Pin into position. Make a loop the size required to fit the button. Leave approximately 0.6cm ($\frac{1}{4}$ *inch*) between the loops. Work a few stitches through the rouleau and garment on the stitch line

Figure 13

116

and remove pins (figure 14). With right sides together tack and stitch the facing to the garment with the loops in between (figure 15). Trim and layer the turnings and turn the facing to the wrong side. This will make the loops extend from the garment edge (figure 16). Where a continuous line of loops is needed the rouleau can be used in one long piece.

Buttonhole stitch loops

Work two or three fairly loose straight stitches on the edge of the garment to form a loop. Work buttonhole stitch over these threads (figure 17).

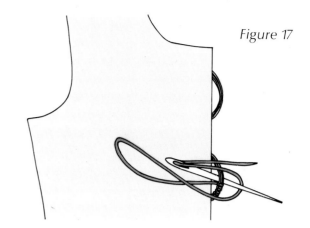

Figure 17

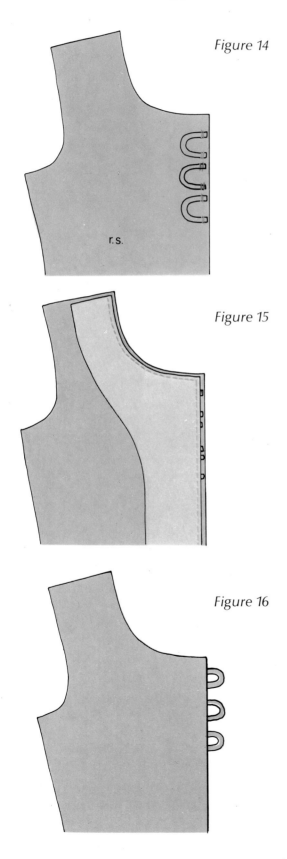

Figure 14

Figure 15

Figure 16

Buttonholes set in seam lines

Stitch to the marks given (figure 18). Press seams open. From the wrong side insert two pieces of interfacing in between the turning and garment. These should be the same length as the buttonhole and 1.3cm ($\frac{1}{2}$ inch) wider either side (figure 19). Tack into place and from the right side stitch at an equal distance from the seam on either side (figure 20). Finish off on the wrong side as with the bound buttonhole facing.

Figure 18

w.s.

Figure 19

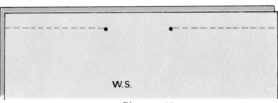

interfacing

Figure 20

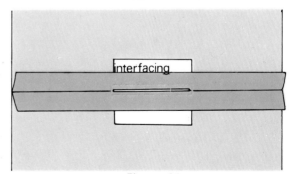

r.s.

Buttonholes for heavy leather, suede and sheepskin

If using sheepskin cut off all fur on the strip to be used as a binding. Cut a piece of skin approximately 5cm (2 inches) longer than the buttonhole and 5cm (2 inches) wide. Cut a piece of interfacing 0.3cm ($\frac{1}{8}$ inch) smaller than the rectangle on all sides. Tack on to the wrong side of the rectangle. Fine down the edges of the rectangle with emery paper and round off the corners. With right sides together attach the facing to the garment over the buttonhole with sticky tape (figure 21). Work in the same way as the bound

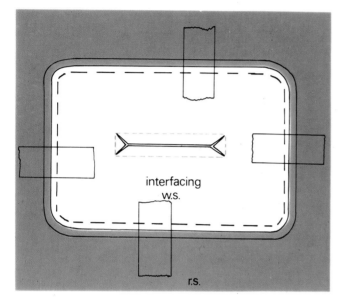

Figure 21

buttonhole. Before turning through trim the turnings if possible. With a warm iron and dry cloth press the facing flat on the wrong side. Spread glue between the facing and wrong side of the garment. Press again and then stitch around the edge of the facing through both thicknesses and 0.6cm ($\frac{1}{4}$ inch) from the button-hole (figure 22).

Figure 22

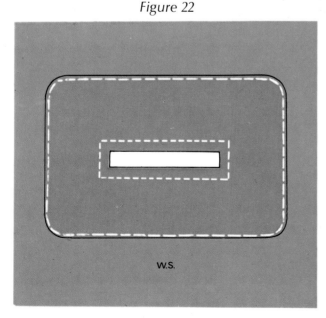

Decorative buttonholes

Cut the interfacing to the shape required. Place on fabric and cut out the same shape, allowing 0.6cm ($\frac{1}{4}$ inch) extra on all edges. Fold the edges on to the interfacing and tack (figure 23). Place binding centrally

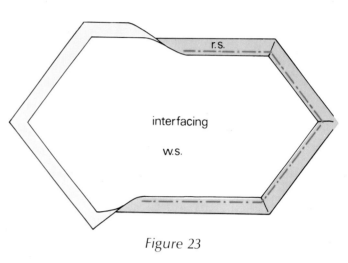

Figure 23

on the buttonhole mark with right side of binding to wrong side of garment. Stitch 0.3cm ($\frac{1}{8}$ inch) away from either side of the mark and across the ends. Cut as for the bound buttonhole and turn on to the right side. Tack around buttonhole and press on the wrong side. Tack and stitch around the edges of the shape (figure 24). Remove tacking.

Figure 24

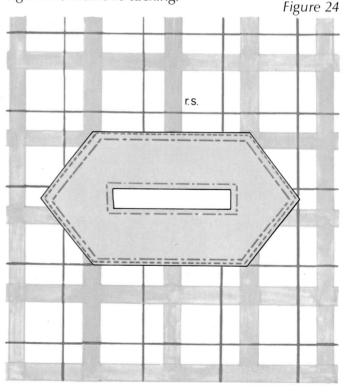

Pretty pockets

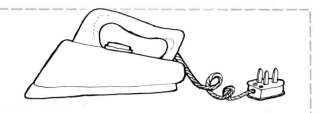

Making and attaching pockets and pocket flaps

It is always advisable to fit a garment before deciding on the position of any pockets. Pockets should be in a flattering position for the figure, i.e. flap, welt or patch pockets should not accentuate a large bust or hips, and hipline pockets should be at the correct height for the style and length of skirt. On a tall, slim figure two sets of pockets can be flattering but are not suitable for a short figure.

Mark in the pocket line on the garment with tacking stitches. Cut flap, welt or patch pocket out of paper and pin in position. Try on the garment and adjust if necessary. Mark any alteration with a new line of tacking.

Patch pocket

This pocket is placed on to the outside of a garment. **When using a light-weight fabric** a patch pocket is often cut in one piece. After attaching interfacing to the wrong side, fold the pocket in half with right sides together and stitch on the seam line leaving a small section open at the lower edge. Trim and layer turnings, clip curves and turn through to the right side (figure 1). Tack the edges, slip-stitch the

opening and press on the wrong side. Tack pocket into position on garment and attach by top-stitching (figure 2). Alternatively, work back stitches from the wrong side, taking the stitches through the garment, under-pocket and turnings only, as near to the edge as possible. No stitches should show on the right side (figure 3).

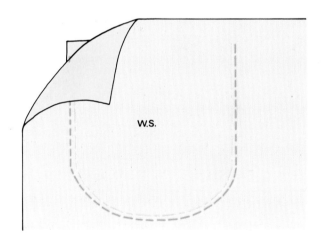

Figure 2

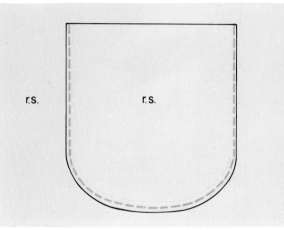

Figure 3

When using a heavy-weight fabric cut a piece of interfacing to the size of the actual pocket and attach to the wrong side of the upper-pocket. One of the following methods is then used:

(A) Cut lining the same size as the interfacing and tack into position on top of the interfacing, right side up. Turn pocket hem over and sew by hand on to the lining. Turn in and tack the remaining pocket edges, easing fullness evenly around curve. Sew to lining.

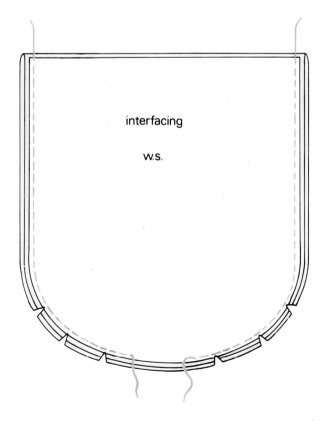

Figure 1

Press pocket on the wrong side and attach to garment (figure 4).

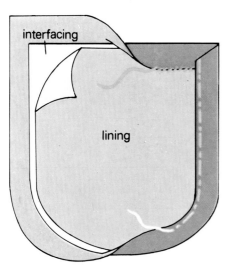

Figure 4

(B) Turn in and tack the hem and other edges of pocket on to interfacing mitring the corners where necessary. Press on the wrong side. Turn in and press the raw edges of lining. Place lining on pocket with wrong sides together and hem-stitch into position (figure 5). Attach the pocket to the garment.

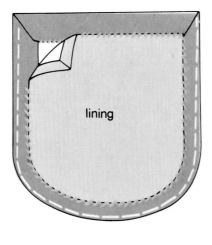

Figure 5

If a flap is to be attached above the patch pocket place right sides of the two flap pieces together and stitch along the seam line on three sides, leaving the top edge open. Start and finish stitching 0.6cm ($\frac{1}{4}$ *inch*) inside the seam line at the top edge working diagonally to the crossing point at top seam line. This gives a neater appearance when the flap is stitched into place, as no ends will show at the edges. Trim turnings and corners, clipping where necessary (figure 6). Turn flap through to right side, tack the edges and press on the wrong side. Top-stitch if

required. Place raw edges of flap to the top of the patch pocket and stitch on the seam line (figure 7). Trim turnings, turn down flap to the correct position and press. Either top-stitch 0.6cm ($\frac{1}{4}$ *inch*) from the

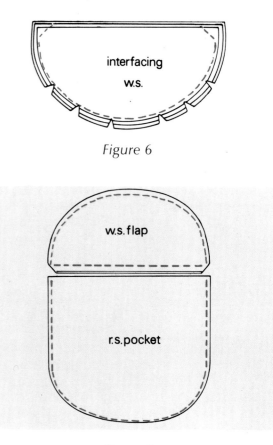

Figure 6

Figure 7

fold line (figure 8): or trim off as much of the under-flap turning as is practicable, turn in a small hem and hem-stitch down on to the wrong side of the top flap. The stitches should not show on the right side.

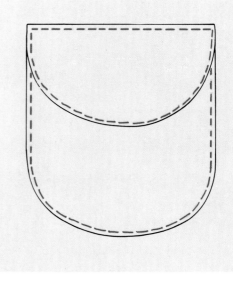

Figure 8

Work safety bars on the wrong side of the garment (figure 9).

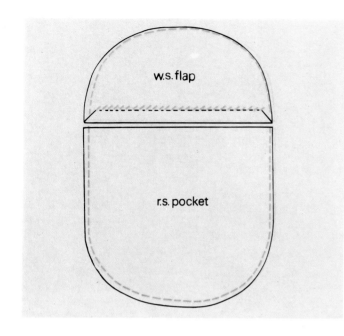

Figure 9

Welt pocket

This pocket is always on the inside of a garment and the opening neatened with a stiffened band. The welt is usually made from one piece of fabric.

After attaching interfacing, fold welt in half with right sides together and stitch both ends. Trim turnings and corners and turn through to right side. Tack the edges and press on the wrong side (figure 10).

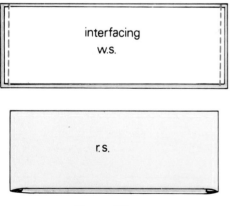

Figure 10

With raw edges uppermost and right sides together, place the welt to the pocket line on the garment and tack into position. With right sides together tack lining into position, with the pocket line of lining on the raw edges of the welt. Stitch around the pocket line 0.6cm ($\frac{1}{4}$ *inch*) on either side and across both ends, stitching diagonally across the top corners. This prevents the lining from showing when the welt is stitched into place (figure 11). Cut on pocket line to

0.6cm ($\frac{1}{4}$ *inch*) from each end. Cut diagonally into the corners almost to the stitching through lining and garment (figure 12). Turn lining to the wrong side. Work two or three stab stitches through the lining and triangle at each end. Press on the wrong side (figure 13).

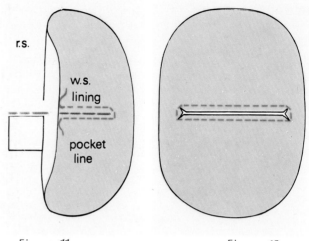

Figure 11   *Figure 12*

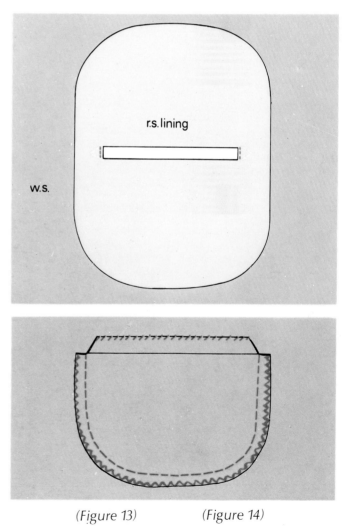

(Figure 13)   *(Figure 14)*

Fold the top lining down over the bottom lining. Stitch the two together on the seam line and neaten the turnings together (figure 14).

On the right side, tack the welt into position and top-stitch or stitch by hand from the back, as for the patch pocket. From the wrong side, work safety bars at the corners of the pocket, ensuring that no stitches show on the right side.

If using a different fabric for the pocket lining a strip of matching fabric approximately 7.5cm (3 inches) wide must be stitched on to the right side of the lining before tacking this on to the pocket line (figure 15). When using weak or loosely woven fabrics, it is advisable to stitch a stay on to the wrong side of the garment behind the pocket opening. This is a strip of suitable interfacing cut on the straight grain, usually 3.8cm ($1\frac{1}{2}$ inches) wide and 5cm (2 inches) longer than the pocket line (figure 16). The stay is stitched into position on the wrong side of the garment before the welt is tacked on. When the pocket has been completed, any excess of the stay can be trimmed off.

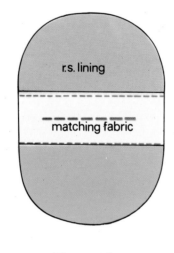

(Figure 15)

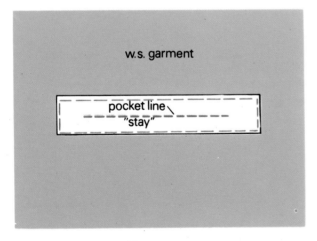

Figure 16

Welt pocket with flap
This is a pocket on the inside of a garment with a flap on the outside to conceal the opening. It is worked and attached in a similar way to a welt pocket but the flap is placed to the other side of the

pocket line and the diagonal stitching worked at the lower corners (figure 17). Safety bars are worked across each corner on the wrong side before the top lining is folded on to the lower lining.

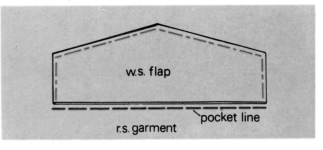

Figure 17

On some welt and flap pockets the lining is cut in two pieces. Work the pocket in the same way as for a welt pocket as far as the stab stitching and pressing. The other piece of lining is then placed on top. With right sides together tack and stitch the two pocket pieces all round and neaten turnings together (figure 18). To give extra strength, a row of stitching is sometimes worked on the right side (figure 19).

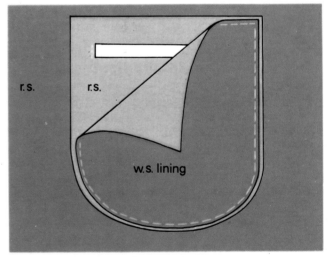

Figure 18

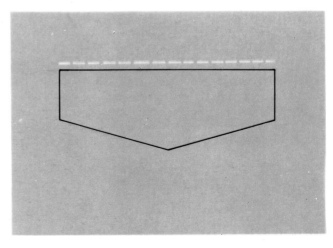

Figure 19

Pockets with a purpose

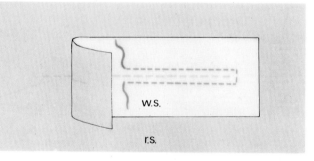

Making more complex pockets and flaps
Bound or slot pocket

This is a neat pocket for suits and coats. The pocket is on the inside of the garment and the pocket opening is strengthened with matching fabric.

When using matching fabric for the lining the pocket is worked with one piece only. If using a different fabric four pieces are required, two strips of matching fabric for the binding and facing and two pieces in another material for the lining.

For the one piece method tack lining to pocket line on the garment with right sides together. Work a row of stitching 0.6cm ($\frac{1}{4}$ inch) on either side of the pocket line and across the ends. Cut on pocket line to 0.6cm ($\frac{1}{4}$ inch) from the ends and then diagonally into the corners almost to the stitching (figure 1). Turn lining

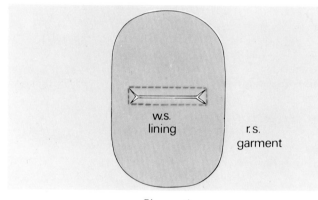

Figure 1

through to wrong side of garment and work two or three stab stitches through lining and triangles underneath. Fold lining over the turnings either side so that the folds touch, forming an inverted pleat at each end. Work a row of diagonal tacking to hold in position and press on the wrong side. Work a row of stitching on the lower edge and the sides (figure 2).

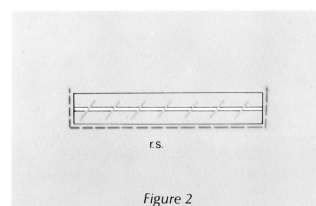

Figure 2

Stitch the edges of the lining on the seam line and neaten the turnings together. For extra strength work safety bars through the lining and wrong side of the pocket at both ends (figure 3). On right side, work a row of stitching on the top edge of opening.

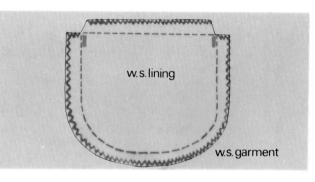

Figure 3

If using lining of a different fabric with right sides together tack matching strip of facing on to the pocket line on the garment. Stitch 0.6cm ($\frac{1}{4}$ inch) on either side and at the ends (figure 4). Cut on the pocket

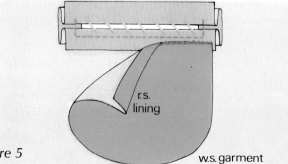

Figure 4

line and diagonally into the corners. Turn facing through to the wrong side of the garment and work as far as the diagonal tacking. Press on the wrong side and stitch on the lower edge and sides.

Turn in a narrow single hem on the smaller piece of lining and hem into place just below the bottom row of stitching (figure 5).

Figure 5

With right sides together stitch the larger piece of lining to the facing strip. With right sides together stitch the edges of the pocket lining pieces and neaten the turnings together.

From the wrong side work safety bars at each end of the pocket (figure 6).

On the right side, work a row of stitching on the top edge of the opening (figure 7).

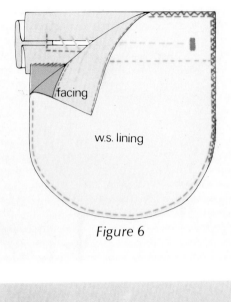
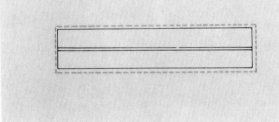

Figure 6

Figure 7

Piped pocket

This is similar to a bound pocket, but two pieces of piping or interfacing are used for strength. Piped pockets are usually wider than bound ones and are often used as a design feature.

Cut two strips of iron-on interfacing 2.5cm (*1 inch*) wide by length of pocket plus 5cm (*2 inches*). Cut two strips of matching fabric the same length and 6.5cm (*2½ inches*) wide. Iron interfacing on to the edge of each strip of fabric on the wrong side (figure 8). Fold

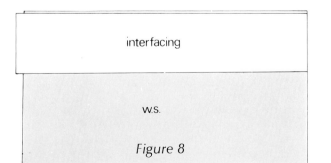

interfacing

w.s.

Figure 8

remaining fabric over the interfacing as tightly as possible. Work a row of stitching on the edge through the three thicknesses. Trim off the excess fabric and press (figure 9).

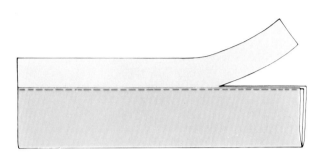

Figure 9

Place the raw edges of the strips together along the pocket line and stitch 1.3cm (*½ inch*) on either side of this and across the ends (figure 10).

Cut on pocket line of garment to 1.3cm (*½ inch*) from each end and diagonally into the corners, almost to the stitching. Turn piping through to the wrong side and work stab stitching at the corners through the piping and triangles underneath. Tack diagonally across the pocket mouth, to hold in position (figure 11). Attach small and large pieces of lining, as for a bound pocket using a lining of a different fabric, with a strip of matching fabric stitched on to the larger piece of lining as a facing.

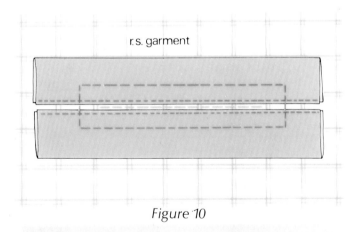

r.s. garment

Figure 10

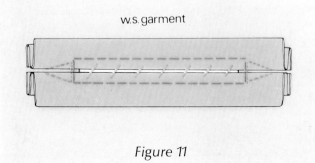

w.s. garment

Figure 11

Simple concealed pocket in a seam line

This type of pocket is frequently used in skirts or trousers, but unless reinforced at the top and bottom, it can drag and pull the seam undone.

With right sides together and matching all notches, stitch along seam line (figure 12). If using fine fabric

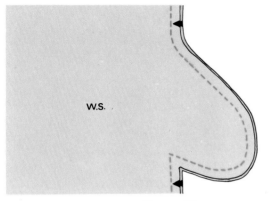

Figure 12

press turnings towards the centre-front and neaten together. With thicker fabric clip across the back seam allowance almost to the stitching line above and below the pocket. Press open and neaten seams and clipped edges. Neaten turnings of pocket together

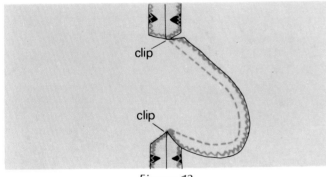

Figure 13

(figure 13). Cut a strip of iron-on interfacing the depth of the pocket plus 5cm (*2 inches*) and 3cm (*1¼ inches*) wide. Iron to the wrong side of a piece of matching fabric cut to the same size. Neaten edges. Place strip on top of seam and pocket with interfacing between. Work a row of stitching through strip and edge of the back turning (figure 14).

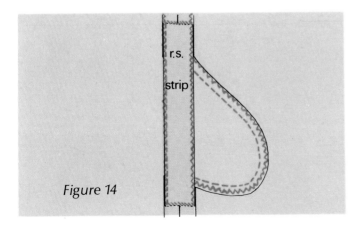

Figure 14

If the turnings of the seam and pocket have been neatened together, the interfaced strip may be cut narrower and the corners lying towards the back may be rounded off.

On the right side of the garment work a small safety bar with matching thread at the top and bottom of the opening through all thicknesses.

Catch down the edge of the strip lying over the pocket lining with slip hemming. No stitches should show on the right side (figure 15).

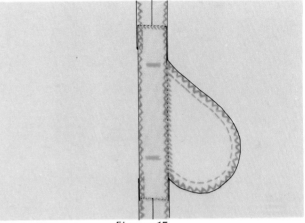

Figure 15

If a pocket is not included in the pattern and one is required, cut out the pocket shape twice in paper and glue or pin to the seam line in the same position on the back and front pattern pieces (figure 16).

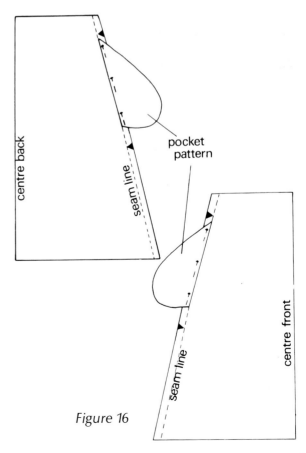

Figure 16

Pocket for a yoke

This type of pocket can be set into a side front panel or yoke: for the lower edge of a side front panel, the pocket and side panel are cut in one. The pocket lining is cut separately.

With right sides together and dots matching position lining on front panel. Stitch between the dots (figure 17). Trim turnings and clip to dot at corner. Turn lining to wrong side and edge-tack. With right sides

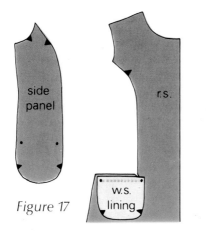

Figure 17

together tack and stitch the side panel to the front panel as far as the dot. With right sides together tack and stitch the pocket lining to the side panel from one dot around to the other dot. Work safety bars over the dots. Press on the wrong side. Trim and neaten turnings (figure 18).

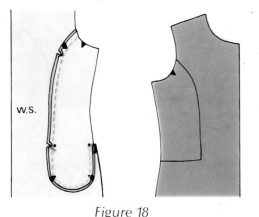

Figure 18

For a yoke line a pocket flap is made separately. Iron interfacing to the wrong side of one flap piece. With right sides together tack and stitch the two flaps together around seam line except for the top edge. Trim and taper the turnings. Turn through, tack around the edges to hold in place and press. Top-stitch if required and remove tacking (figure 19).

Figure 19

With right sides together and matching notches stitch top pocket lining on to top edge of bodice. Trim turnings and clip to dots. Turn lining on to the wrong side and press (figure 20). Position flap between notches on the bodice and tack into place (figure 21). With right sides together and matching notches, tack and stitch the yoke to the bodice from the centre-front to the dot and from the armhole to the dot (figure 22). With right sides together place under-

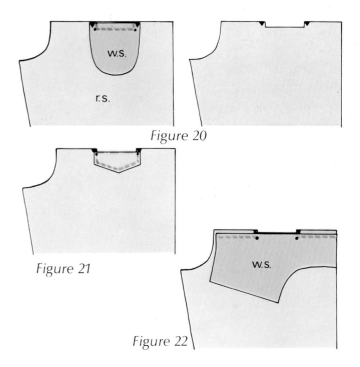

Figure 20

Figure 21

Figure 22

pocket lining to dots on turning and stitch on edge. Press turnings upwards. Match notches on the two linings and stitch on seam line (figure 23). Work a row of top stitching above the seam line to hold down the turnings (figure 24).

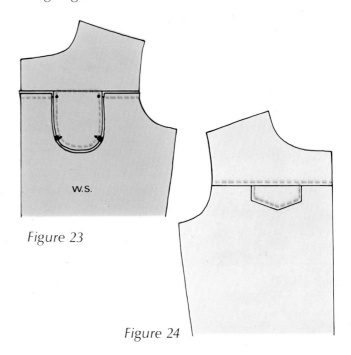

Figure 23

Figure 24

126

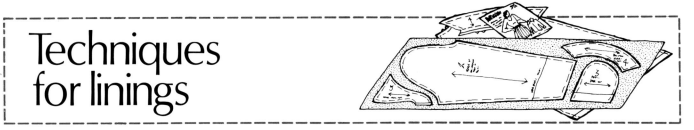

Mounting and Lining

When deciding whether to mount or line a garment there are several factors to consider. The weight and texture of the main fabric and the style chosen usually determines whether mounting or lining is most suitable, or if a combination of both methods is recommended, i.e. a mounted bodice with a lined skirt.

A coat or jacket is generally lined as this gives a neater appearance to the wrong side of the garment and prevents it clinging to the garment worn underneath. Loosely woven and fine fabrics are often mounted in order to give body. Mounting a sheer fabric prevents it being transparent and the seams do not show through to the right side. If a very full or flared skirt is lined it should have a loose lining i.e. attached at waist only, so that it hangs correctly. The lining must be appropriate to the main fabric being used: a washable, non-iron fabric should be lined with a fabric having the same properties; if ironing is necessary then the temperature needed for both fabrics should be the same.

The weight of the lining should be correct for the style and fabric of the garment. A heavy lining would detract from the appearance of a soft, flowing style in chiffon, whereas it could give a tailored look to a loosely woven tweed.

Mounting is a form of backing which gives more support than a lining and is attached when making up a garment. It is used mostly on coats, dresses and trousers and is cut the same size as the pattern piece. In order to prevent pulling at the seams, it is advisable to add 0.3cm ($\frac{1}{8}$ inch) to each seam line on the outer fabric. This allows for the roll of the fabric when it is stitched together. Test allowance on spare fabric and mounting each cut into three panels, allowing 0.3cm ($\frac{1}{8}$ inch) extra on seam edges of main fabric. Working with fabric and mounting together, tack and stitch panels together. Press. The centre panel should not pull. On some very stretchy fabrics no extra is needed if a firm, tight fit is required. Where the fit of the garment is uncertain it is helpful to cut out the mounting fabric first. Tack together and fit, making the necessary alterations before cutting out the main fabric. Re-pin paper pattern on to the mounting ensuring that the grain line is correct. Place pattern and mounting together on to the main fabric, checking that the grain lines on mounting and garment fabric correspond. Cut out, allowing for the roll of the fabric. Lay each piece of garment with the corresponding mounting piece on to a large flat surface

with wrong sides uppermost. Work a row of tacking through centre-front and centre-back if there is no centre-front and centre-back seam.

Pin all edges together and work a row of diagonal tacking approximately 2.5cm (1 inch) in from each edge (figure 1). On fabrics such as lace it is advisable to work several rows of diagonal tacking all over each piece to hold the mounting firmly in place.

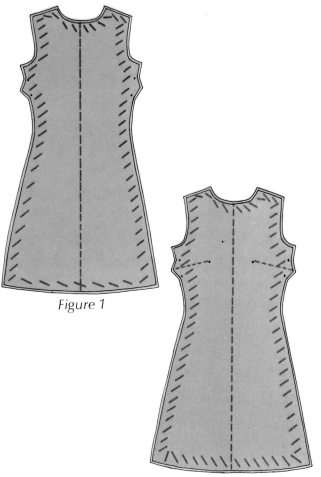

Figure 1

Figure 2

Use a fine needle with fine thread. If the garment is to be decorated at given points with sequins, beads, etc., it is easier to sew these on while the garment pieces are flat and firmly tacked in position. Sewing them on at this stage also avoids the risk of pulling.

Tack a line through the centre of each dart from the top edge to the point. This prevents slipping and ensures that the main fabric is stitched through properly when machined (figure 2). Where darts are rather bulky when worked in two fabrics, cut through the centre almost to the point and press open.

Neaten edges of fabric and mounting together (figure 3). With a very wide dart, trim to about 1cm ($\frac{3}{8}$ inch) at the wider end for a neater finish.

Join seams as directed, press open and neaten fabric and mounting together, trimming if necessary to make both edges even. The mounting fabric may be used for facings when the garment is of lace or a bulky fabric.

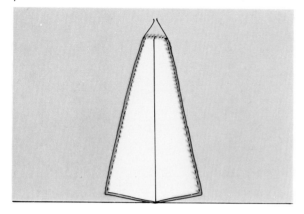

Figure 3

Finish hems by trimming off 0.6cm ($\frac{1}{4}$ inch) from the mounting, turning top fabric over this and working a row of machine stitching through all thicknesses approximately 0.3cm ($\frac{1}{8}$ inch) from the fold (figure 4). Turn up hem and slip-stitch into place.

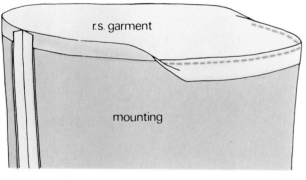

Figure 4

When using lace or fabrics which fray badly, the raw edges can be neatened with binding cut from the mounting fabric. For straight edges straight binding can be used, stitched 0.6cm ($\frac{1}{4}$ inch) in from the raw edges (figure 5). Use crossway binding for all curved edges. With harsh or thick fabrics the mounting fabric can be used for neckline and sleeve hem facings.

When a zip is to be inserted across an overlaid or lapped seam, it can be very bulky if the edges of the turning are neatened together. Leave 3cm ($1\frac{1}{4}$ inches) either side of the seam line, clip one side of the turning almost to the seam line and press this open. The seam line will then be flat when it is turned under for the zip (figure 6). Hem the edge of the zip tape down to the clipped edge of the turning.

Remove all tacking from the garment before the final press.

When using mounting of a contrasting colour a colourless pearl thread is available for pale shades and a grey one for darker colours. If this is used to stitch the seams together do not neaten edges with it as it scratches the skin. Instead use a thread that tones with both fabric and mounting or matches the fabric as this will show on the seam turnings.

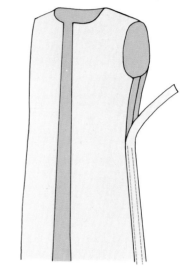

Figure 5

Lining

Lining is made up separately from the garment and is then attached with permanent tacking to hold it in place. When making a coat or jacket, the pattern often allows for the lining to be slightly smaller to prevent wrinkles. If no lining pattern is given it is always advisable to make a pleat at the centre-back at the neck edge as most linings have no stretch in them at all, whereas the outside fabric often has. This pleat allows for stretching the shoulders and bending forward etc. The pleat should be approximately

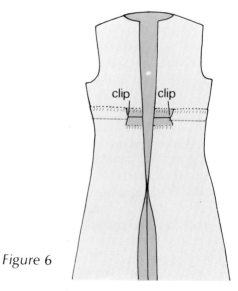

Figure 6

3.8cm ($1\frac{1}{2}$ inches) wide. The paper pattern of the back should be placed 2cm ($\frac{3}{4}$ inch) from the fold of the fabric at the neck edge and to the fold at the hem edge (figure 7).

The garment is usually stitched together first and the seams pressed open. The back neck and centre-front facings are often stitched to the lining. When this has been attached the rest of the lining can be stitched and the seams pressed open. The collar is then either sandwiched between the garment and the lining or the upper-collar stitched separately to the garment and the under-collar stitched to the lining and then the two stitched together round the outer edges (figure 8).

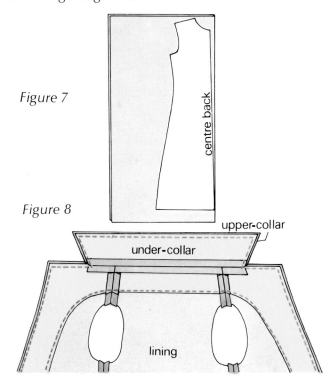

Figure 7

Figure 8

Sleeves are either lined after stitching into the armholes or set into the garment and lined separately before the centre-front and collar are joined.

If the sleeves are to be stitched in after the centre-front and collar have been attached permanently, tack the garment and lining together at the armhole and machine stitch sleeve into the armhole through all thicknesses. This method is recommended on some treated fabrics as they can easily tear and the lining gives added strength at this point when the shoulders and arms are moved (figure 9). Turn in

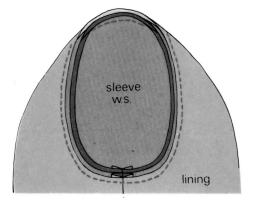

Figure 9

the seam allowance of the lining and hem to the stitching line. Trim off any excess lining at hem of sleeve, turn under and hem-stitch to sleeve hem of garment (figure 10).

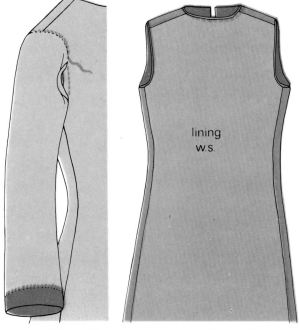

Figure 10   *Figure 11*

The hem of the lining can either be loose or attached to the garment. In either case the seam lines on the garment and lining are permanently tacked together to within approximately 2.5cm (1 inch) from the top of the hem of the garment. Match notches and use small tacking stitches and a synthetic or pure silk thread (one that has elasticity). Place raw edges of garment and lining together and work stitches approximately 0.6cm ($\frac{1}{4}$ inch) from the seam line through both thicknesses. Start and finish with three back stitches. When using stretch fabric and lining leave loops at intervals, working three back stitches before and after each loop. The stitches will then stretch with the fabric.

If lining is attached at the hem, trim off excess lining at lower edge to hem fold line, turn under and pin approximately 2.5cm (1 inch) above hem line and tack into place. Slip-stitch lining by working from right to left and working the stitches about 0.3cm ($\frac{1}{8}$ inch) underneath the fold of the lining.

When lining a sleeveless dress or blouse, the lining can act as a facing for the neckline and armholes. For a garment with sleeves, the lining can act as a neck facing.

Lining a garment with sleeves

Join all shoulder and underarm seams on garment and lining and press open. Trim off 0.3cm ($\frac{1}{8}$ inch) on neckline of lining. With right sides together and matching seam lines and notches, stitch neckline of garment to neckline of lining. Trim and clip turnings. Turn to right side, tack the edge and press on the wrong side (figure 11).

If a zip is to be inserted stitch zip to main fabric only. Trim some of the lining fabric away if necessary, fold under and hem to the stitch line at the back of the zip tape. At the lower edge of the zip make two diagonal cuts in the lining and fold under raw edges to form a square. Tack remaining seams together with permanent tacking as described. Tack lining and garment together round armholes and insert sleeves (figure 12).

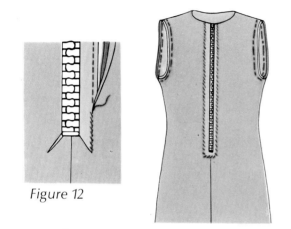

Figure 12

Lining a garment without sleeves

For a garment with a centre-front or centre-back opening, join shoulder seams of lining and garment and press open. Trim off 0.3cm ($\frac{1}{8}$ *inch*) on neckline and armholes of lining. With right sides together and matching notches and seams tack and stitch neck-

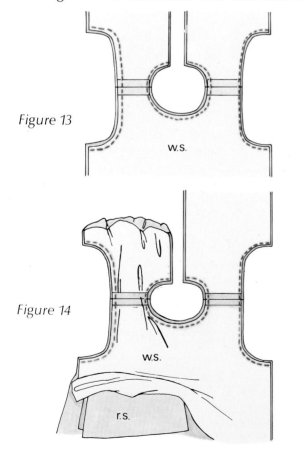

Figure 13

Figure 14

line and armholes of lining to garment. Trim and clip turnings (figure 13). Turn through to the right side by pushing each piece either side of the open seam line separately. Tack the edges and press on the wrong side whilst the garment is flat (figure 14). To join side seams open out garment, with right sides together pin armhole seam, then tack and stitch from lower edge of garment to lower edge of lining (figure 15). Make a clip almost to the stitching on either side of the armhole seam. Press open and permanently tack turnings together part of the way down towards the hem. On opening, stitch lining and garment seams to point indicated. Clip almost to the seam line and press open. Tack raw edges of garment and lining together for the opening. Permanently tack remaining turnings together almost to the hem.

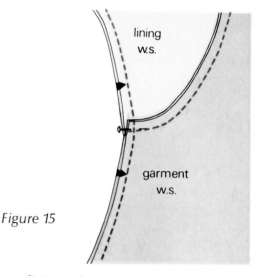

Figure 15

Loose lining a lower edge

Permanently tack seams to within 5cm (*2 inches*) of top of hem of the garment. Trim off excess lining below the fold line, turn up lining hem and stitch by hand or machine. To hold the lining in place, French tacks should be worked between the lining and the garment approximately 2cm ($\frac{3}{4}$ *inch*) from the fold line. Make three or four stitches about 0.6cm ($\frac{1}{4}$ *inch*) long between inside seams of garment and lining and work blanket stitch over these (figure 16).

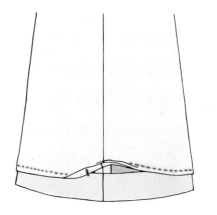

Figure 16

Ways with hems

Hems and edges

Hem allowances given on patterns are usually 5cm (2 inches). Often it is advisable to make the hem deeper, as this will add weight to the garment and make it hang better. To do this, pin the pattern to the fabric in its correct position. Place the end of a tape measure or ruler on the hemline and mark the extra hem allowance required with pins or tailor's chalk, following the shape of the pattern (figure 1). Cut along this line.

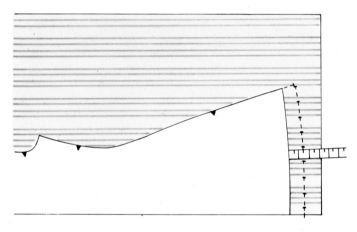

Figure 1

The hem is usually the last part of the garment to be worked. When trying on make sure you are wearing the shoes you intend to wear with the garment as different shoes can alter the angle of the body and the heel height will affect the length of the hem.

Using a yardstick or any long ruler, mark the hem all round with a row of pins placed at the required length (figure 2). When marking a hem on yourself use a hem marker, which is a ruler on an upright stand which is placed on the floor. Some hem markers will mark a hem with chalk. Even with a marker, however, it is useful at this stage to have the help of a friend. It is important to let the garment hang for at least a day as often the hemline will drop to different levels, especially on fine fabrics and circular skirts. With some fabrics it helps to place weights such as paper clips or spring-type wooden clothes pegs at evenly-spaced distances on the raw edge whilst the garment is hanging. Place a piece of paper between fabric and peg to prevent damage to the fabric.

On fine fabrics, after placing the pins or needles, which are finer, work a row of small tacking stitches on the line and let the garment hang for another day, then check length again using your yardstick or ruler.

Work a row of tacking stitches on the adjusted hemline (figure 3). Fold on this tacking line and work

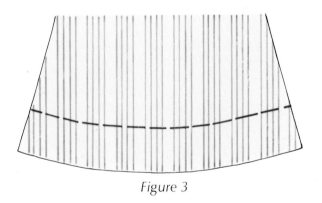

Figure 3

another row of tacking stitches approximately 0.6cm ($\frac{1}{4}$ inch) from the edge through both thicknesses (figure 4). Lay the garment on a flat surface, right side

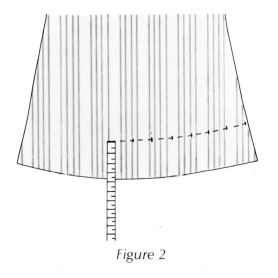

Figure 2

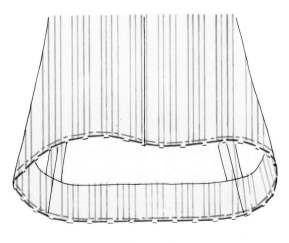

Figure 4

131

up, and using a ruler or tape measure, measure from the fold up towards the raw edge and mark out an equal distance from this all round the hem. Trim away any excess fabric (figure 5).

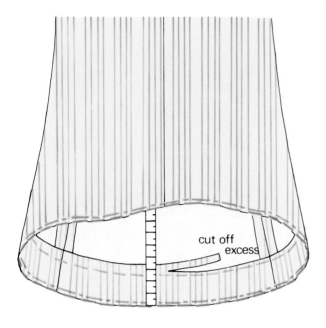

Figure 5

The method of finishing the hem depends on the fabric used and the style of garment.

On a straight hemline a small single hem may be turned on to the wrong side and a row of machine stitching worked approximately 0.3cm ($\frac{1}{8}$ *inch*) from the edge. Placing pins vertically, pin up the hem, first at the seams, then at the centre-back and centre-front (if there are no seams at these points). Pin half-way between each pair of pins, and repeat until there are pins at 5cm (*2 inch*) intervals (figure 6).

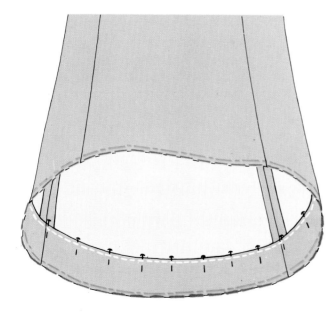

Figure 6

If the hemline is flared make a small single hem and place pins as for a straight hemline. Then pat the fold of the fabric gently with the palm of the hand. Press fingers on the hem and small folds will appear on the neatened edge. Pin in these folds but do not have any fold larger than 0.6cm ($\frac{1}{4}$ *inch*) or the hem will be bulky. Make sure that the edges of these small folds are together or a dip will appear in the hemline (figure 7).

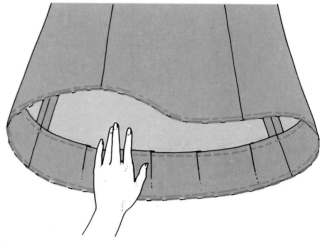

Figure 7

With straight or flared hemlines work another row of tacking whilst the fabric is flat approximately 0.6cm ($\frac{1}{4}$ *inch*) from the hemline. Check the length of garment again, then tack 0.6cm ($\frac{1}{4}$ *inch*) from the neatened edge. Slip-hem into place in the following way: fold hem away from garment along the line of tacking; work three back stitches on the wrong side of this fold; pick up one thread from the garment then slide the needle through the fold and continue in this way all round the hem (figure 8). Always start and finish with three small back stitches on the fold.

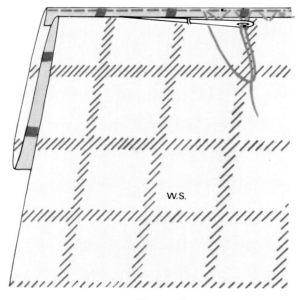

Figure 8

Press the hem on the wrong side using a steam iron and dry cloth or a damp cloth and dry iron. If the hem is flared and there are small folds on the neatened edge place a piece of paper or cloth under the folds before pressing to prevent marking the right side. Let the garment hang until it is completely dry, then work two or three small back stitches over the folds on to the fabric beneath (figure 9).

Figure 9

On a tight skirt in a stretch fabric it is best to leave a loop of thread approximately every 7.5cm (*3 inches*) when working the slip hemming. Work three back stitches on either side of this loop on the fold, then push the loop under the fold. This prevents the thread from breaking if the hemline is stretched (figure 10).

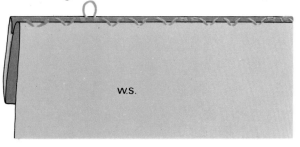

w.s.

Figure 10

On heavy fabrics a straight binding can be stitched 0.6cm ($\frac{1}{4}$ *inch*) from the raw edges and the hem pinned as for a straight hemline and hemmed into place in the following way: pick up one thread from the garment then take needle through the binding down again on to the garment. Always begin and end with three back stitches worked on the binding (figure 11).

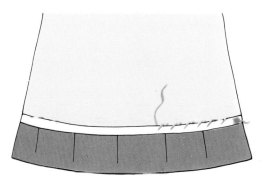

Figure 11

Shrinking an edge to reduce fullness. On some fabrics the raw edge may be shrunk to reduce fullness but it is not advisable to do this if the garment is likely to shrink when cleaned making it necessary to let down the hem.

Work a gathering thread 0.6cm ($\frac{1}{4}$ *inch*) from the raw edge. Place pins in hem as for a straight hemline. Pull up thread until edge fits the garment and wind thread round a pin in a figure-of-eight to hold it in place (figure 12). Place garment on ironing board with wrong

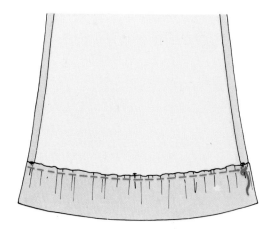

Figure 12

side up, place cloth or paper between garment and hem and press gently with the nose of the iron, a small section at a time. Use a dry iron and damp cloth or steam iron and dry cloth (figure 13). Do not

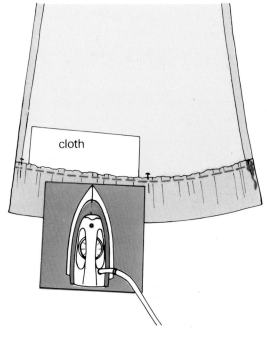

cloth

Figure 13

move the iron from side to side. As each piece is pressed pat the fold with the palm of the hand and press gently with the fingers from hemline towards the raw edge. Continue in this way until the complete hem has been shrunk. Remove cloth from beneath hem and leave garment on a flat surface to dry out. Place straight binding on the gathering thread and work a row of stitches on the edge. Tack into place and hem.

On fine and sheer fabrics a triple hem gives a neat appearance and adds weight. On long, full-skirted dresses however a very narrow hem or binding may be used on the hemline. Shell edging can be used on a fine fabric (figure 14) or, on a completely straight edge

Some fabrics, even though only one thread has been picked up, tend to show an indentation where the stitches have been worked. In such cases a decorative finish by machine is often advisable. This can be achieved by: quilting the hem; using rows of twin stitching and repeating this feature on another part of the garment; or working rows of very small zig-zag stitches as part of the design. Test these methods on a spare piece of fabric before starting the garment to see if any is suitable. If not it may be necessary to mount the top fabric on to a lining to prevent indentations showing on the top fabric.

Interfaced hems On some fabrics it is best to insert an interfacing between the hem and the garment. This is attached to the wrong side of the part of the garment to be turned up (figure 16). The interfacing

Figure 14

threads can be drawn out and the hem hem-stitched on to one side (figure 15).

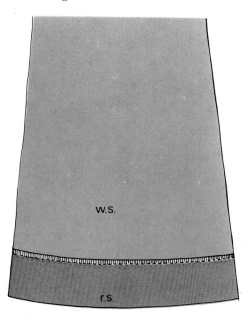

Figure 15

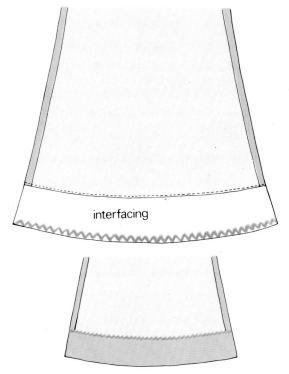

interfacing

Figure 16

should be cut 0.3cm ($\frac{1}{8}$th inch) narrower than the hem to allow for the roll of the fabric. The edges can be neatened with a zig-zag machine, or another 0.6cm ($\frac{1}{4}$ inch) can be trimmed off the interfacing at the raw edge and the fabric stitched down over this. This type of finish is suitable for the hems of trousers and for straight-cut jackets made in stretch fabrics to prevent the hem from stretching.

A double-sided iron-on interfacing is available which does not need stitching, but care should be taken that the fabric is not stretched when this is being ironed on and that no wrinkles are pressed in. Test on a spare piece of fabric first as this type of interfacing does make a very stiff finish and if the garment is washed and ironed frequently and the fabric shrinks wrinkles will appear on the right side.

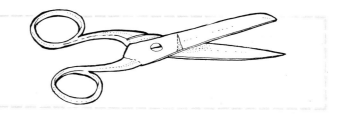

Pretty pleating

Tucks, Pleats and Godets
Tucks

These are often used as decoration on a particular section of a garment, such as the centre-front of a blouse or the centre of a sleeve.

On paper patterns the tuck is usually indicated by two lines. When transferred to the fabric the lines are pinned together and stitched to the indicated depth parallel to the fold of the fabric (figure 1A). Most tucks are stitched and then pressed to one side (figure 1B). With larger tucks, especially when using heavy fabrics, tack on the indicated line and press the tuck to one side. From the right side stitch through the three thicknesses, just catching in the underfold (figure 1C). This keeps the tucking flat. In order to avoid stretching, tucks are usually on the straight grain. To achieve a more pronounced effect a corded embroidery thread can be inserted between the stitching and the fold of the tuck either before or after stitching. Piping cord is satisfactory on a heavy fabric. Use the zipper or cording pressure foot if the cord is being inserted whilst stitching (figure 1D).

Machine worked shell tucks

These can look most attractive on baby clothes or a blouse front. Practise making them on a spare piece of fabric before working on a garment. The tuck should not be wider than the largest depth on the dial of a zig-zag machine. Tack tuck on indicated line and stitch with either zig-zag or broken straight stitch. The zig-zag or largest stitch must go just over the tuck fold to draw it in to form a shell (figure 2A). Tucks may also be worked with a twin needle. The larger the space between the needles, the larger the ridge of the tuck will appear. This type of tucking can transform a man's plain shirt into an evening shirt or give a luxury look to a blouse or dress. The broken straight stitch can be used as well as straight or double zig-zag stitch. Experiment to produce the most pleasing effect. Make several rows of tucks, an equal distance apart, on either side of the front strap or opening (figure 2B).

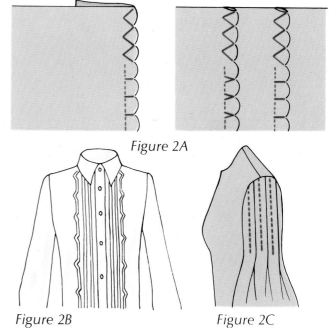

Figure 2A

Figure 2B   Figure 2C

Using tucks to replace gathers

Tucks may also be used instead of gathers to control fullness at the top of a sleeve. These may be worked on the right or wrong side. When working tucks on the right side take all the ends of threads through to the wrong side and fasten off with three back stitches (figure 2C). If making tucks as a design feature on a tailored garment it is advisable to insert an interfacing as far as the fold of each tuck. This gives a crisp, neat finish.

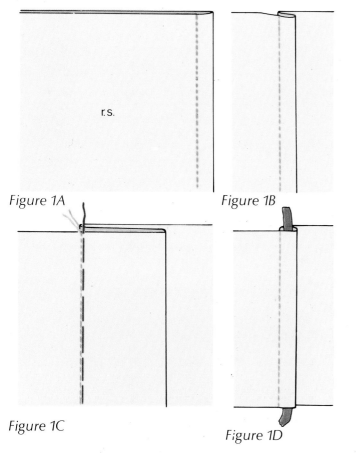

Figure 1A   Figure 1B

r.s.

Figure 1C

Figure 1D

Pleats

There are various methods of marking out pleats on to the fabric. Where there are several pleats to be marked it is often sufficient to make tailor's tacks on the fold lines at the waist and hem and at intervals lengthways (figure 3A). Pin the pleats into place, press and tack near the fold on the right side. Work a row of tacking through all thicknesses at the waist (figure 3B).

Pleating can be worked on a sewing machine using a special pleating foot.

On the right side place the centre fold on to the seam line, tack the outer folds of the pleat to the garment and top-stitch from the waist to the hip line or below. The end of the stitching can be reinforced by working a row of stitching diagonally towards the centre of the pleat (figure 4B), or making a sprat's head or arrow head in buttonhole thread (figure 4C). Sometimes part of the pleat is cut away to prevent bulk. In this case work safety bars on the wrong side at the end of the stitching where the two sides meet (figure 4D).

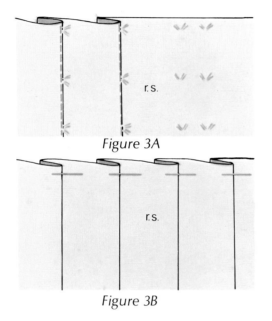

Figure 3A

Figure 3B

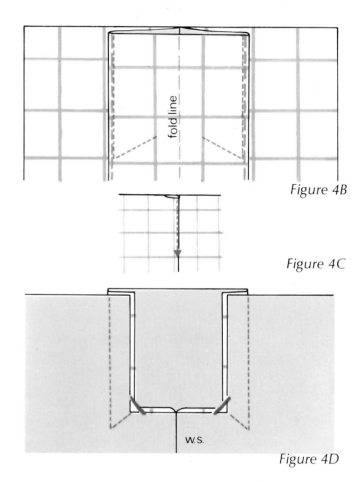

Figure 4B

Figure 4C

Figure 4D

Box pleat

This type of pleat is visible on the right side of the garment and is usually indicated on the pattern by lines. When transferred to the fabric pin lines together, tack and stitch to required depth (figure 4A).

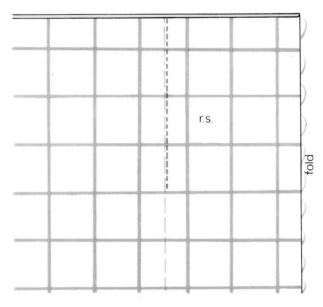

Figure 4A

Inverted box pleat

This is not visible on the right side of the garment. On the wrong side pin the lines together and stitch to the length indicated (figure 5A). Place fold line on to the

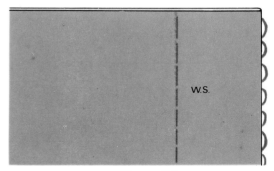

Figure 5A

stitching line, tack into position and press. A row of stitching may be worked from the right side near the edge of the seam line, or a diamond stitched to hold the pleat in place. Alternatively a sprat's head may be worked on the right side (figure 5B). When the pleat is not cut away on the inside a row of machine stitching worked part of the way down the folds will help to hold the pleat in place (figure 5C).

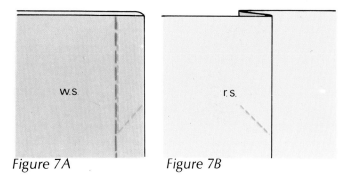

Figure 7A   *Figure 7B*

Double inverted or fan pleat

This type of pleat can be cut in one piece or two and is made in the same way as the inverted pleat (figure 8A), but it is tacked on the central line with one pleat on top of the other (figure 8B). A stay or support is necessary at the top of the pleats on the wrong side. Reinforce with any of the methods mentioned before (figure 8C).

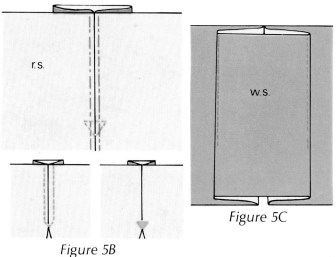

Figure 5B   *Figure 5C*

Two-piece box or inverted box type pleat

This pleat has had the top part cut away on the pattern and the back of the pleat is attached separately. Stitch on line to indicated point. Press seam open on the wrong side. Place right side of back pleat to the back of front pleat and stitch along top and each side. When turning up a hem on this type of pleat the turnings are usually neatened together first. Clip almost to the stitching just above the top of the hem and oversew the raw edges of the clip (figure 6).

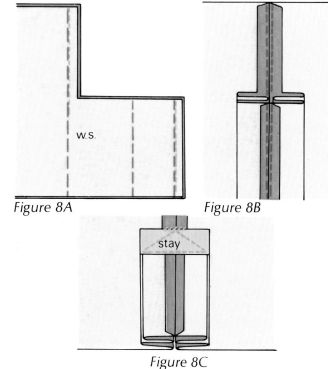

Figure 8A   *Figure 8B*

Figure 8C

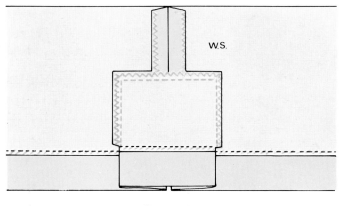

Figure 6

Single knife pleat

On the wrong side stitch on lines to the indicated point. Press to one side. On the right side work a line of stitching diagonally towards the fold of the pleat underneath (figure 7A), or a row of stitching on the pleat itself and work a safety bar on the right or wrong side as preferred (figure 7B).

Loose drape pleats

These are often on the shoulder or waist line and are frequently on the cross. The pleats are usually held in position at the seam line only and a stay of fabric or lining placed underneath, extending some way down under the loose pleats. To hold pleats in position work small stitches beneath the folds through to the stay underneath (figure 9). These stitches should not be visible on the right side. Where fabric is to be draped on top of a garment, stitch on the edge of the inside folds for part of the way. Working from under the folds, stitch drapery on to the garment with just enough hand stitches to hold in position.

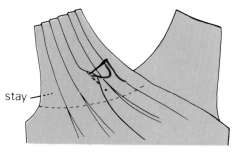

Figure 9

Fish tail pleat

This is often a design feature on bridal or evening wear. The pleat is usually inverted with a centre seam line and shaped at the lower edge (figure 10A). The top of the pleat is cut away on the inside of the garment and replaced with a stay which is caught into the side seams (figure 10B).

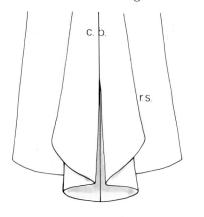

Figure 10A   *Figure 10B*

Godet

A godet is an extra piece of fabric, usually triangular in shape, inserted to add width at a certain point in a garment, for example at a hem line or in a sleeve. This is not really suitable for a stiff fabric, a soft, flowing material gives the best results. Godets are set either into a seam line, or into a slit cut on the straight grain.

Setting a godet into a seam line

Stitch seam to point indicated. Press seam open and neaten (figure 11A). Place point of godet to end of

Figure 11A   *Figure 11B*

stitched line and with right sides together stitch down to the hem line on each side. Hem-stitch point of godet to skirt seam allowance. Neaten turnings on either side of godet together. Care must be taken not to stretch turnings of the godet as they may be on the cross grain (figure 11B).

Setting a godet into a slit

Cut to the point indicated (figure 12A). Place the centre point of the godet to the top of the slit with right sides together and stitch down to the hem on both sides (figure 12B). Start at the top of the slit each time, graduating the seam out to about 0.6cm ($\frac{1}{4}$ inch). Neaten turnings together. Hem raw edge of garment on to the godet at the top. If the godet is cut on the cross it is advisable to let the garment hang for one or two days before turning up the hem as it may drop.

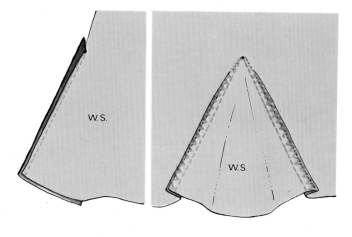

Figure 12A   *Figure 12B*

Permanently pleated fabric

This is usually sold with paper covering both sides. Use one of the pleated paper lines as the straight grain and cut out fabric whilst it is still on the paper. Cut two pieces each measuring half the width of the hips plus turnings and ease by the centre back length plus turnings and hem. Some of the new fabrics do not require neatening at the hem line. Make a row of stitching at the top of both pieces. This is the waist line. Tie ends of the stitching thread to prevent them coming out whilst paper is removed from the fabric. Remove paper. With right sides together join side seams leaving opening for a zip. Trim turnings and neaten together. Pull up waist line thread to the required waist size and tack to the waist band or petersham. Try on skirt with the shoes to be worn with it and check the hang of the pleats. On some figures it is necessary to move the waist band down approximately 0.6cm–2cm ($\frac{1}{4}$ inch–$\frac{3}{4}$ inch) at the centre front and 0.6cm–0.9cm ($\frac{1}{4}$ inch–$\frac{3}{8}$ inch) at the side seams. If this is necessary make another row of stitching on the new line and ease into the waist band or petersham. Let the skirt hang for a day or two before finishing off the hem line.

Decorative braids & cords

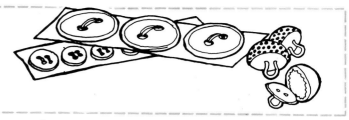

Using rouleau, braid and cord
Rouleau
This is a tube of fabric cut on the cross to any required length. Fold the strip of fabric in half widthways and stitch the long raw edges together. Trim the turnings to 0.3cm ($\frac{1}{8}$ inch) narrower than the width of the tube. Turn through. Piping cord or wire can be threaded through the tube to give it extra strength and shape, or the rouleau can be pressed flat.

Rouleau edging with insertion stitches (faggoting)
Used in this way rouleau forms a decorative edge for neck and sleeves. Tack the edge of the garment on to paper with the right side up. Place the rouleau on the paper approximately 0.6cm ($\frac{1}{4}$ inch) away from the edge of the garment (figure 1). Work three buttonhole stitches through the edge of the garment and then three buttonhole stitches on the edge of the rouleau. The last stitch of each three stitches on the garment should be in line with the first stitch on the rouleau (figure 2).
Rouleau can be worked in a design and held in place by insertion stitches.

Rouleau with twist stitch
Work faggoting from left to right in a matching or contrasting thread. Run the needle through the fold of the garment edge and work a back stitch. Insert the needle from wrong side to right side over the back stitch. Make sure that the thread is to the left hand side of the needle and under the point of the needle. Pull through. Insert needle into rouleau from wrong side to right side with the thread under the needle and towards the right hand side. Pull needle through and continue in this way (figure 3). To make the stitch firmer work three or four blanket stitches after the twist stitch but before inserting the needle into the fabric again.

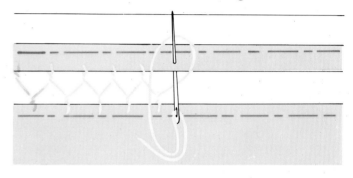

Figure 3

Rouleau with knotted stitch
Work from left to right starting as for rouleau with faggoting. Insert the needle from right side to wrong side and pull through. Place both threads under needle and then the needle under the threads. Pull again and this will form a knot (figure 4). To strengthen this, blanket stitch can be worked over the stitches (figure 5).

Figure 4

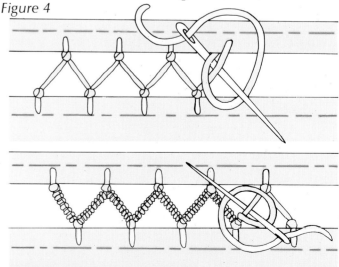

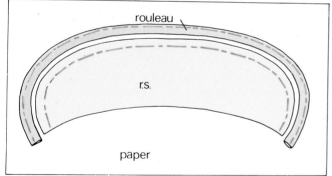

Figure 1

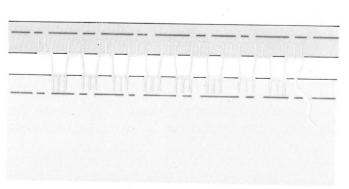

Figure 2

Figure 5

Rouleau inset with faggoting Draw the shape of the inset and design on paper (figure 6A). Tack rouleau into place and work stitches as before. Circles and ovals can be worked with long stitches crossing each other and then buttonhole stitch worked over these stitches to keep the shape (figure 6B). When the design

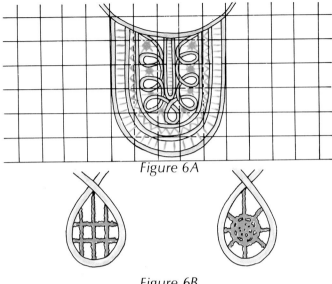

Figure 6A

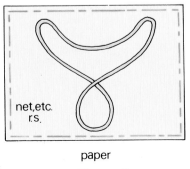

Figure 6B

is completed face or turn in the edge of the garment where the rouleau is to be attached. Tack this edge on to paper approximately 2cm (¾ inch) from the edge (figure 7).

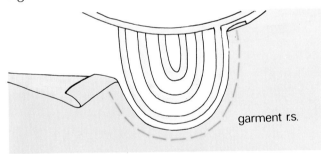

Figure 7

Rouleau on fine fabric Draw the design on paper. Place the fabric on top and tack around edges. Tack the rouleau on to the fabric following the design lines underneath (figure 8). From the wrong side work

net, etc.
r.s.

paper

Figure 8

small back stitches through paper, fabric and rouleau but making sure that no stitches show on the right side of the rouleau. One row of stitches is usually sufficient but two rows may be needed on sharp curves. When completed, with right sides together tack and stitch the fabric to the garment. Then remove the paper very carefully from the back of the work.

Rows of rouleau can be attached to the top of a garment in the same way, on collars and cuffs for example.

To attach rouleau as an edging, slip stitch through the fold at the edge of the garment and the rouleau (figure 9).

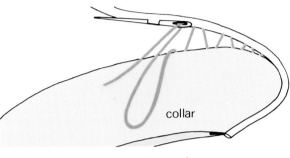

collar

Figure 9

Decorative loop edging with rouleau This can be made by marking out equal distances along the edge of the garment and equal distances of one and a half times this amount on the rouleau.

For example, mark every 2.5cm (*1 inch*) on the garment and at 4cm (*1½ inch*) intervals on the rouleau. With marks matching stitch the rouleau to the garment at the marks (figure 10).

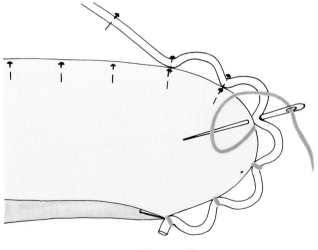

Figure 10

Rouleau frogs Make the rouleau in the normal way and then insert piping cord to strengthen. Form the central loop and secure with stitching where the rouleau crosses. Form another loop to one side of the first and stitch down. Then make a larger loop and stitch down. Take rouleau under existing loops and form another the same size as the second loop.

Stitch down. Make sure that no stitches show on the right side. Stitch the frog into place leaving the long loop free. Attach a button or toggle on the other side of the garment to correspond with the long loop (figure 11).

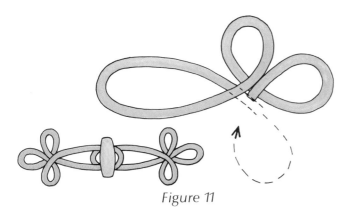

Figure 11

Rouleau hooks and eyes Make the rouleau as above. Insert wire and bend to the correct shape. Split curtain rings can be covered in the same way and used as rings.

Cording

This is available in most stores in various sizes and colours or can be made quite easily with embroidery thread or wool. To do this use three or four strands of three times the required length. Knot the threads together at either end. Attach one end over a hook and place a knitting needle above the knot. Hold the threads taut and turn the needle in a clockwise direction (figure 12). Continue this until the cords curl

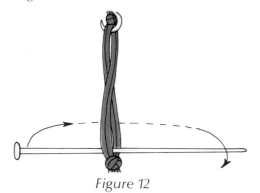

Figure 12

up if the threads are slackened. Keeping the threads as taut as possible fold the cord in half and the threads will automatically twist together. Tie a thread tightly around the cords above the knot and cut off the knot. Cording can be used for tie belts, edging on a garment, loop buttonholes and frogs but in all cases make sure that the ends are securely finished off to prevent the cords unravelling. If a design is being worked on top of the garment in cording make two small holes in the fabric so that the ends of the cords can be finished off on the wrong side. Transparent sticky tape is a good way to finish off the ends and also makes them easier to thread through the fabric.

Tassels

Wind threads around a piece of cardboard of the required depth. Insert a matching thread under the threads on one edge (figure 13). Pull together and tie a single knot. Cut through the threads on the other edge. Place a round or oval bead under the threads on the knotted end. Thread the ends of the tying thread through a needle, and insert them from bottom to top through the bead (figure 14). Spread the threads evenly over the bead and tie a piece of matching thread tightly beneath the bead. Fasten off in between vertical threads. An acorn shape can be used in a matching colour. Insert a thread under the vertical threads as above, then pull up through hole in top of acorn (figure 15).

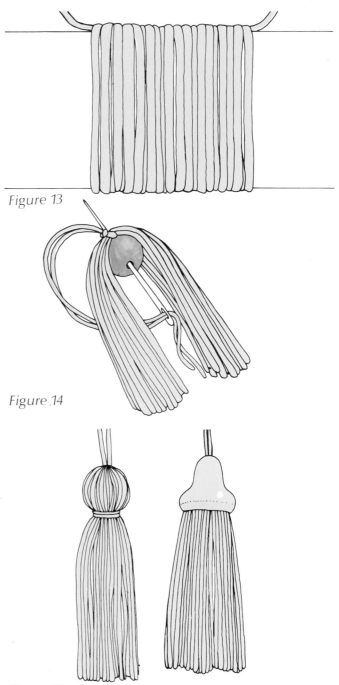

Figure 13

Figure 14

Figure 15

Braid

Military braid This is a plaited braid that will stretch in the same way as a bias strip and can be used in the same way. As a binding, tack and stitch braid on to the required edge 0.6cm ($\frac{1}{4}$ inch) from the edge. Then take over to wrong side and hem on to stitching line (figure 16). This braid stretches both ways. For this reason run a gathering thread across the folded short end and ease it to the correct width (figure 17). It is a soft braid so it is possible to cover buttons in it to match the trimming.

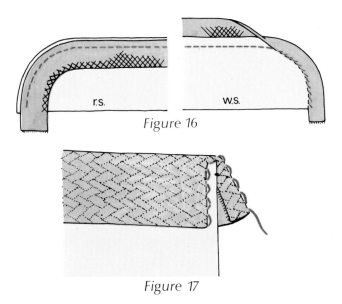

Figure 16

Figure 17

Russia braid This is a narrow braid made up of two cords joined together. It can form an attractive design feature if used on top of a garment, perhaps in several rows at an equal distance apart. For guide-lines, work rows of tacking on the right side of the garment or use transfers which can be purchased at most large stores. To attach the braid work stitches by hand or machine between the two cords or work zig-zag stitch over both cords on the right side (figure 18). For a rigid effect, stand the braid on its side and hem-stitch the lower cord to the garment (figure 19).

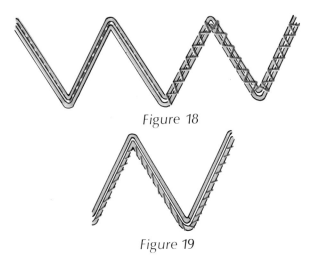

Figure 18

Figure 19

Straight braid This can be purchased either embroidered or plain. When applying straight braid to a curve slip-stitch the braid along one edge to the widest side of the curve. Using a pin, pick up a thread on the free edge of the braid and pull gently until the braid fits the smaller side of the curve. Be sure that the braid lies flat and is not pulled to one side. If possible press this edge of the braid before stitching down, to shrink away any fullness (figure 20). Ribbon can also be attached in this way.

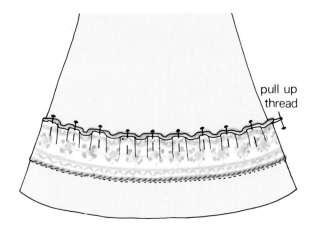

pull up thread

Figure 20

Ric-rac braid This can be attached with a machine straight stitch through the centre of the braid (figure 21A) or by using zig-zag stitch to follow the curves. If following the curves adjust the stitch length so that it fits the depth of the braid exactly (figure 21B).
Corded patterned braids A line of straight stitching down the centre usually holds this in place or zig-zag stitch worked over the corded edges.

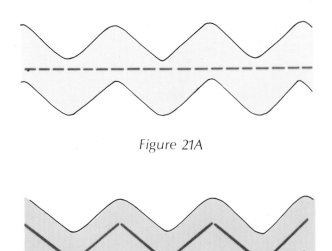

Figure 21A

Figure 21B

4

Problem fabrics

Jersey polyester

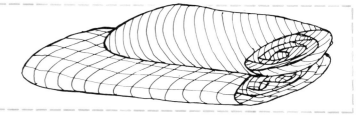

Working with jersey polyester fabrics

Jersey polyester is one of the easiest of the easy-care fabrics. Polyester is a man-made fibre, crease-resistant, colour-fast, shrink-proof and easy to wash. Jersey polyester, i.e. knitted polyester, has an added advantage for the home dressmaker, as its slight elasticity makes it easy to work with. There are various weights of jersey polyester fabric, and it is important to choose the right one for the garment required.

Light-weight crepe polyesters are suitable for blouses, but being semi-transparent they will probably require an anti-static lining or mounting. Other heavier fabrics including plain polyester crepe and twill finishes are suitable for most garments. However some ribbed fabrics are produced with the rib running horizontally and it is not advisable to cut trousers from this with the rib running vertically, in the usual way, as the fabric will stretch at the knees and the creases will not hang properly. Any piled jersey fabric should be cut so that the pile runs the same way on all pieces.

Jaquard patterned jerseys again are suitable for most garments but try always to match the pattern at the seams.

Many jersey polyester fabrics, especially polyester knit backed velvet will need to be lined with anti-static jersey.

Making up jersey polyester fabrics

Most jersey polyester fabrics are thermoplastic which means that creases pressed into the fabric with a hot or steam iron are often difficult to remove. Therefore it is essential to fit the garment with the creases tacked in to check that they are positioned correctly before pressing.

Often the edges on a length of fabric are stretched out of line, so before laying the pattern, square off the edges by using a set square or by measuring equal distances from the fold line and cutting off the excess (figures 1A and B).

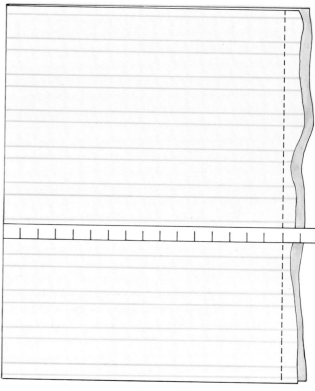

Figure 1B

Polyester fabrics can be bought in the form of a tube and if the fabric is patterned the pattern can be used as a guide for cutting a straight edge. If the fabric is not patterned turn to the wrong side, note where the stitches run vertically and cut through these (figure 2). When stitching jersey fabrics use a ballpoint needle or a 'perfect stitch' needle. These are special needles for use on jersey man-made fibres. The ballpoint needle has a rounded point and will slide between stitches preventing laddering and damage to the threads. The perfect stitch needle is similar to a ballpoint needle but finely ground and highly polished.

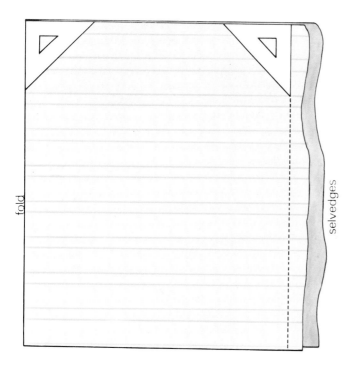

Figure 1A

This is the most suitable needle for top stitching. Both types of needle are available in most large stores and advice is given on the packet on choice of size.

The turnings on seams will often curl up. To prevent this trim the turnings to 0.6cm ($\frac{1}{4}$ inch) and neaten together with a zig-zag stitch, large both in depth and width (figure 4).

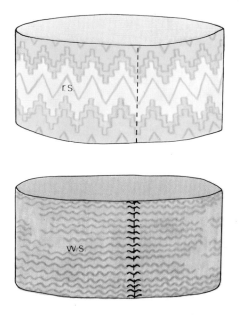

Figure 2

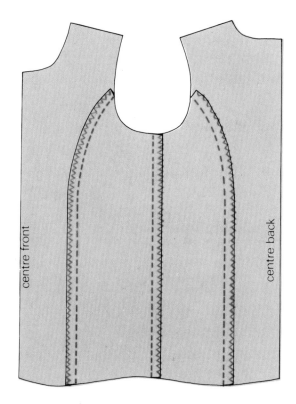

Figure 4

Stitching jersey polyester fabrics Use a synthetic or pure silk thread for stitching these fabrics. Feed the fabric under the machine foot so that it is not stretched at all. Often it is advisable to work a row of stay stitching along a raw edge to prevent stretching. Work a row of large stay stitches, tie the threads together at both ends and then work the actual stretch stitching close to the stay stitching (figure 3). Then pull out the stay stitches.

For a flat stitched seam, with right sides together tack and stitch on the seam line. Trim turning to 0.3cm ($\frac{1}{8}$ *inch*) on one turning. Press the larger turning over

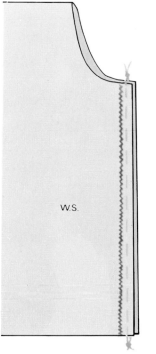

Figure 3

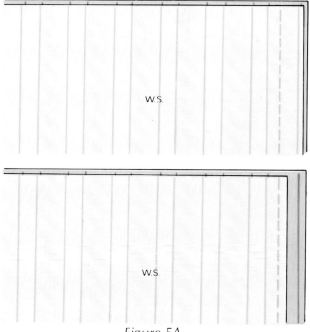

Figure 5A

this and from the right side work a row of stitching 0.6cm ($\frac{1}{4}$ *inch*) from seam line. Trim off excess fabric close to stitch line on wrong side (figures 5A and B).

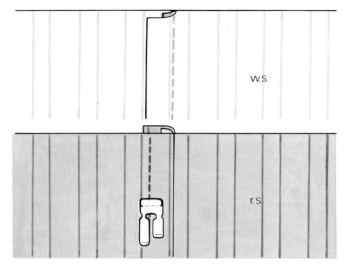

Figure 5B

Interfacing jersey polyester fabrics Light-weight sew-in or iron-on interfacing can be used to add body to the fabric on collars, cuffs and pockets. A woven polyester lawn or light-weight fabric should be used as interfacing on a tight fitting garment that may be stretched in wearing. If no light-weight fabric is available use industrial nylon cut on the cross grain of the fabric.

Hems should be stay-stitched and then machined into position using stretch-stitch, or work zig-zag stitch along the raw edge and slip-stitch into position by hand. On tight fitting hems leave a loop at intervals between the stitches to prevent the thread from breaking if the hem is stretched (figure 6).

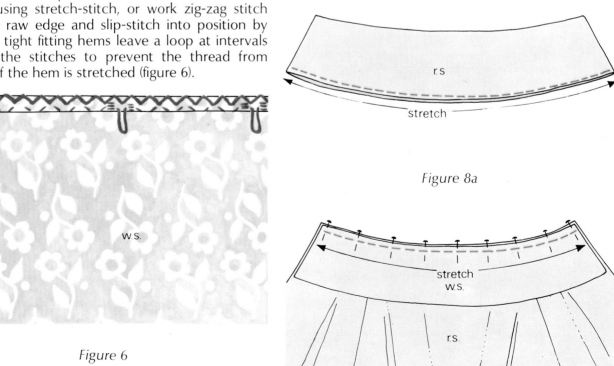

Figure 6

Braid, trimming and lace attached to polyester jersey should have the same washing and pressing qualities as the fabric.

To obtain a close fitting neckline with a jersey fabric cut a piece of fabric on the horizontal grain approximately 6.5cm ($2\frac{1}{2}$ *inches*) wide plus turnings. Measure neck 3cm ($1\frac{1}{4}$ *inches*) above the base and cut out the strip this length plus turnings (figure 7). With right sides together fold strip in half lengthways and stitch

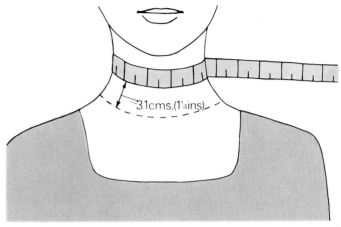

Figure 7

across the ends. Trim turnings and turn on to right side. Stitch the long raw edges together stretching them slightly as you do this (figure 8A). With right sides together pin the collar on to the neckline. Pin at centre-front and centre-back first, then pin on the rest of the collar stretching it on to the neckline between centre-front and each shoulder seam

Figure 8a

Figure 8b

146

(figure 8B). Tack and stitch. Trim turnings to 0.6cm ($\frac{1}{4}$ inch) and neaten together. Press on wrong side towards garment (figure 8C).

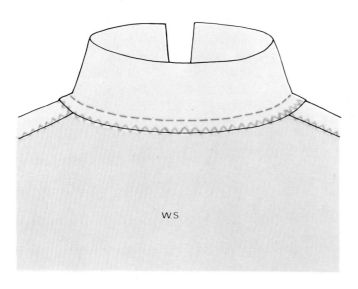

Figure 8c

The care of garments made in jersey polyester fabrics

Once the garment is completed and pressed it should need little or no pressing after washing. Never place the iron directly on to the fabric. Always use a cloth, even when using a steam iron, or the fibres in the fabric could be permanently damaged.

Polyester fabrics need frequent washing. Hand-hot water should be used (very hot water can cause permanent creases in the fabric). Nearly all detergents and washing powders are suitable but generous rinsing is needed to prevent scum forming. A fabric softener added to the last rinse will prevent polyester knits from clinging to the body or underwear. Antistatic underwear is available in most big stores to help overcome this problem. Follow instructions carefully for machine washing and do not over spin-dry as this will cause permanent creases. Hang garments in the fresh air or in a well-ventilated room to drip-dry, as man-made fibres absorb smells.

When sending a garment to the dry cleaners attach a note stating what the fabric is so that harmful chemicals are not used.

Stain removal

Never use bleach, nail polish remover or a nail brush on polyester fabrics as this can damage the fibres. Washing up liquid rubbed in on the wrong side with a circular movement will remove most marks. Pen marks can be removed with methylated spirits. Blood and alcohol stains should be immediately washed in detergent or immersed in hand-hot salted water. Grease, oil, tar, glues and waxes can usually be removed with a strong hand detergent.

Always test first on a spare piece of fabric and then wash the garment immediately after stain removal.

Accessories

On light-weight fabrics where a heavy zip would pull on the fabric use a nylon or polyester zip. If a heavier zip is required in trousers make sure it is securely fastened and locked at the top before machining.

Metal buttons and fastenings can pierce threads in the fabric and cause laddering. To prevent this, cut out circles of nylon and secure over attachments with an elastic band or a piece of thread during washing (figure 9).

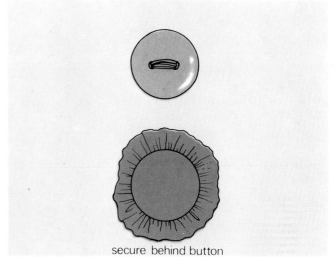

secure behind button

Figure 9

If creasing occurs near a button, remove the button or cut a small piece of foam rubber with a slit in the middle and place this over the button. Press garment on the wrong side (figure 10).

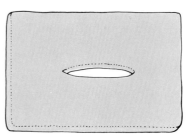

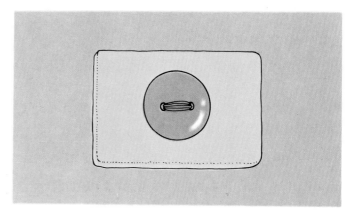

Figure 10

Sheer know-how

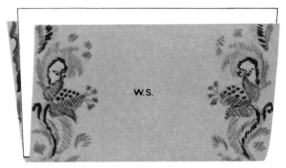

Working with sheer fabrics

Pin the material on to a thick blanket when cutting out. Fine pins and needles should always be used to prevent leaving holes in the fabric. So wherever possible the pins should be placed on the seam allowance.

It is essential to use very sharp shears as sheer fabrics tend to stick to the blade when cutting. Rub the blades with a good spray silicone polish and then clean and polish them well before use.

To prevent the teeth marking the fabric when machine stitching use a layer of tissue paper between the teeth and the material. Tissue paper is also a help when used between the fabric while stitching the seams. It provides extra thickness and stops the seam from puckering. To prevent either of these things happening on an extremely fine fabric, use a piece of transparent paper folded under and over the seam. Tear away the paper from the stitch line carefully after machining (figure 1).

Pleated sheer fabrics are usually sold between two pieces of paper to hold the pleats in place. Use one of the pleat folds as the straight grain line and cut out the material while it is between the paper. Where cutting lines cross the pleats, such as waistlines and the tops of sleeves, work a row of machining 1.3cm ($\frac{1}{2}$ inch) from the cutting line before removing the paper (figure 3).

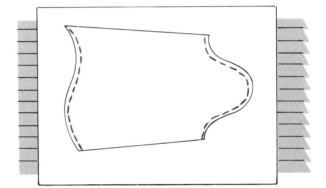

▲ Figure 2　　　　　　　　　　▼ Figure 3

Figure 1

Pattern laying and cutting out

Pin the fabric on to the thick blanket and place the pattern on top of it. It is always advisable to leave larger turnings than usual to allow for any fraying. Also allow enough material to form a triple hem. This adds a little more weight which helps the garment to hang well.

Decide whether or not the body part is to be mounted or if a separate underslip will be worn. If the mounting method is used add an extra 0.3cm ($\frac{1}{8}$ inch) on the underarm and shoulder seams to allow for the roll of the fabric.

If using embroidered sheer fabric, place some tissue paper between the right sides as this prevents the threads catching on to each other and pulling (figure 2).

Marking and tacking

Work all markings in fine synthetic threads or pure silk, using a fine needle. Trace tacking is the best method to use on all seams as tailor and thread tacking are inclined to fall out when worked on fine fabrics. Tacking stitches should be kept very small. Do not work any machining before the garment is fitted as it can leave a permanent mark if it is not correct.

Machining

A layer of tissue paper placed between the fabric and footplate prevents the threads catching to the teeth and the fabric from slipping around. A machine needle no larger than a number 80 (11) should be used. Test the machine stitch on a piece of fabric. There should be no pulling on the stitch line, so it is best to use a small stitch with a slightly loose tension.

Neatening seams

A French seam is the best method of neatening on a straight stitch machine. With wrong sides together, tack and stitch 0.6cm ($\frac{1}{4}$ inch) on the outside of the trace-tacked seam line. Press the seam and trim the turning to 0.3cm ($\frac{1}{8}$ inch) (figure 4A). Turn so that the right sides are together and tack and stitch on the seam line. Press the seam towards the back of the garment (figure 4B).

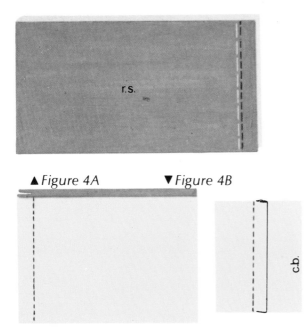

▲ Figure 4A   ▼ Figure 4B

Zig zag

Test on a piece of fabric. After straight stitching the seam, it should be trimmed to 0.3cm ($\frac{1}{8}$ inch). This is so that the depth of the stitch just touches the straight stitches, and the length of the stitch is close enough so that the raw edges are barely visible (figure 5). If the turning tends to stretch place a double line of the machine thread through the hole, on the foot, or centrally under the foot, and machine over this. The thread can then be pulled up slightly when the seam is neatened, and finished off with a few back stitches. Or alternatively use an overlocking foot.

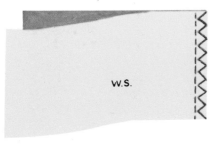

Figure 5

Interfacing

This is seldom used as it is not very attractive. If it is essential however use either a thickness of the same fabric, very fine organdie or a very fine net. Always check the interfacing for its appearance on the right side before deciding which one to use.

Fastenings

Use a light-weight nylon zip where necessary and be sure that turnings on the wrong side are turned in towards the zip tape and stitched at the very edge (figure 6). Loop buttonholes and covered buttons are often used instead of a zip.

Fasteners should always be nylon ones. Buttonhole-stitch over hooks and bars and preferably handmake the loops. Press studs should also be worked over in buttonhole stitch.

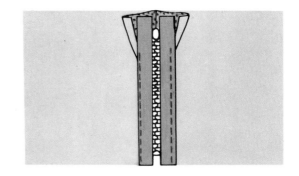

Figure 6

Hems

For very narrow hems use either a rolled, shell-stitched or corded edge.

A rolled hem is an extremely narrow hem, which should not be pressed. It is used on very sheer fabrics such as chiffon, silk and organdie on which the hem will show. The edge of the material is taken between the index finger and the thumb and rolled as you stitch. The stitches should be small catch stitches but not tight and not visible on the right side.

For a plain hem, a triple hem is best. This means that the fabric is turned in 7.5cm (3 inches) once and the same amount again and then carefully slip-stitched down (figure 7). A neat finish can be achieved by using a small straight stitch with a double or triple needle, a zig-zag stitch or an embroidery stitch. The stitch used should be repeated on another part of the garment as a design feature, the sleeve hems for example.

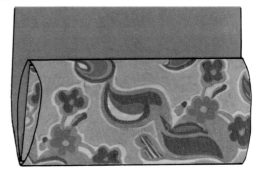

Figure 7

Decorative hems
Shell stitching

The same method is used for this as for rolled hems. Instead of catching the roll on to the wrong side however, the needle is passed through the roll and at regular intervals brought out on the wrong side. Then the thread is taken right over the roll and the needle is passed from the right side back to the wrong side. When the thread is pulled up it creates a loop in the material between the stitches (figure 8A). On some sewing machines it is possible to adjust the stitch pattern to an automatic shell stitch (figure 8B).

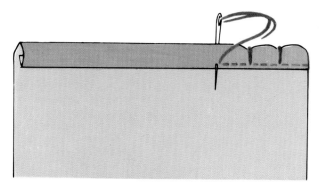

Figure 8A

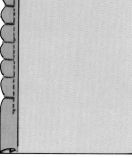

Figure 8B

Corded edging

This is a neat and rather decorative finish. Some matching or contrasting cord will be needed. It should be threaded through the hole in the machine foot on a zig-zag machine. Working on the right side of the fabric zig-zag the raw edges and the cord together (figure 8C).

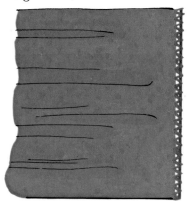

Figure 8C

Mantua seam

A mantua seam should be used to attach a flounce or frill to the hemline. The frill should be gathered evenly on to the garment with right sides and raw edges together and tacked. The turning of the frill should be trimmed to 0.6cm ($\frac{1}{4}$ *inch*) (figure 9A). The untrimmed edge should be turned on to the tacking line with the raw edge turned in, giving the effect of a binding or piping. Stitch along the tacking line (figure 9B). This method can also be used on the right side as a decoration and threaded to make it look more like a piping (figure 9C). A quick knit nylon yarn is very suitable for this as it is light in weight and the fibres fluff out to form a piping. This yarn can also be used between fabrics with a double or triple needle. The thickness of the yarn then depends on the distance between the lines of stitching.

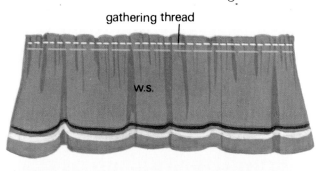

gathering thread

w.s.

r.s.

Figure 9A

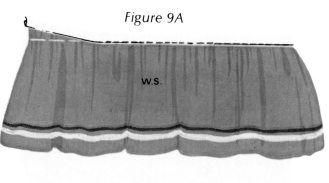

w.s.

r.s.

Figure 9B

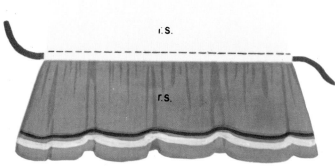

r.s.

r.s.

Figure 9C

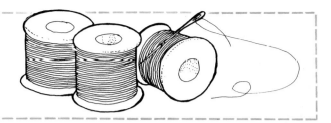

Working with lace

Making a garment in lace

Lace can be bought from the roll in the same way as other fabrics and in various widths from 69cm to 152cm (27 to 60 inches). The lace can be made from rayon, terylene, nylon, wool or cotton, and some lace can be bought with a scalloped border for use as a hemline or the scallops cut off and used as decoration on another part of the garment.

Care should be taken when choosing a pattern for a lace fabric as too many seams will break up the pattern of the lace. Also try and match up the pattern at seams as with ordinary patterned fabrics. The method of sewing lace together at seams applies to all types of lace. Use a heavy needle on the wrong side. Work two rows of straight stitch fairly close to each other. Trim the turnings very narrowly and oversew together.

Fine cotton lace is inclined to go limp with washing and needs starching to retain a crisp look.

Rayon lace can crease so it must be mounted to help prevent creasing and to add body to the fabric. Allow an extra 0.3cm ($\frac{1}{8}$ inch) on seams to allow for the roll of the fabric.

Terylene and nylon lace fabric is stiff when new and so it is advisable to wash and rinse it with a fabric softener before making up into a garment.

Wool lace often stretches badly when stitching. To prevent this stitch on the wrong side using a large straight stitch. Tie the threads together at one end of the seam. At the other end pull up the lower machine stitch until the seam is the correct length and tie off ends. Work stretch stitch alongside the straight stitch feeding the lace under the machine foot. When completed remove the row of straight stitch (figure 1).

Making lace insets

Draw the shape of the inset required on paper. Place this on the wrong side of the garment and a piece of lace larger than the inset on the right side. On the wrong side straight stitch around the motif through all the thicknesses. On the right side go over the straight stitching using a small zig zag (figure 2). Trim

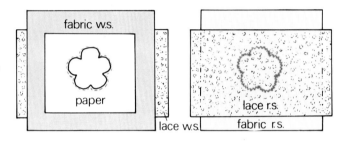

Figure 2

off the excess lace close to the edges. Trim away fabric on the wrong side of the lace motif. Place another piece of paper on to the wrong side of the garment. On the right side work another row of zig zag over the original row but using a slightly larger stitch (figure 3). (The paper holds lace and fabric firm while stitching.) Remove paper and fasten off all ends

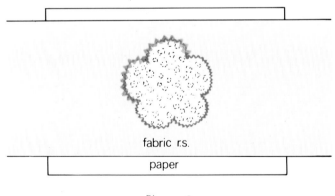

Figure 3

on the wrong side. If the lace motif is very fine a permanent backing of fine jersey nylon can be attached in the same way as the paper. This will give the motif extra strength but retain the transparency. If you cannot work zig zag stitch on your machine, work the first row of stitching using straight stitch. Then work another row of straight stitch close to the first on the outside. Remove paper in the same way as before. Work satin or blanket stitch over the two rows of machining in the same thread. To make

Figure 1

the edge more pronounced, the stitching in both methods can be worked over a thin cord or crochet thread (figure 4).

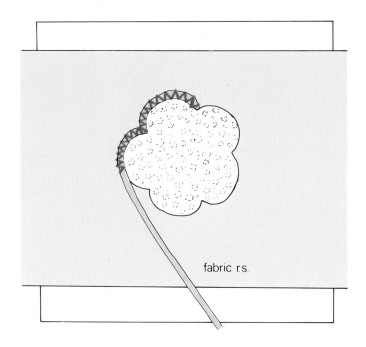

Figure 4

Lace can be decorated in various ways for evening wear by using sequins and lurex thread. Study the pattern of the lace and you will see the repeat in the pattern. Heavier types of lurex thread can be placed on the outside of a pattern and whipped on with ordinary thread (figure 5). Another effect can be made by backing the lace with a glitter fabric such as lurex.

Figure 5

Appliqué with lace

Garments can be decorated with lace motifs: cut a piece of lace larger than the motif required. Draw the shape required on paper and place on the wrong side of the lace. Work a row of straight stitches around the shape from the wrong side (figure 6). From

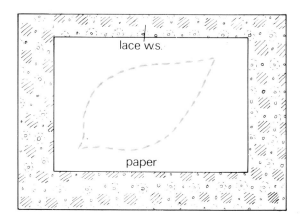

Figure 6

the right side work a row of small zig zag stitches over the straight stitches. Cut off excess lace and remove paper. Place another piece of paper beneath the main fabric and the motif on the right side. Work another row of slightly larger zig zag stitches over the first and remove the paper (figure 7).

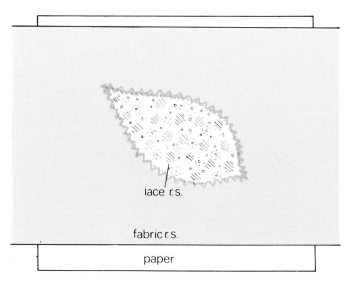

Figure 7

Lace trimmings

Cluny lace is a heavy crochet type of lace trimming made of cotton. It can be used as an insertion feature.

Guipure lace is a cotton trimming available in many different widths, designs and colours. The motifs can be cut out and stitched on separately or the trimming stitched on in a continuous line.

152

Insertion lace has two straight edges and can be stitched on by machine or hand. The fabric can then be removed from underneath. Insertion lace is available with eyelet holes already worked through which to thread ribbon (figure 8).

Figure 8

Galloon lace has one straight edge and one scalloped edge and is therefore used as border lace with the straight edge stitched to the garment (figure 9).

Figure 9

Flouncing lace like galloon lace has a straight edge with a cord and is attached in the same way.

To join lace

If it is possible overlap the lace at corners by stitching around a motif through all thicknesses. Trim away the excess lace underneath (figure 10). Otherwise work a row of straight stitches across the corner and trim away excess lace (figure 11).

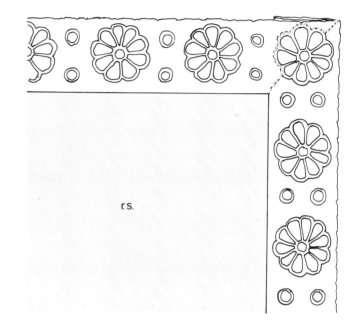

Figure 10

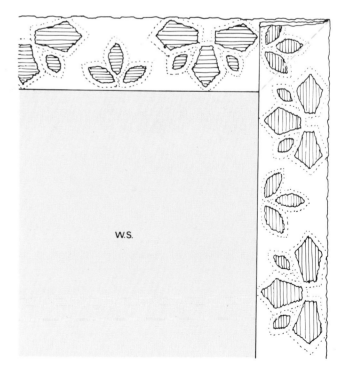

Figure 11

On most straight-edged lace one of the threads can be used as a gathering thread and pulled up so that the lace fits a curve on a garment and lies flat (figure 12). When the entire length of the lace is to be gathered allow approximately one and a half times the finished length. Pin to garment at intervals and pull up the lace in between (figure 13).

If it is difficult to pull up a gathering thread on the edge of the lace, work a small zig-zag stitch along the straight edge of the lace and insert a thin cord or crochet thread through the stitches. Pull up the thread to fit the curve (figure 14).

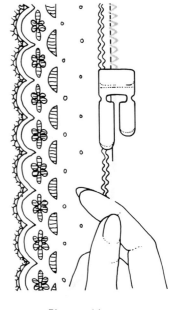

Figure 14

Broderie Anglaise

This is a cotton or cotton/polyester fabric available in a 91cm (*36 inch*) width or as a lace trimming. Wide trimming can be attached to the garment with a seam. With right sides together and raw edges facing the same way tack and stitch the trimming to the garment. Trim and press turnings. From the right side work zig-zag stitch over the seam line. This will hold the turnings down underneath (figure 15).

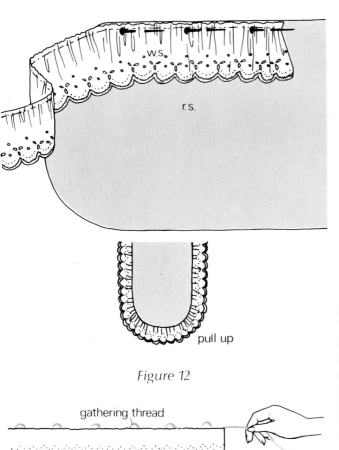

Figure 12

Figure 13

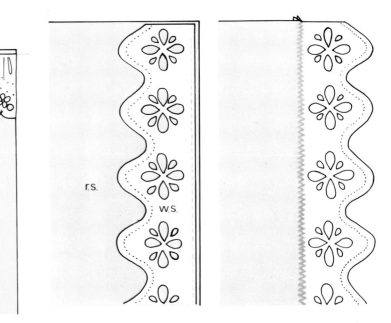

Figure 15

The luxury of fur

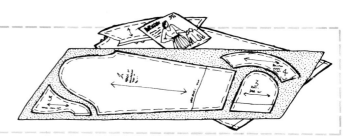

Handling fur fabric

Working with fur fabrics can be as simple as working with any other fabric. There are many different types of fur fabric but the method of cutting and sewing is basically the same for all.

Some fur fabrics can be washed quite easily and are therefore practical for children's clothes where frequent cleaning is necessary. This is a point to check when buying. Apart from coats, jackets, collars and cuffs, fur fabric has many other uses – toys, catsuits and bedspreads to mention a few.

After several washings, the pile may mat or flatten down. To restore this, use a teasle brush or 'poodle brush', the latter is less likely to damage the hands (figure 1). Lay the garment on a flat surface and brush the pile in one direction only, using long strokes. This will often change the appearance of a patterned textured fur, making it more fluffy and the pattern less pronounced.

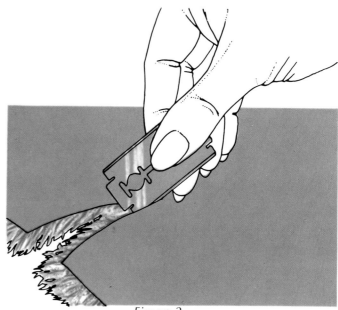

Figure 2

On the main part of a garment, i.e. back, front or sleeves, the pile should lie down towards the hem and on collars and cuffs it should lie upwards. If in doubt as to which way the pile is lying, hold the fabric up to the light with the wrong side facing you. The pile will extend beyond one of the cut edges and this is the lay of the pile (figure 3).

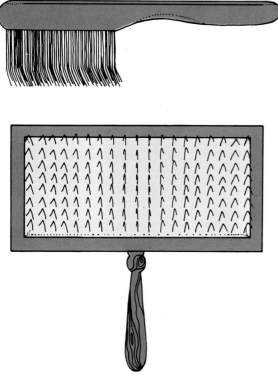

Figure 1

Figure 3

Cutting fur fabric

Always cut one layer at a time, cutting the fabric backing only and not the pile. Try to fold the fabric on the cutting line and, following the pattern or marking, cut through the fabric backing with a razor blade or unpicker (figure 2).

There are various depths of pile and the thicker the depth the greater the roll of the fabric. Extra turnings must be left on all seams to allow for this, from 0.3cm–1.3cm ($\frac{1}{8}$ inch–$\frac{1}{2}$ inch). Test on a piece of fabric first, together with the lining. Cut two small pieces of fur fabric and two of lining. With wrong sides together pin edges of lining to the edges of the fur fabric (figure 4). With right sides together stitch the

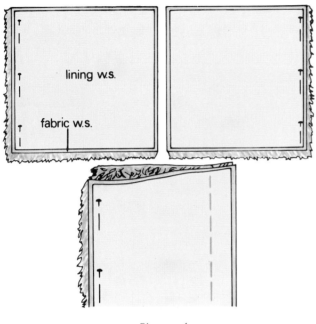

Figure 4

four thicknesses together along one edge. Open out flat on the wrong side. If the fur fabric is pulling up the lining unpin the edge and measure how much extra turning is required (figure 5).

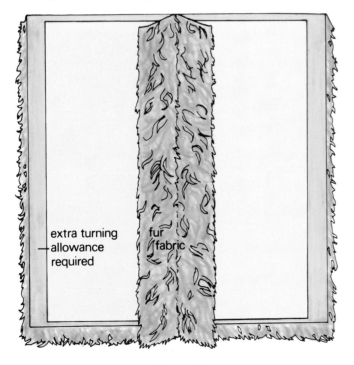

Figure 5

Making up

On some close pile fabrics it is difficult to stitch by machine without catching in the pile. To pull out the pile, after stitching use either a needle, pin or teasle brush along the seam on the right side, brushing in the direction of the lay of the pile.

When using a firm backed fabric, it is sometimes more satisfactory to stitch the seams by hand, as with real fur. Test first as the seam allowances must be cut off before stitching if using this method. Using pure silk or synthetic thread and a fine, sharp needle, work small oversewing stitches first in one direction and then back in the other direction. Whilst working use spring-type clothes pegs to hold the edges together, keeping all the pile tucked down on the right side (figure 6).

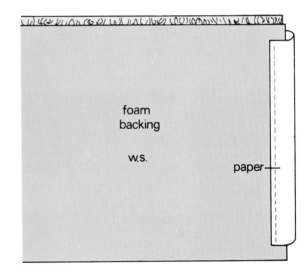

Figure 6

Some fur fabric is foam backed and may be difficult to stitch on a machine. Spraying the throat plate with silicone is often sufficient to overcome this. Alternatively use a Teflon coated machine foot, or fold strips of paper over the two edges, stitch through this and then remove the paper (figure 7). This type of fabric tends to hang away from the body and adds width to it.

If making a lined garment that is to be washed, make sure that the lining has the same properties as the fur fabric.

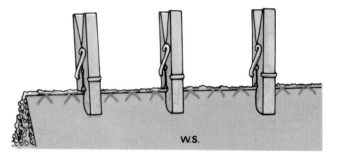

Figure 7

Fur collars and cuffs

Making and attaching collars and cuffs in fur fabric
Making up collars

Collars are usually backed with matching lining or contrasting fabric.

For a full thick collar cut a piece of foam the exact collar size but without turnings. Place this on to the wrong side of the fur fabric collar. Turn the seam allowance of the fur fabric on to the foam and slip-stitch down (figure 1). On a curve the fur fabric may need pinking to eliminate bulk.

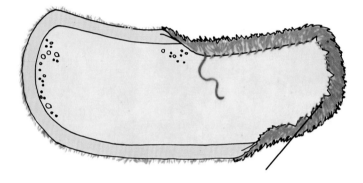

Figure 1

Cut a piece of interfacing the size of the collar, but without turnings. Then trim off another 0.6cm ($\frac{1}{4}$ *inch*) all around. Tack interfacing on to the wrong side of the lining using large diagonal stitches. Turn the seam allowance of the lining on to the interfacing and tack close to the fold. Then trim 1.6cm ($\frac{5}{8}$ *inch*) off the lining turning so that it lies flat (figure 2).

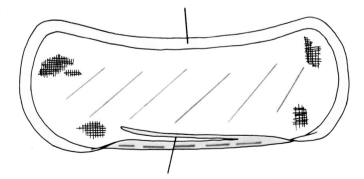

Figure 2

With wrong sides together slip-stitch the lining to the collar (figure 3). Remove all tacking.

For a flat collar use interfacing rather than foam and work in the same way.

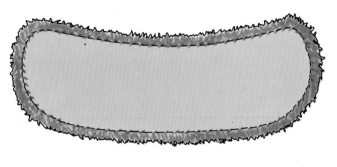

Figure 3

Making up cuffs

Cuffs do not need to be backed with lining as they are slip-stitched directly on to the sleeve.

Work the fur fabric cuff in the same way as the collar but without any lining. Position cuff on to sleeve and slip-stitch along both edges 0.6cm ($\frac{1}{4}$ *inch*) in from the edges (figure 4).

Figure 4

Attaching a collar

Here are methods for attaching three basic collars.

When altering the collar pattern, cut out the shape required in paper and pin on to the neck edge of the garment. The neck edges should match so adjust the pattern, where necessary, allowing turnings. It is advisable to cut a full collar pattern piece as the fur fabric should not be doubled when cutting out. A collar should be made up completely before it is attached to a neckline.

A roll collar is so called because it can be placed on top of another collar on a ready made garment. Slipstitch all around so that the inside edge lies along the highest point of the original collar (figure 5).

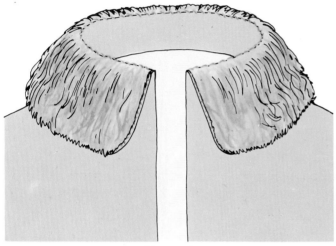

Figure 5

A Peter Pan collar is a collar which is also laid flat on top of the garment, but without a ready made collar underneath. It should be attached with button loops and buttons or French tacks (figure 6A).

French tacks: These are straight stitches approximately 1cm ($\frac{3}{8}$ *inch*) long worked between the collar and garment neck edges, at regular intervals and strengthened with buttonhole stitch worked over them.

Button loops: Work hand button loops at intervals along the neck edge of the finished collar. Sew on buttons to correspond on the inside of the neck line on the garment (figure 6B).

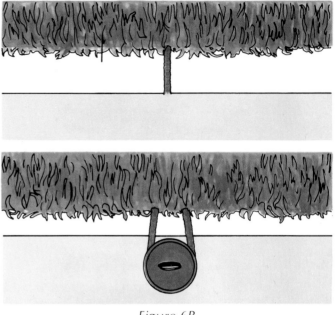

Figure 6B

A rever collar is again attached on the right side so that when the neck is fastened, the revers will stand up a little and when it is unfastened the revers will spread out and lie flat either side of the centre-front. To do this, stand the neck edge of the collar vertically on the seam line of the garment matching centre-fronts and centre-back. Insert the needle through the fold of the garment neck edge and then through the fold of the collar neck edge directly opposite. Pull the thread taut and continue in this way. When it is completed the collar will fold down on to the right side (figure 7).

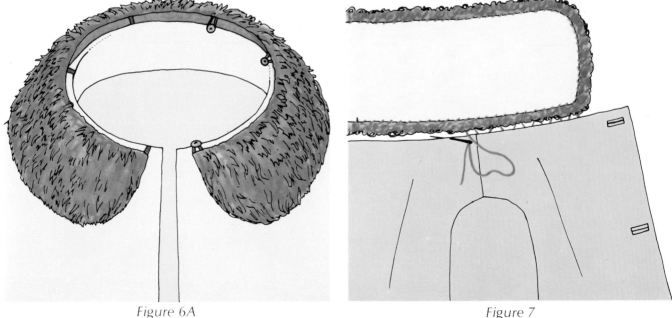

Figure 6A

Figure 7

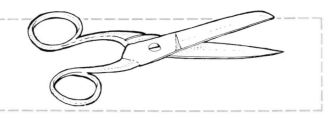

The leather look

Sewing suede and leather
Choosing a pattern
When choosing a pattern for a garment to be made in suede or leather, it is important to note the size of the pattern pieces. If the pattern pieces are too large for the size of the skins available, it may be necessary to insert seams on the pattern, for example at centre-back and centre-front. Seam allowances should be included before cutting out.

Choosing skins
There are many skins available to the home dress-maker in varying sizes and colours. Be sure to avoid skins with weak or stretched areas and be certain that the skins match exactly in colour and that there are no dye markings which look like water marks.
Feel the weight of the skin when choosing. For garments that will need regular washing, use a light-weight skin. Heavier skins are suitable for outer garments such as coats and jackets and should be dry cleaned, also for accessories – bags, hats and belts. Soft skins which will stretch but will also retain their shape are available for glove-making.

Cutting out
Never fold a skin but always lay it out flat. Secure pattern pieces with sticky tape, not pins which leave marks. Draw around the pattern pieces with chalk and mark in any notches and lines on the wrong side. Treat suede skins in the same way as napped fabrics by positioning the pattern pieces in one direction only and so that the top of the pattern is nearest the neck of the skin.
If you wish to line suede or leather garments to prevent stretching, cut out the lining from the pattern first and make up. Any adjustments necessary are more easily made on the lining as alterations on the skins are not always possible. (Holes made by stitching will remain in suede and leather when stitches are unpicked.)
Interfacing can be used, but should be applied with a hot, dry iron over brown paper.
Special leather and fabric glue is available, other glues should not be used as they will damage skins.

Sewing by hand
Use a special leather needle and synthetic thread or pure silk. Work back stitches along the seam lines but do not pull the stitches tight, as this will make the seam pucker.

Sewing by machine
Use a special leather needle or an unused needle size

14–16. Loosen the top tension slightly and adjust the foot pressure so that the skin can slide easily underneath. A special leather foot is available for machines. Use synthetic thread or pure silk. Spray some silicone polish on to the underside of the foot so that it slides along the skin easily, or fold a piece of tissue paper over the edges to be stitched and tear it away after stitching. Raw edges can be held together with sticky tape, paper clips or clothes pegs (figure 1).

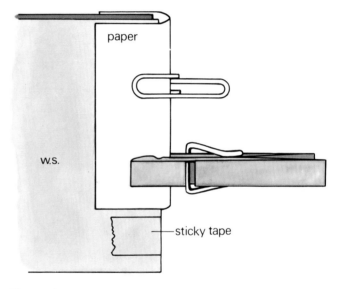

Figure 1

Stitching darts
Mark the dart on the wrong side with solid lines. Stitch in the normal way, but finish off the threads at the point by hand rather than reversing the machine stitch as this could stretch the skin (figure 2). Cut

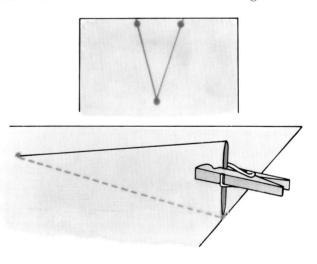

Figure 2

through the fold almost to the point. Trim off excess turnings and glue on to the garment (figure 3).

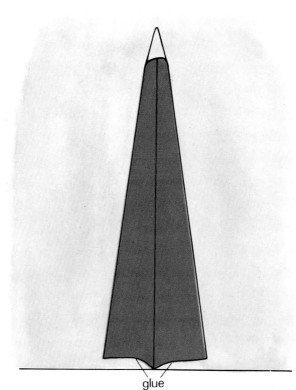

glue

Figure 3

Finishing seams
Fasten off threads by hand and glue down the turnings. One turning can be trimmed and the other laid over it and then top-stitched on the right side (figure 4). This must be done accurately as stitches taken out

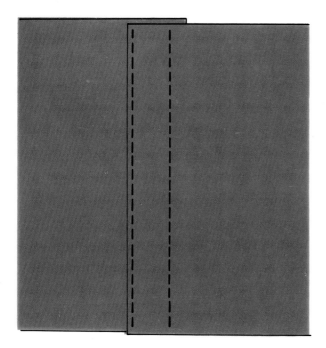

Figure 4

leave marks. Curved seams should be pinked before glueing to avoid bulk (figure 5).

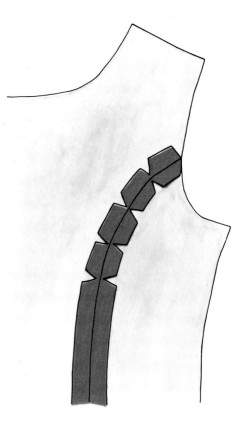

Figure 5

Raw edges on an unlined garment can be bound for a neater appearance. Straight tape should be attached to the back of any seam which will bear a lot of strain. For example, welt or set-in pockets should have a strip of tape or iron-on interfacing placed over the seam line on the wrong side, then stitching worked through all thicknesses (figure 6).

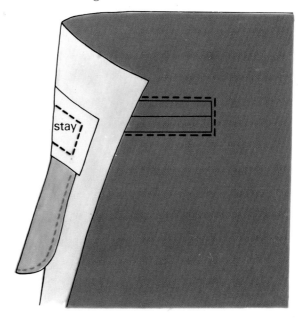
stay

Figure 6

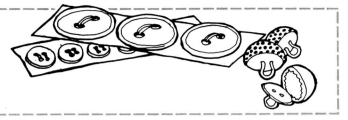

More ways with leather

Advanced work on suede or leather
Bound buttonholes

Bound buttonholes on leather and suede are worked in the same way as on fabric garments but after turning through the edges are glued down. Cut a slot out of the facing slightly larger than the buttonhole and instead of turning in the edges, glue into place. This slot may need interfacing on the wrong side before cutting to prevent it from stretching (figure 1).

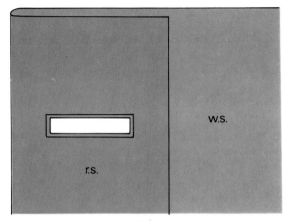

Figure 1

Machine worked buttonholes

To avoid stretching when stitching, work the buttonhole stitches over a thin cord or crochet thread (figure 2). On a very heavy suede decorative buttonholes can be worked. Cut out the shape required and stitch on to the wrong side through the garment and facing. Cut down the centre of the buttonhole (figure 3). Turn through to right side and glue down.

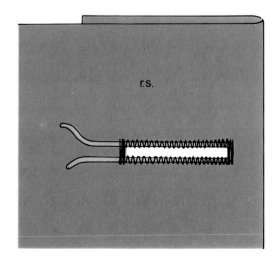

Figure 2

Stitch around the outside edge of the shape (figure 4). Interfacing may be used on the wrong side of the shape to prevent stretching.

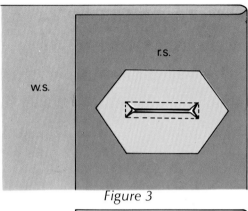

Figure 3

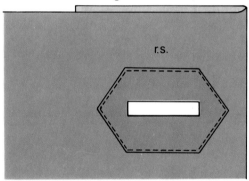

Figure 4

Sleeves

Before inserting sleeves into a lined garment tack the lining to the garment around the armhole. A small reduction may be necessary on the sleeve head to make the sleeve fit the armhole. Mark approximately 0.6cm ($\frac{1}{4}$ *inch*) down from the sleeve edge from the centre dot. Draw in a line tapering from either side of this dot to the notches (figure 5).

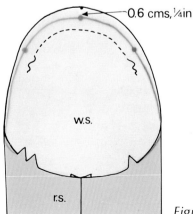

Figure 5

Work a row of gathers and fit the sleeve into the arm-hole before cutting off excess.

On a lined garment, work another row of stitching 0.6cm ($\frac{1}{4}$ inch) from the first. On an unlined garment the turnings can be bound together.

Hems

Hems are unnecessary on suede or leather garments, but if required turn hem allowance to the wrong side and glue into position. On a shaped edge the hem will need pinking (figure 6).

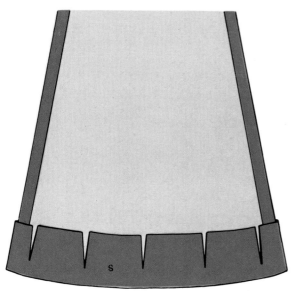

Figure 6

Top stitching

Trim off the seam allowance on one piece of the garment and place the edge on to the right side of the corresponding piece along the seam line. Hold in position with sticky tape. Work a row of top-stitching close to the edge and another row 0.6cm ($\frac{1}{4}$ inch) from the first (figure 7).

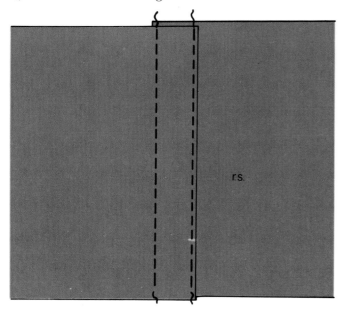

Figure 7

Collars and pockets can be worked in the same way before they are attached to the garment. Interface the pattern piece and hold the suede and interfacing together with sticky tape. Work a row of top stitching just inside the stitch line and another row 0.6cm ($\frac{1}{4}$ inch) from this (figure 8).

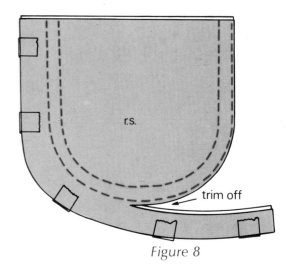

Figure 8

Buttons

When attaching buttons to a garment it is advisable to sew a small flat button on to the wrong side directly behind the main button and work stitches through both. This will prevent the button from pulling on the skin (figure 9). If the skin is torn, place the edges together on an ironing board and iron sticky woven tape on the wrong side to hold the edges together permanently.

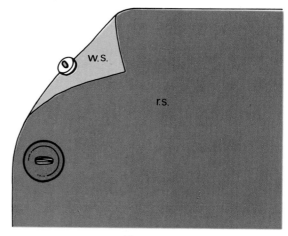

Figure 9

Cleaning

Leather soap can be bought for cleaning smooth leathers. Using a sponge, apply the soap to the leather with warm water using circular movements. Suede can be freshened up by holding the garment in front of a steaming kettle and then brushing with a suede brush or a piece of dry sponge. To remove bad grease marks rub the area with a piece of crocus paper (fine emery paper) always with a circular movement.

Using velvet fabrics

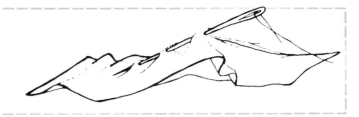

Working with Velvet, Velveteen, Needlecord, Corduroy

Velvet, velveteen, needlecord and corduroy are fabrics with a raised pile which usually runs in one direction only. When making a garment in one of these fabrics all pattern pieces must be placed one way. As a general rule the pile should lie upwards on chiffon velvet, etc., and downwards on velveteen, needlecord and corduroy. The fabric will feel smooth when the hand is run over it in the same direction as the pile. On crushed velvet and man-made jersey backed velvet it is possible to lay the pattern pieces either way as the pile does not run in a particular direction.

When attaching pattern pieces to the fabric use fine needles and not pins as these often leave permanent marks.

Pure silk or a fine man-made thread should be used for tacking, to avoid marking. Use very small tacking stitches as the fabric is inclined to slip when under the machine foot.

To avoid puckering on the seam line it may be necessary to loosen the tension and adjust the pressure foot. On machines where this is not possible, tissue paper placed underneath the fabric will prevent the teeth of the throat plate marking the fabric. Most velvet garments hang better with a lining and this prevents them clinging. When using a synthetic fabric, use anti-static lining or wash the lining in one of the new fabric softeners before using.

Pressing

Ideally, velvet fabrics should be pressed on a needled velvet board (available at a haberdashery) (figure 1). Velveteen, corduroy and needlecord can be pressed flat with a slightly damp cloth and iron. Use very light movements with the nose of the iron. Never place the iron down flat or leave it in one spot for any period of time. It is essential to test the fabric before any kind of pressing is done.

Figure 1

A substitute for a velvet board is a cover made of close-piled velvet fixed over the ironing board or table. Place the right side of the fabric on to this and on a test seam try pressing very lightly with the iron set at the correct temperature for the fabric. Place a piece of tissue paper between the seam and the garment to avoid a ridge appearing.

Another method of pressing is to stand the iron on its heel and, holding the seam open, pass the wrong side over the iron (figure 2). Paper pinned at each end will help to avoid burning the fingers or attach the paper to each end of the seam and, with the wrong side of

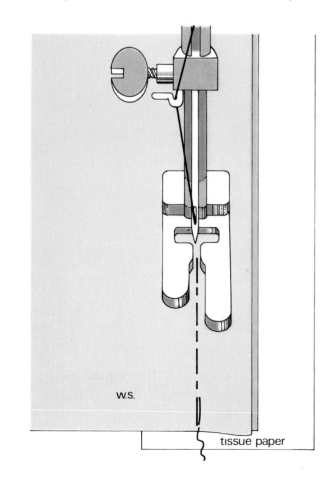

w.s.

tissue paper

163

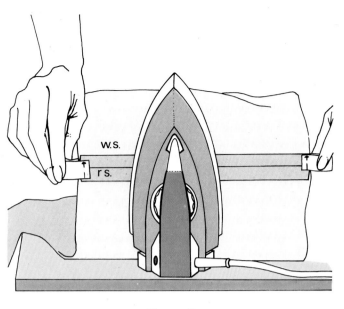

Figure 2

the garment facing a kettle that is steaming, move it backwards and forwards through the steam. Place the seam on to a flat surface with the wrong side up and, with a round piece of wood covered with a cloth and slightly padded, gently roll the seam out, keeping paper between the turnings and the garment (figure 3).

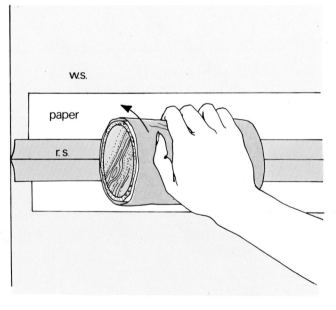

Figure 3

When pressing armhole seams it is advisable to insert a pressing mitt or a pad into the armhole whilst the garment is wrong side out. Steam in front of a kettle and use the round pad to roll the seam out towards the sleeve (figure 4). Always press all seams before neatening, to prevent marking. To freshen up a velvet garment, hang it in the bathroom with the steam penetrating it for a short while, then hang it to air. Velvet fabrics are inclined to hold fluff, dust and powder. The easiest and least expensive way to clean

this off is to use a small piece of dry sponge, brushing in the direction of the pile.

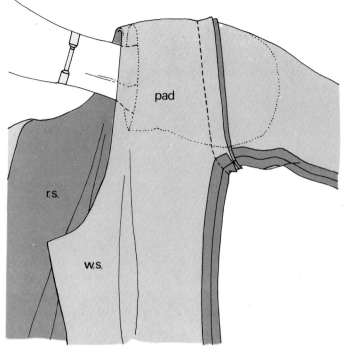

Figure 4

Hems

When the garment is unlined, hems can be turned up with crossway binding or a silky-type straight binding, depending on the amount of flare. Alternatively the edges can be zig-zagged or oversewn by hand and then slip-hemmed into place. Pick up one thread only when working this as indentations may appear on the right side. Do not stretch the binding too much on the edge of the hem as it may pull on the right side.
Most velvet fabrics should be dry-cleaned, but if the manufacturers give instructions for washing, follow these to avoid damaging the fabric. Top-stitching is not generally advisable as it crushes the pile and breaks the line of corduroy or needlecord.

Interfacing

Iron-on interfacing can be used on facings for corduroy and needlecord, but it is not suitable for other velvets. Usually a woven type is most satisfactory and it is essential to use the correct weight. If the interfacing is too heavy it will spoil the line of the garment and may wear away the fabric.

Zips

It is advisable to use an invisible zip if possible, which can be inserted by machine. All other zips should be inserted by hand, using small stitches, as machine stitching breaks the pile and looks ugly. Use the correct weight of zip for the fabric; the teeth of a too heavy zip could wear through the material.

5

Making your
own patterns

The basic block

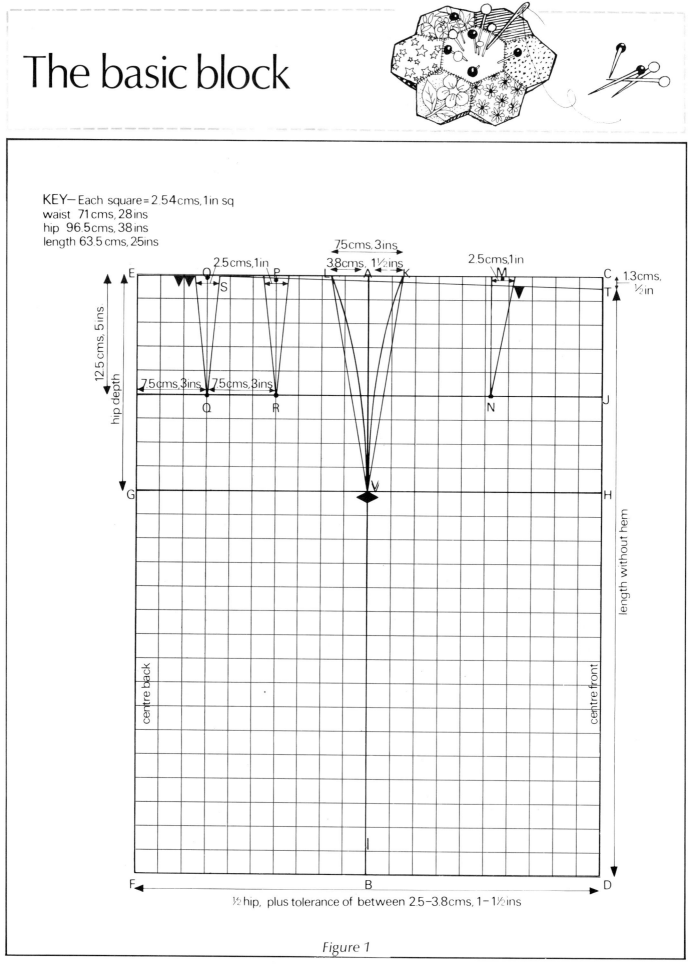

KEY—Each square=2.54cms, 1in sq
waist 71cms, 28ins
hip 96.5cms, 38ins
length 63.5cms, 25ins

Figure 1

Why make a basic block?

A basic block is invaluable if you wish to make your own patterns, or adapt an existing pattern to incorporate your own ideas and to obtain a perfect fit, especially if you are not stock size.

Making a basic skirt block

You will need the following basic equipment: graph paper, tape measure, pins, ruler, metre or yard stick, pencil and tape.

Taking the measurements

It is necessary to take accurate measurements of waist, hips, centre-back length and the depth between waist and hips.

Measure the hips while standing and when sitting, to decide on the amount of tolerance needed. An allowance of up to 7.5cm (3 inches) should be made for ease of movement.

The waistline on the garment is usually made a little larger than the actual waist measurement and is then eased into a waistband of the exact waist measurement.

To measure the depth between waist and hips tie a piece of tape around the waist and measure down from this to the fullest part of the hips, usually between 15cm and 20cm (6 inches and 8 inches). To measure the length, place one end of the tape measure on the waist tape at the centre-back, let it hang straight down and decide the required length.

Making the block

Cut a piece of graph paper to the length of the skirt without a hem and half the hip width with approximately 2.5cm–3.8cm (1 inch–1½ inch) allowance for tolerance. Do not include any seam or hem allow-

ances at this stage as these are added later.

Fold the pattern in half lengthways, crease, unfold and draw a line on the crease for the side seam A–B. Mark in centre-front and back lines C–D and E–F. Measure down from C and E to the hip level and draw a horizontal line across the pattern, G–H. Measure down again from C and E 12.5cm (5 inches) and draw another horizontal line I–J.

Measure 3.8cm (1½ inches) either side of point A and mark K and L. Draw a line from K and L to meet at the hipline on A–B. Mark this V and draw a balance mark just below V. Draw a curved line from V–K and from V–L.

Mark M half way between C and K. Measure the distance from C–M and mark a point at the same distance from J on the line I–J, add 1.3cm (½ inch), and mark with a dot, N. Mark 1.3cm (½ inch) either side of M and draw two lines to meet at N.

Measure from E towards L 7.5cm (3 inches) and 15cm (6 inches) and mark O and P. Repeat this on line I–J and mark Q and R. Measure 1.3cm (½ inch) either side of O and P. Draw lines to meet at Q and R. Mark the point where the inside line of dart O meets line E–L, point S. The waistband usually dips at the centre front. Draw a line from the inside line of the dart O marked S to 1.3cm (½ inch) below C marked T. Mark in balance marks next to M and O (figure 1).

Waistband Cut a strip of paper the length and the width required for the waistband. Fold in half widthways, crease, open out and draw a line 2.5cm (1 inch) from the creaseline on one side only. Mark this line U (figure 2). Fold ends of strip to this line, crease and open out. Mark centre-front on the crease line on the larger half and centre-back on the creaseline on the smaller half (figure 3). Place centre front line of waist-

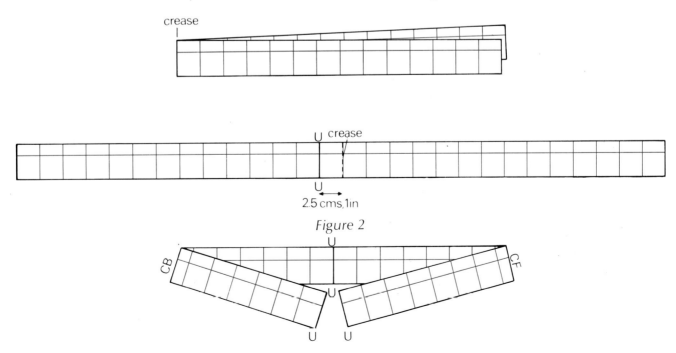

crease

U crease

2.5 cms, 1 in

Figure 2

CB   U   CF

U   U

Figure 3

band on line T–K and mark in balance mark. Place centre back line of waistband on to line E–L and mark in balance mark (figure 4).

This pattern can be used to make a two or four panelled skirt.

For a two panelled skirt mark in 'place to fold' on centre-front and centre-back. Write 'Skirt Front' and 'Skirt Back' in large letters and '(cut 1)' on pattern (figure 5). Cut pattern along line B–V, and from V–L and V–K on the curved lines. Cut off excess above T–S.

For a four panelled skirt mark in a straight grain line on each half on a vertical line. Write in large letters 'Skirt Front' and 'Skirt Back' and '(cut 2)'.

Mark in balance marks on centre front and centre back and on side seams approximately 7.5cm (3 inches) above the hem line (figure 6). Cut pattern along line B–V, and from V–L and V–K on the curved lines. Cut off excess above T–S.

When the block has been completed, it is advisable to make a toile. This is the garment made up in calico to check the fit before making up any garment in fabric. Allow turnings when cutting out and

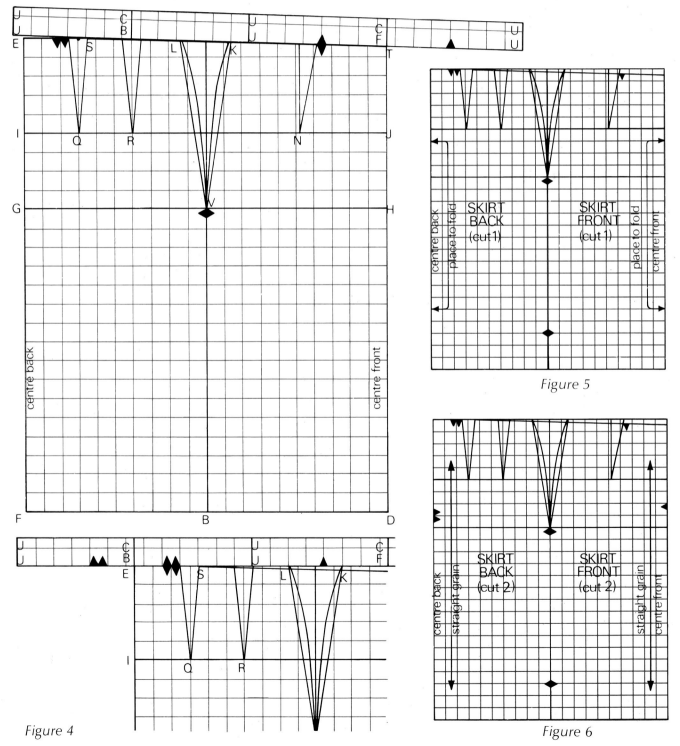

Figure 4

Figure 5

Figure 6

stitch together. Try on and fit. Transfer any alterations on to the graph paper block.

A permanent pattern can be made from the toile, in Vilene or in paper.

If the pattern is to be used many times, the toile makes a strong, permanent pattern. Unpick the made-up toile and fold it in half at the centre-front and centre-back. Work coloured stitching to indicate darts and seam lines, a straight line of stitching an equal distance from the centre-front and centre-back as the straight grain line, and another row on the hem fold.

When using Vilene or paper for the pattern, place the graph pattern on to it and mark in seam allowances on all seam lines and 5cm–7cm (2 inches–3 inches) for the hem. (Use coloured thread or pencil to mark Vilene.) Add an extension to either end of the waistband, for lapping, plus turnings. Add seam allowance to one long side only, then mark out twice this width and mark in the fold line and the balance marks (figure 7).

It is essential to make all markings clear and accurate. Keep the original graph pattern without turnings as this can be adapted for other designs.

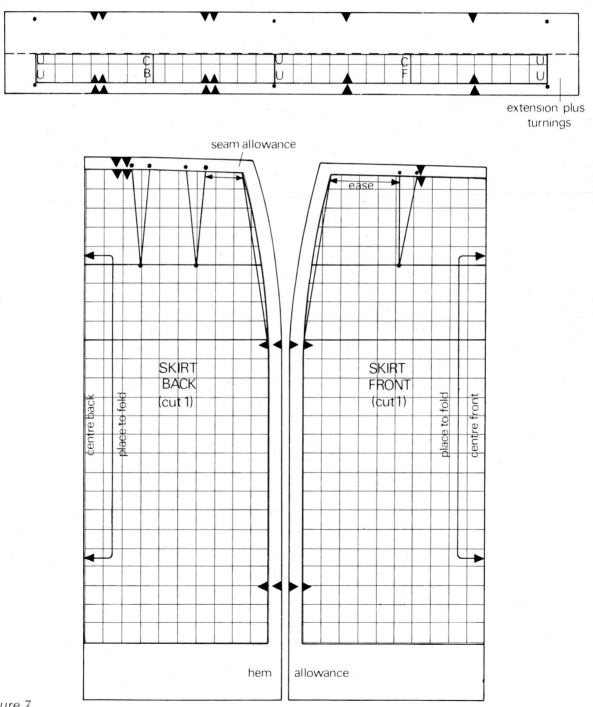

extension plus turnings

seam allowance

ease

SKIRT BACK (cut 1)

centre back   place to fold

SKIRT FRONT (cut 1)

place to fold   centre front

hem   allowance

Figure 7

Making skirt patterns

To make a shaped, yoked or gored skirt, you will be using the basic skirt block on page 166.

Shaped skirt without waist darts

Trace out the original skirt block omitting the waist darts and side seam. Draw in a horizontal line at hip depth and a new hip line 2cm ($\frac{3}{4}$ inch) above this. Mark in waistline A−B, new hip line C−D and hemline E−F. Fold the paper in half vertically and then in half again, making three equally spaced creases. Open up the paper and draw lines on the crease marks G−H, I−J and K−L (figure 1). Cut on these lines almost to line C−D. Fold out three darts of equal measure-

ment at G, I and K, so that the line A−B equals half the waist measurement plus a little ease if desired. H, J and L will then open up on the hemline. Place paper beneath the gaps and pin or paste the pattern into position. Mark H1, J1 and L1. Draw in the side seam from the centre of the dart at I to line C−D and centrally between J and J1 on line E−F. Cut the pattern on the side seam and draw in balance marks (figure 2). Mark A−E Centre-back (place to fold) and B−F Centre-front (place to fold). Both are (Cut 1). Re-cut the pattern, add turnings and hem allowance (figure 3).

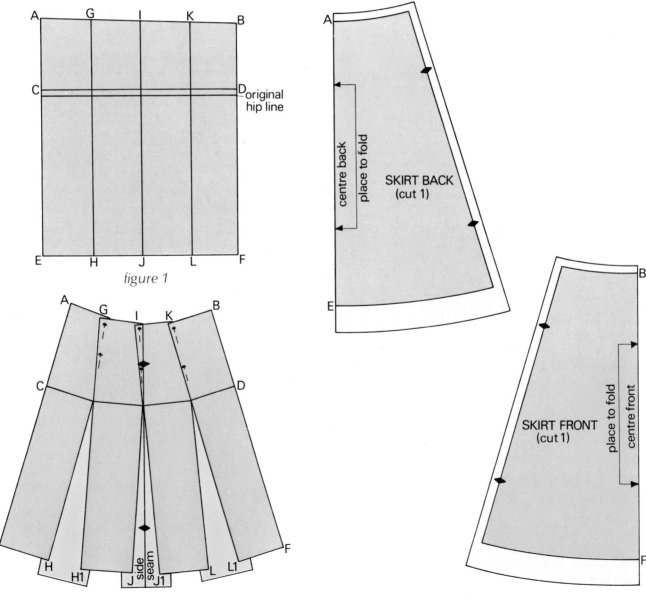

figure 1

figure 2

figure 3

Gored skirt

Trace out the basic block as before with lines A–B, C–D and E–F marked. Fold paper in half vertically and mark I–J. Measure from A–I and divide equally into three. Mark G one third from A and two thirds from I. Mark K two thirds from I and one third from B. From these points draw parallel lines to H and L on line E–F. Cut on these three lines almost to line C–D. Fold out darts at G, I and K as before. Place paper under the gaps and mark H1, J1 and L1. Draw lines centrally on darts G, I and K as far as line C–D and continue to points half way between H–H1, J–J1 and L–L1. Draw in balance marks on all these lines and cut on the lines (*figure 4*).

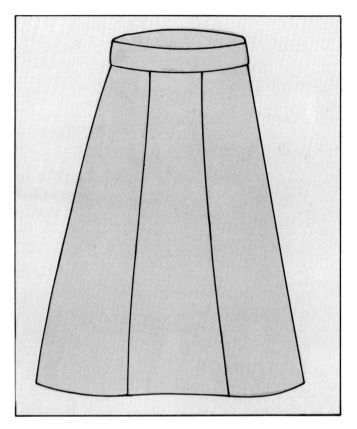

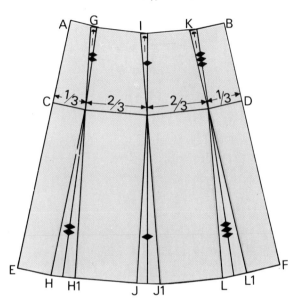

figure 4

Re-draw the pattern and mark A–E Centre-back (place to fold) and B–F Centre-front (place to fold). Both are (Cut 1). On piece G–I draw a straight grain line centrally and mark Skirt side back (Cut 2). On piece I–K draw a straight grain line centrally and mark Skirt side front (Cut 2). Cut on lines G–H, I–J and K–L. Add turnings and hem allowance (*figure 5*).

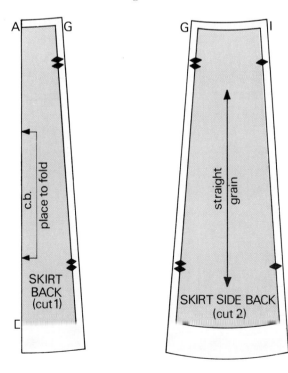

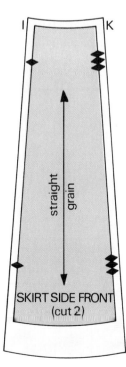

figure 5

Yoked skirts

There are various yoke styles that can be made from the basic block pattern. Before deciding on a style, the height of the wearer and the length of the completed skirt should be considered, in order to obtain the most flattering effect. A deep yoke on a short skirt will appear out of proportion. The general ruling is that the yoke can be up to a quarter of the total length of the skirt on a tall figure, this decreasing to one sixth for a shorter figure.

Trace out the basic block and mark in the original darts, side seam, centre-back and centre-front. Decide on the depth and design of the yoke desired and draw in on the pattern, making sure that the lines match on the side seam L–B and K–B.

Draw in balance marks on the yoke line and on the side seam above and below the yoke line. The lower points of the darts Q, R and N must be lengthened or shortened so that they touch the yoke line (*figure 6*).

On the front skirt and yoke mark in the Centre-front – place to fold (Cut 1). On the back skirt and yoke mark in the Centre-back – place to fold (Cut 1). Add turnings and hem allowance (*figure 7*).

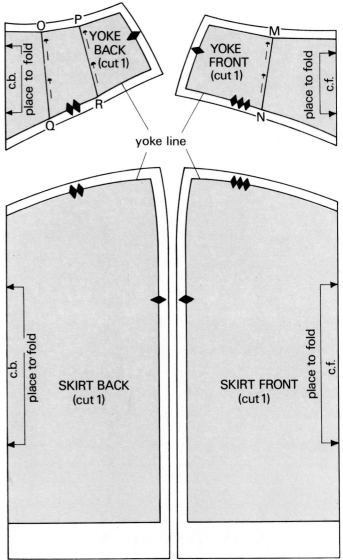

figure 7

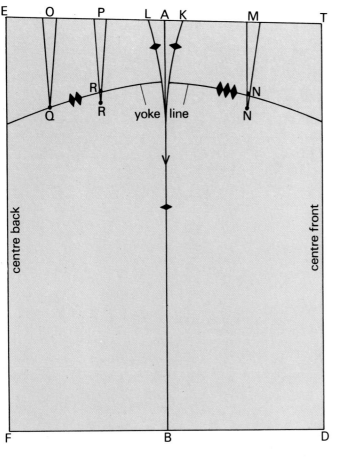

figure 6

Cut on line B–L and K through V. Cut on the yoke line back and front. Fold out the darts at the waistline at O, P and M and pin into position.

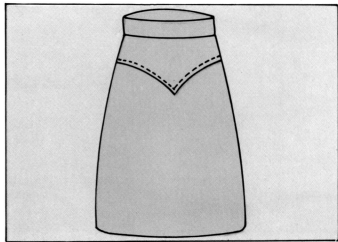

This skirt pattern may be used just as it is or pleats added. Instructions for adding pleats to a pattern are given on page 174, *(figure 8)*.

To make the skirt into a flared style draw equally spaced vertical lines from the yoke line to the hem-lime, as for the shaped skirt. Cut on these lines from the hemline almost to the yoke line and open at the lower edge. To give more width, half the measurement inserted in the hemline may be added to the side seams on the back and front. Draw straight lines from B to B1. This is where the side seam starts to curve towards the waist. Add turnings and hem allowance *(figure 9)*.

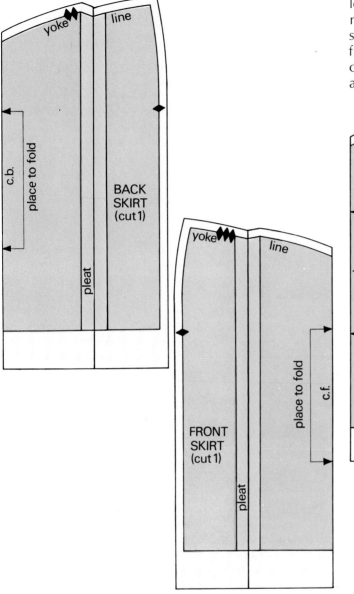

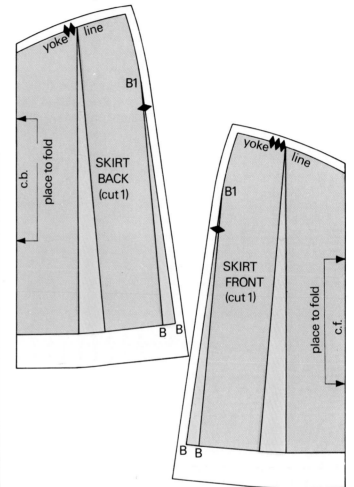

figure 8

figure 9

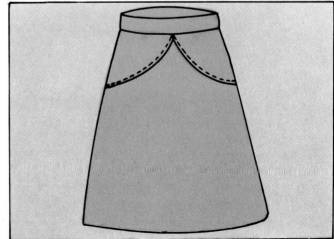

Planning for pleats

Adding pleats to a pattern

Inverted box pleat on a straight skirt

Decide on the depth of pleat required. Place the pattern for the skirt front on graph paper so that the distance between the centre-front edge and the edge of the graph paper equals double the depth of the pleat required. Draw around the pattern and mark notches. Write 'cut 1' on the new pattern.

Mark the original centre-front line AB and write 'fold line' along this line. Draw another line half way between AB and the edge of the graph paper and mark CD. Write 'fold line' along this line and 'centre-front' and 'to fold' on the edge of the graph paper (figure 1).

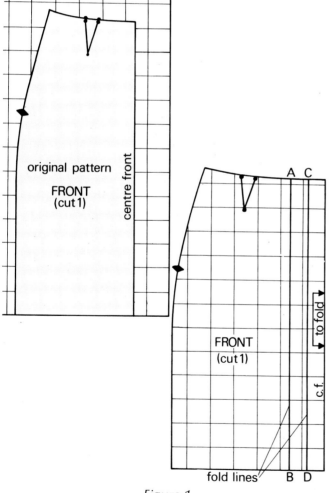

Figure 1

Cut out in fabric and tack along lines AB and CD both sides of the centre-front. Lay the fabric flat with right side facing up. Fold the fabric on the two lines AB and place to the centre-front. Tack down the folds. Turn the fabric to the wrong side and the lines CD will automatically form folds. Tack down these folds

through all thicknesses and press (figure 2).

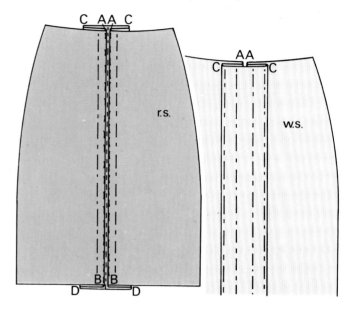

Figure 2

On the right side tack across the top of the pleat and across the bottom which should be approximately half way between the hip and knee levels. Top-stitch down the folds and across the bottom of the pleat. Work a safety bar or arrow head at the bottom end of the pleat. Make up the garment in the normal way leaving the tacking in the pleats until the garment is completed (figure 3).

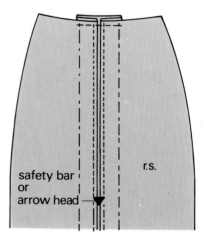

Figure 3

Visible box pleat

Draw a new pattern incorporating fold lines for pleats, as for inverted pleat.

Cut out the fabric and with wrong sides together fold the fabric on the centre-front line so that the lines AB lie on top of each other. Tack down AB through both

174

thicknesses. Machine stitch from A towards B starting at the waist and finishing at hip level (*figure 4*). Lay the

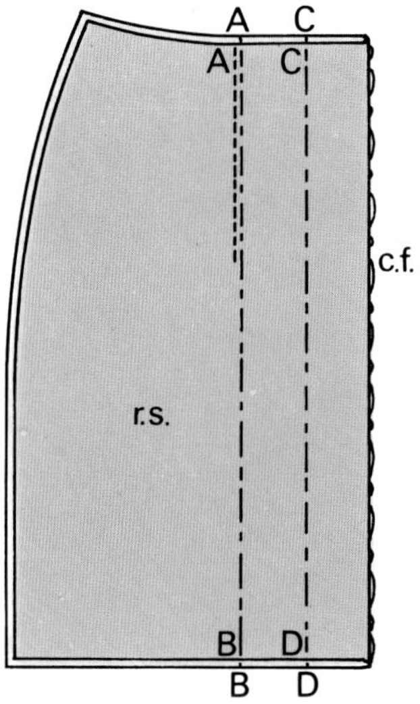

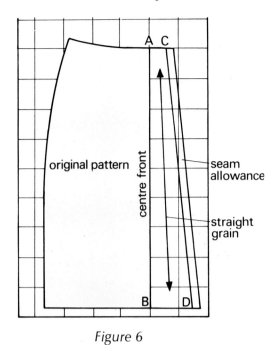

Figure 4

fabric flat and flatten the pleat so that the lines CD automatically form folds on the right side. Tack down the folds through all thicknesses. Top-stitch on the edge of the folds to the required depth. Stitch from the folds across the pleat to the centre-front at an angle (*figure 5*).

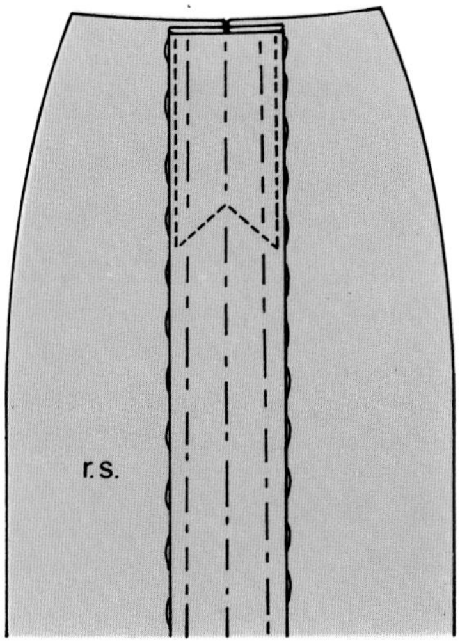

Figure 5

Inverted pleat on a flared skirt
This is a shaped pleat with a separate backing piece to enable the garment to hang well. The lower edge of the pleat is usually 1.3cm (½ inch) larger than double the measurement at the top edge of the pleat.
Place the pattern on to a piece of graph paper so that the centre-front edge lies approximately 10cm (4 inches) from the edge of the paper. Mark centre-front of pattern AB. Measure 3cm (1¼ inches) horizontally from A and mark C, and 7.5cm (3 inches) from B and mark D. Draw a straight line from C to D. Mark the straight grain line between AB and CD. Add a seam allowance to the right side of CD and cut off excess

paper. Fold the pattern on the centre-front line and trim off excess at the waistline (*figure 6*).

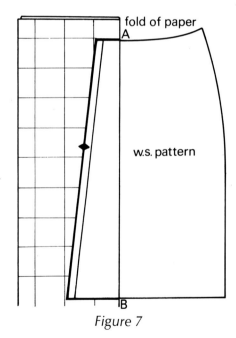

Figure 6

Fold a piece of graph paper in half and place the skirt pattern on this paper so that AB lies on the fold line. Draw around the pattern and mark the notch (*figure 7*).

Figure 7

Remove pattern and cut out the new pattern which is the backing piece for the pleats. Mark 'to fold' and 'cut 1' and mark a straight grain line on the backing piece. Write 'cut 2' on the skirt pattern.
Cut out skirt and pleat backing piece in fabric and tack along AB on the backing piece. This is the centre-front. With wrong sides together fold the skirt along AB on both sides and place these folds to the centre-front of the backing piece on the right side. Tack through all thicknesses. Turn the skirt on to the wrong

side and with matching notches, tack the edges of the skirt and backing piece together. Press (figure 8).

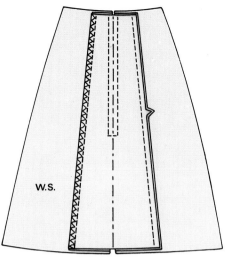

Figure 8

Tack across the top of the pleat. From the right side top-stitch down the folds AB through all thicknesses of fabric and to the depth required. Work a safety bar or arrowhead at the end of the stitching.

Unpick the tacking at the lower edge of the seams on the wrong side. Work the skirt and backing piece hems separately. Then tack and stitch the seams. Trim and neaten turnings together.

Knife pleats on a straight or slightly flared skirt

These are easy to work and can be inserted where required. Cut through the pattern parallel with the centre-front edge at the required place. Place a piece of paper underneath the two separate pieces and spread them open until the gap equals double the width of pleat required.

Draw a line down the centre of the insertion paper and mark CD. This is the fold line of the pleat. Mark the other lines AB and EF (figure 9). Fold the pattern along

AB. Decide which way the pleats will lie and pin the folds in that direction. Trim off excess paper at the waistline.

Cut out in fabric and tack along fold lines. With wrong sides together fold the fabric along AB or EF and place the fold to EF or AB respectively. Tack through all thicknesses. On the wrong side tack through all thicknesses close to line CD. Press. Tack across the top of the pleats. From the right side machine stitch to the required depth close to the fold of the pleat. Strengthen the end of the pleat as above (figure 10).

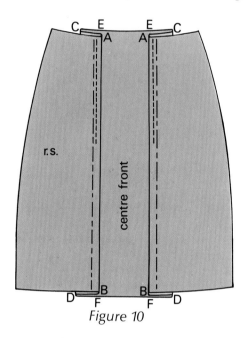

Figure 10

A dart can be worked into the pleat by using the above method. Cut parallel to the centre-front through the centre of the dart to the lower edge of the pattern. Mark the outside points of the dart, E and A at the waistline. Fold along these lines and work as above (figure 11).

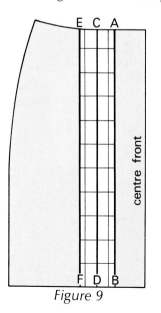

Figure 9

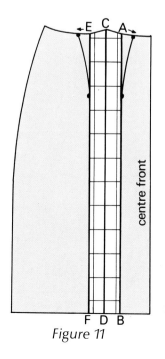

Figure 11

Making a pleated skirt

waistline. Mark the centre of each piece of insertion paper with a straight line and write 'fold line'. Take half the pleat measurement plus turnings and add to each side of the pattern (*figure 1*).

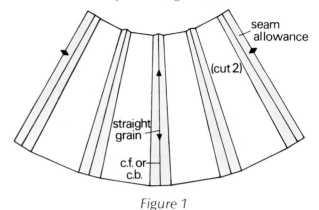

Figure 1

With right side facing up, lay the skirt pattern on a flat surface. Fold each pleat on the centre line towards the right hand side of the pattern so that the edges of the insertion paper lie on top of each other. Mark where the fold line lies on the pattern. Trim off excess paper at the waistline. Mark notches.

Fabric required

This depends on the width and length of the skirt, the width of the fabric and depth of the pleats. It is advisable to measure the lower edge of the skirt pattern before buying fabric as it will then be easier to calculate the quantity required.

To calculate the quantity exactly Mark the width of fabric required on a large piece of paper. Fold the paper in half lengthways as one would with fabric. The edges of the paper represent the selvedges of the fabric. Write 'selvedge' on these edges. Fold the skirt pattern pieces in half down the centre and place to the fold of the paper. Take the length of paper covered by the pattern as the quantity of fabric needed (*figure 2*).

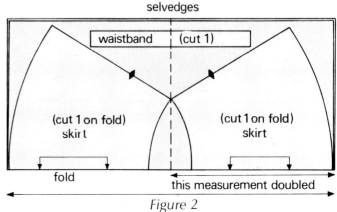

Figure 2

Making a pleated skirt

You will need the basic skirt block on page 166. From the block, cut your skirt pattern without turnings. Join the front and back pattern together at one side seam. Mark centre-back and centre-front. Fold the pattern in half exactly and cut along the fold line. Taking one half of the pattern, draw three vertical lines an equal distance apart at the waist and hem. Cut along these lines and insert paper underneath so that the overall width of the insertion paper at the lower edge is three times the width at the

If the pattern pieces are too wide for the fabric, a centre-front and centre-back seam will be needed. Remove the pattern pieces, cut down the centre lines and glue extra strips of paper on to the centre-front and centre-back edges. Trim the paper to the width of turnings required (figure 3).

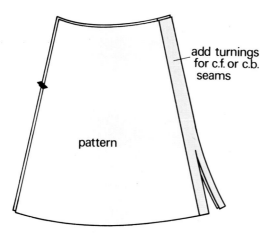

Figure 3

Fold the paper that is representing the fabric in half with the short edges together. Place the pattern pieces with the centre edges to the 'selvedges' of the paper. The quantity of fabric needed will be double the length from the fold of the paper to the short edges (figure 4).

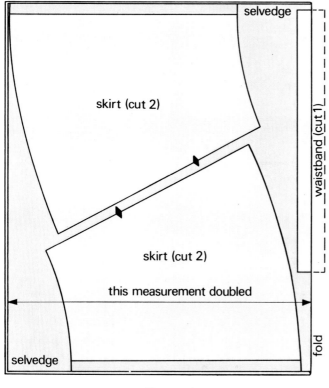

Figure 4

You will also need

Matching thread, 1 × 17.5cm (7 inch) zip; 1 × 1.6cm ($\frac{5}{8}$ inch) button; 1 piece of interfacing the length and width of waistband required.

Cutting out the skirt

Following figures 2 or 4, fold the fabric in half and place the pattern pieces as indicated. For the waistband, cut a strip on the straight grain double the width required plus turnings, by the waist measurement plus 10cm (4 inches). The waistband pattern in figure 4 is the same length but only half the width and it is placed to the fold.

Cut out and transfer all markings, pleat lines and the straight grain line. Work rows of tailor tacking down the pleat lines.

Making up

With right sides together and matching notches tack and stitch all the seams except for the left side seam. Press turnings and neaten together.

Place the fabric on a large flat surface. Working from the right side, fold each pleat on a line and place the fold to the corresponding line. Tack down fold through all thicknesses. Repeat all around skirt.

Using matching thread top-stitch close to the fold of each pleat from the waist for approximately 21.5cm–23cm (8$\frac{1}{2}$–9 inches). Take the ends of the thread to the wrong side and fasten off securely (figure 5).

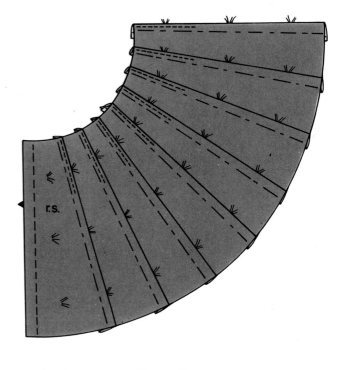

Figure 5

Zip

Taking the length of the zip, measure from the waist down the left side selvedge and clip across the turnings. Fold turning under between this point and the waist.

Place the right hand side of the zip under the fold so that the edge of the fold lies as close to the teeth as possible. Tack and stitch (*figure 6*).

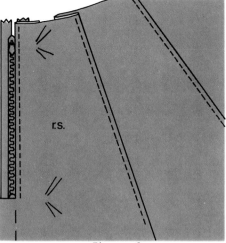

Figure 6

Place the side front pleat over the zip. Tack the selvedge to the zip tape and stitch close to the teeth through single fabric.

With right sides together tack and stitch the left side seam below the zip (*figure 7*).

Zip guard

Cut a strip of fabric on the straight grain a little longer than the zip and approximately 7.5cm (*3 inches*) wide. With right sides together fold in half lengthways and stitch across the short end. Turn through and neaten raw edges together. Press. Place the neatened edges to the edge of the zip tape so that the fold protrudes beyond the zip teeth. Tack and stitch close to the fold through all thicknesses, but allowing enough room for the zip to move freely (*figure 8*).

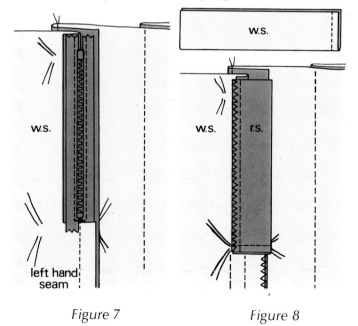

Figure 7   *Figure 8*

Waistband

Cut a strip of interfacing half the width of the waistband. Place to the wrong side of the waistband so that one edge lies along the fold line. With right sides together fold the waistband in half and stitch across the short ends. Trim turnings and turn through. Place the interfaced side of the waistband to the top edge of the skirt. Tack and stitch. Trim turnings and press on to the waistband. Make a turning of 1.6cm ($\frac{5}{8}$ *inch*) on the remaining edge.

Cut two pieces of tape 18cm (*7 inches*) long. Fold each piece in half and place the ends just above the waistband stitch line so that the loops hang down the skirt. One loop should be next to the zip and the other on the side seam. Tack into position. Slip-stitch the remaining folded edge on to the stitch line. Press (*figure 9*).

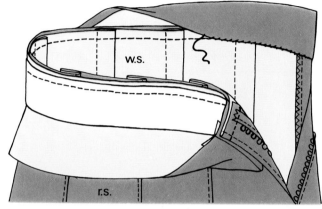

Figure 9

Work a horizontal buttonhole 2cm ($\frac{3}{4}$ *inch*) long and 1cm ($\frac{3}{8}$ *inch*) in from the edge of the waistband. Sew on a button to correspond with the buttonhole.

Hem

Allow the skirt to hang for at least twenty-four hours. Try on the skirt and check the length. Turn up a hem of 4cm (1$\frac{1}{2}$ *inches*). Trim off excess fabric. Neaten the edge of the hem, and slip-stitch into position. Working from the wrong side fold each pleat on the fold line already made and machine stitch close to the fold just for the depth of the hem. This will hold the pleats in place (*figure 10*).

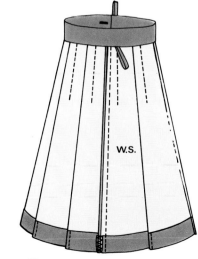

Figure 10

Bodice & sleeve block

Simple basic block for bodice and sleeve

This lesson and the following two lessons describe how to make a straight and shaped bodice block and straight sleeve block. The sizes range from 78cm–135cm ($30\frac{3}{4}$ inch–53 inch) bust and 83cm–140cm ($32\frac{3}{4}$ inch–55 inch) hips. There is a tolerance allowance of 8cm ($3\frac{1}{4}$ inches) on the bust and 6cm ($2\frac{1}{4}$ inches) on the hips. No turnings are allowed on the diagram but should be added after the blocks are drawn. It is advisable to iron interfacing on to the wrong side of graph paper before drawing the pattern. This will preserve the pattern so that it can be adapted to different styles later on.

Following the size required on the graph given, draw in all lines to scale and name them.

Choose the size nearest to personal bust measurement and alter the pattern if necessary by incorporating your measurements if they differ from the standard measurements. To do this measure yourself in the same places as the lines on the pattern: shoulder, across back and across front line. Also measure bust depth and the distance between the bust points. If the distance between the bust points differs from that on the pattern, mark in the correct bust point and re-draw the dart by joining this point to the top edges of the original dart. To alter the centre-back to waist length, insert paper to lengthen or make a tuck on the lines indicated to shorten. The length of the sleeve is adjusted in the same way. Measure the arm while it is bent, from shoulder point over elbow to wrist in line with the little finger. When all alterations are completed on the graph block, trace off the new shape on to another piece of paper and use this as the pattern. The graph block can be kept intact for future use.

Make up a toile in a non-stretch fabric such as calico. Fit the toile and transfer any further alterations on to the graph block.

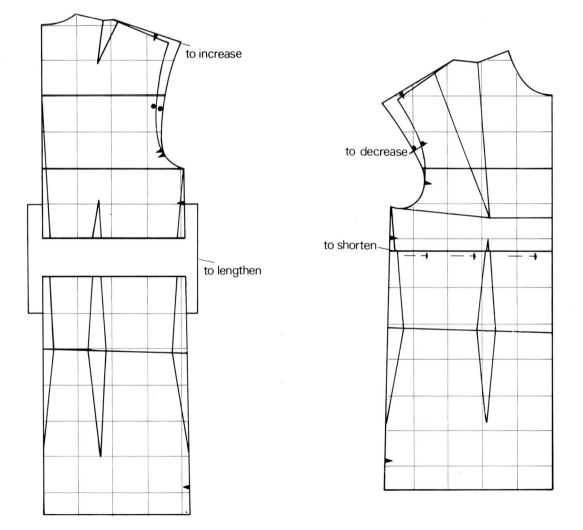

to increase

to lengthen

to decrease

to shorten

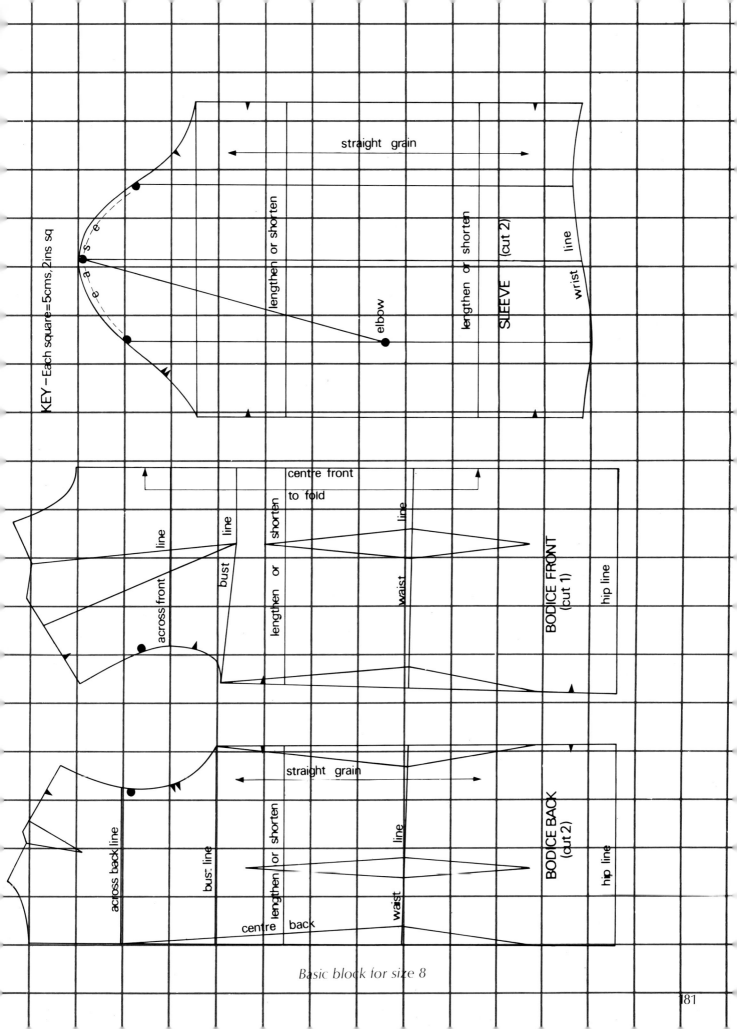

KEY – Each square=5cms,2ins sq

straight grain

lengthen or shorten

elbow

lengthen or shorten

SLEEVE (cut 2)

wrist line

centre front
to fold

across front line

bust line

lengthen or shorten

waist line

BODICE FRONT
(cut 1)

hip line

across back line

bust line

lengthen or shorten

straight grain

waist line

BODICE BACK
(cut 2)

hip line

centre back

Basic block for size 8

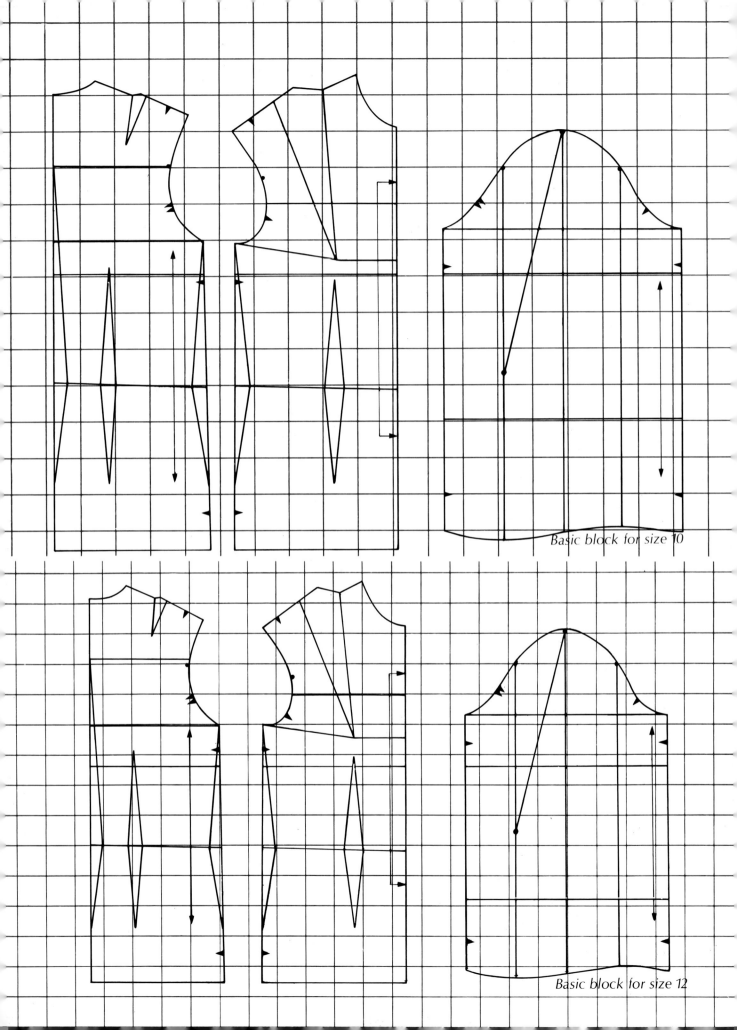

Basic block for size 10

Basic block for size 12

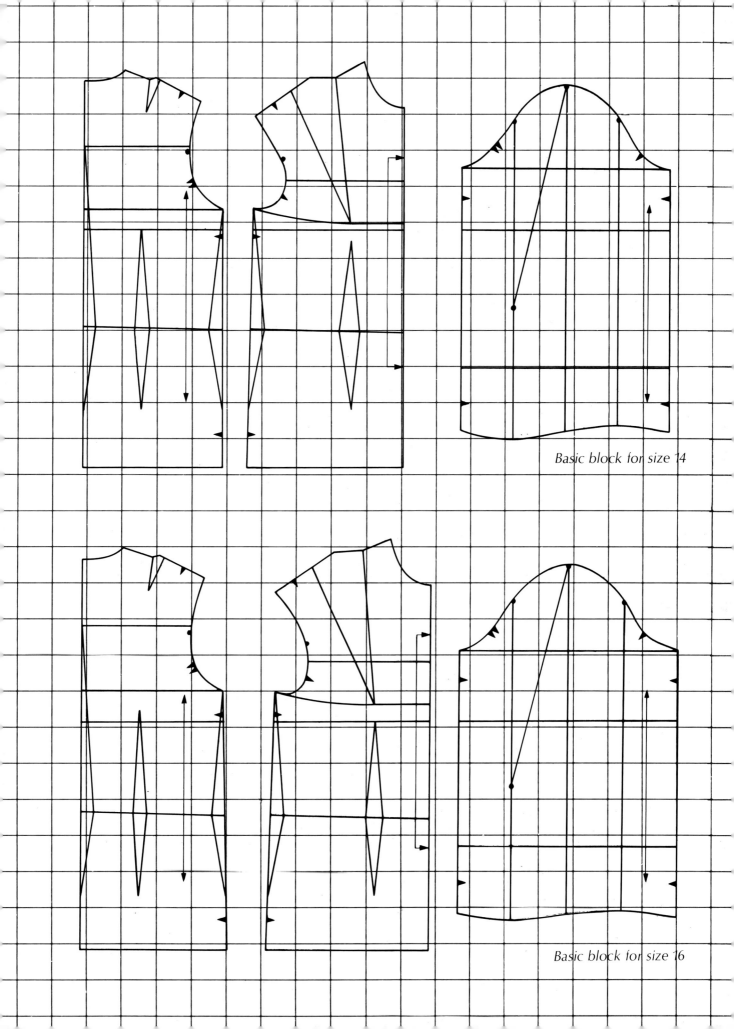

Basic block for size 14

Basic block for size 16

Here are the basic blocks for bodice and sleeve for sizes 18-24. Make your block as shown on page 180.

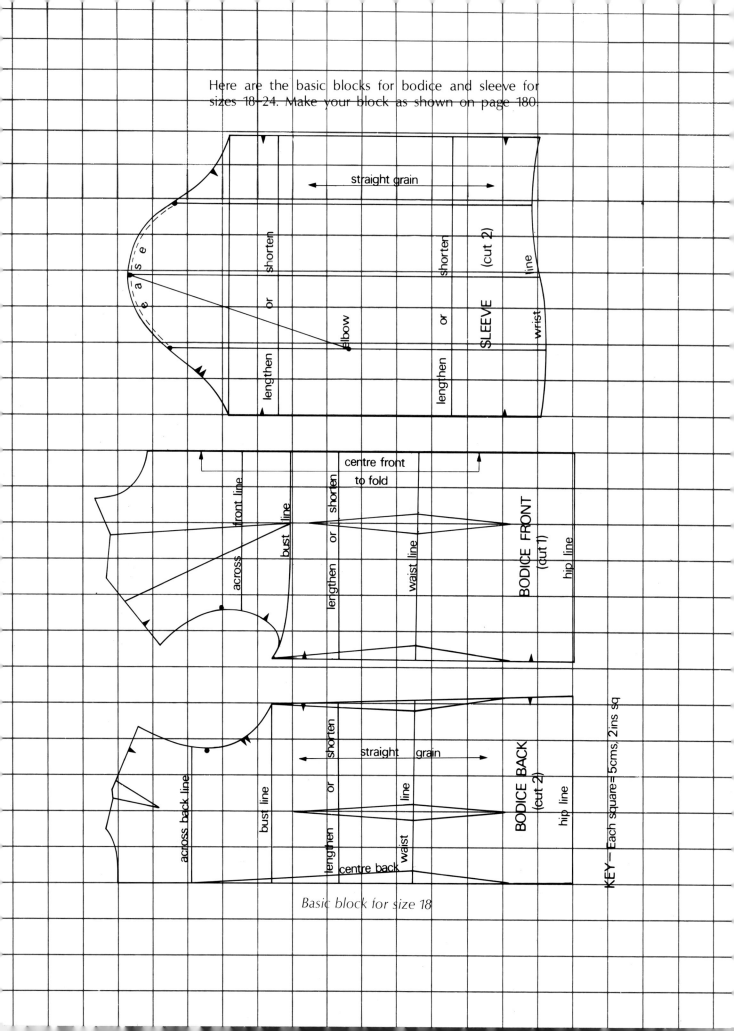

straight grain

shorten

or

shorten

lengthen

elbow

lengthen

SLEEVE

(cut 2)

line

wrist

centre front

to fold

front line

bust line

across

shorten

or

lengthen

waist line

BODICE FRONT
(cut 1)

hip line

shorten

straight   grain

across back line

bust line

or

shorten

line

lengthen

waist

centre back

BODICE BACK
(cut 2)

hip line

KEY—Each square=5cms, 2ins sq

Basic block for size 18

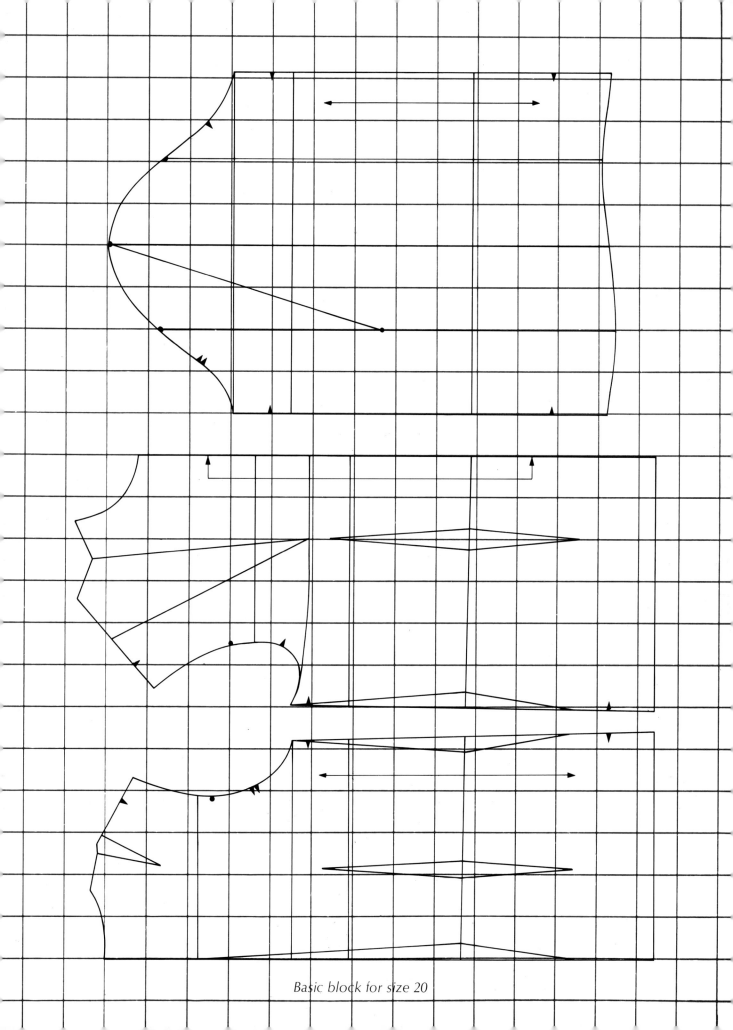

Basic block for size 20

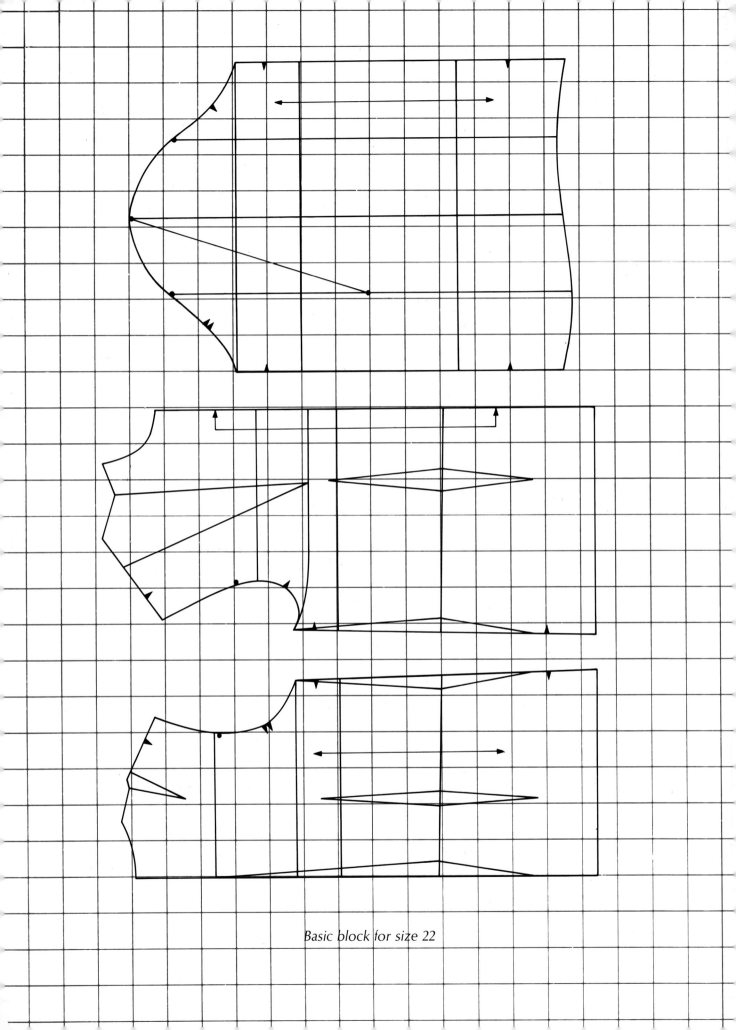

Basic block for size 22

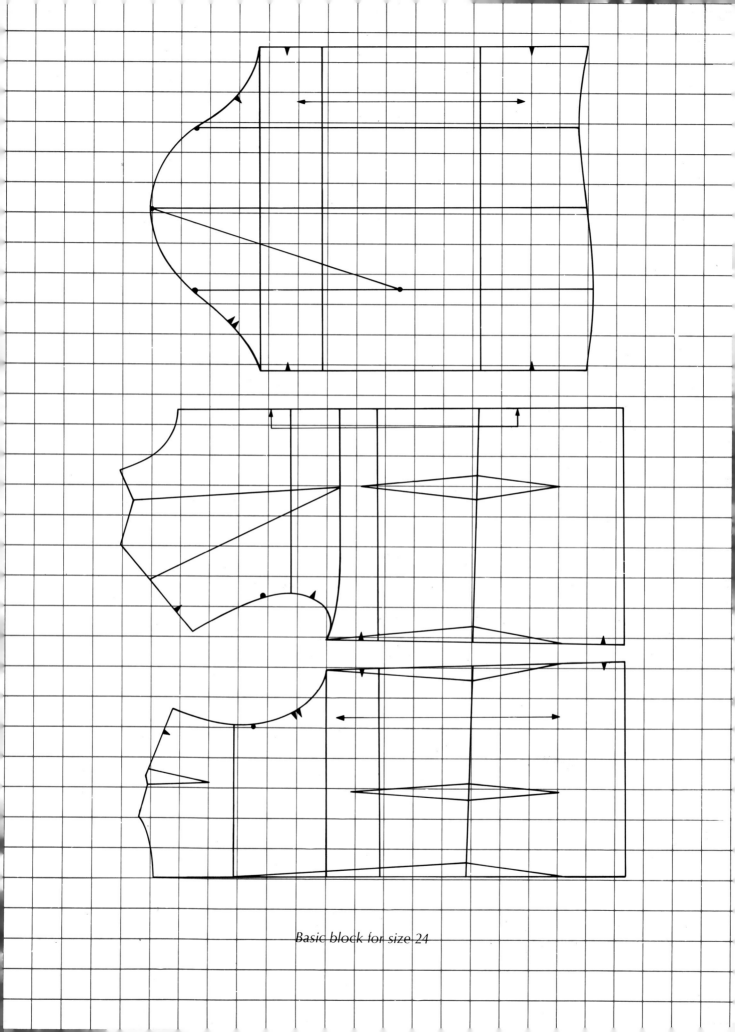

Basic block for size 24

Here are the basic blocks for bodice and sleeve for sizes 26–32. Make your block as shown on page 180.

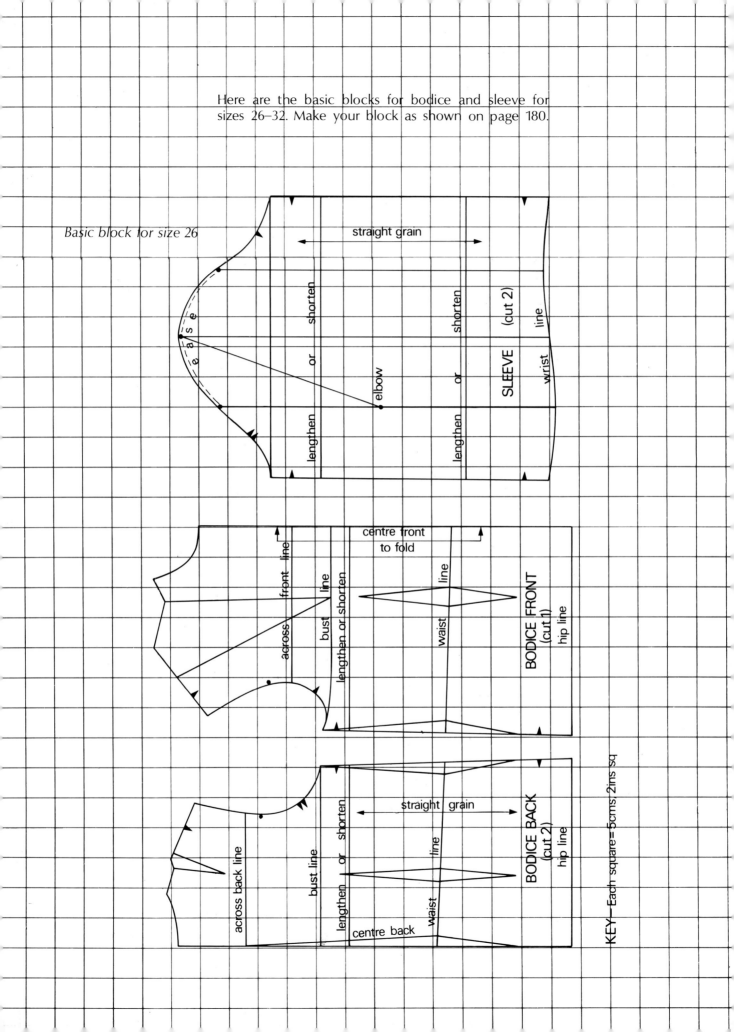

Basic block for size 26

straight grain

shorten

or

lengthen

shorten

or

lengthen

elbow

SLEEVE (cut 2)

wrist line

ease

centre front to fold

across front line

bust line

lengthen or shorten

waist line

BODICE FRONT (cut 1)

hip line

across back line

bust line

lengthen or shorten

straight grain

waist line

centre back

BODICE BACK (cut 2)

hip line

KEY—Each square=5cms 2ins sq

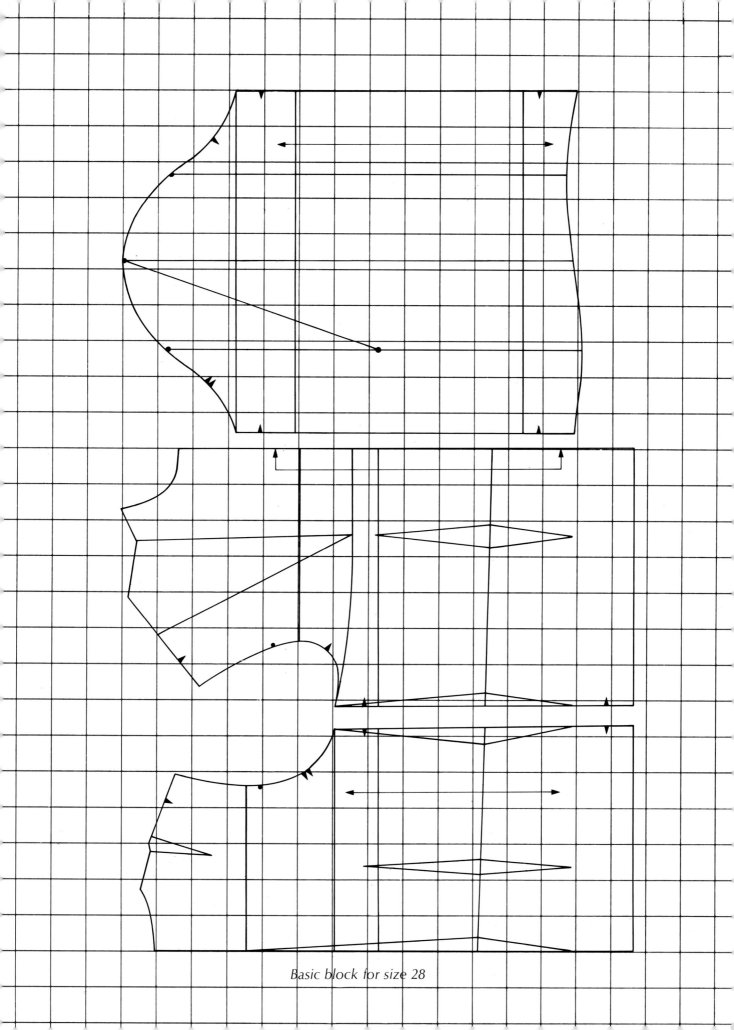

Basic block for size 28

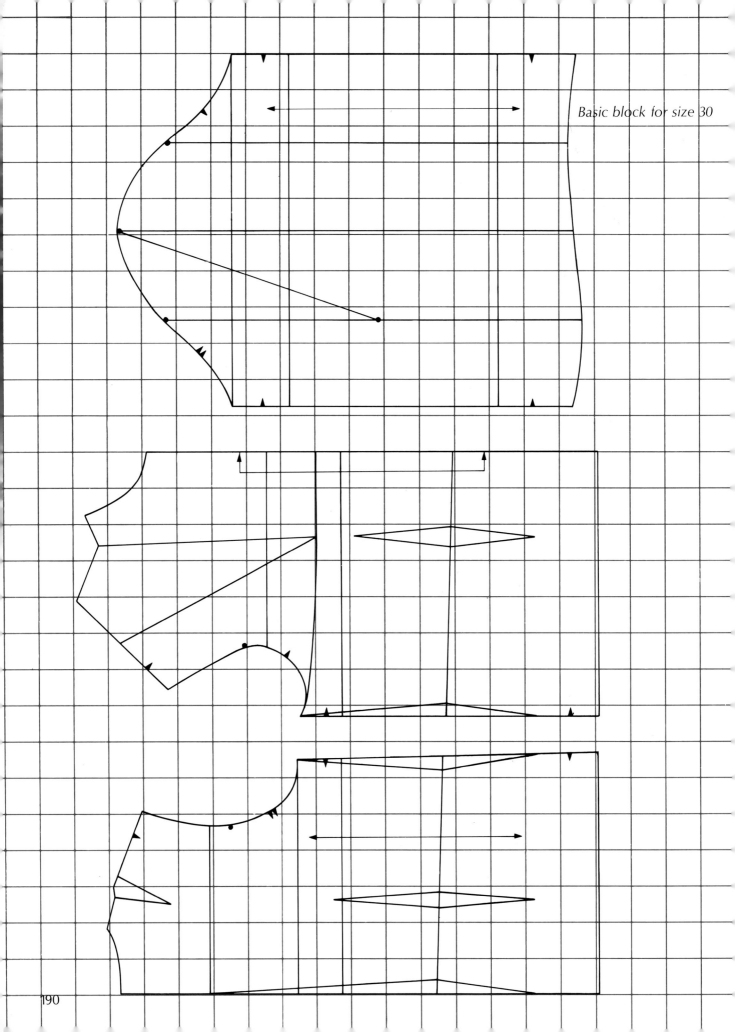

Basic block for size 30

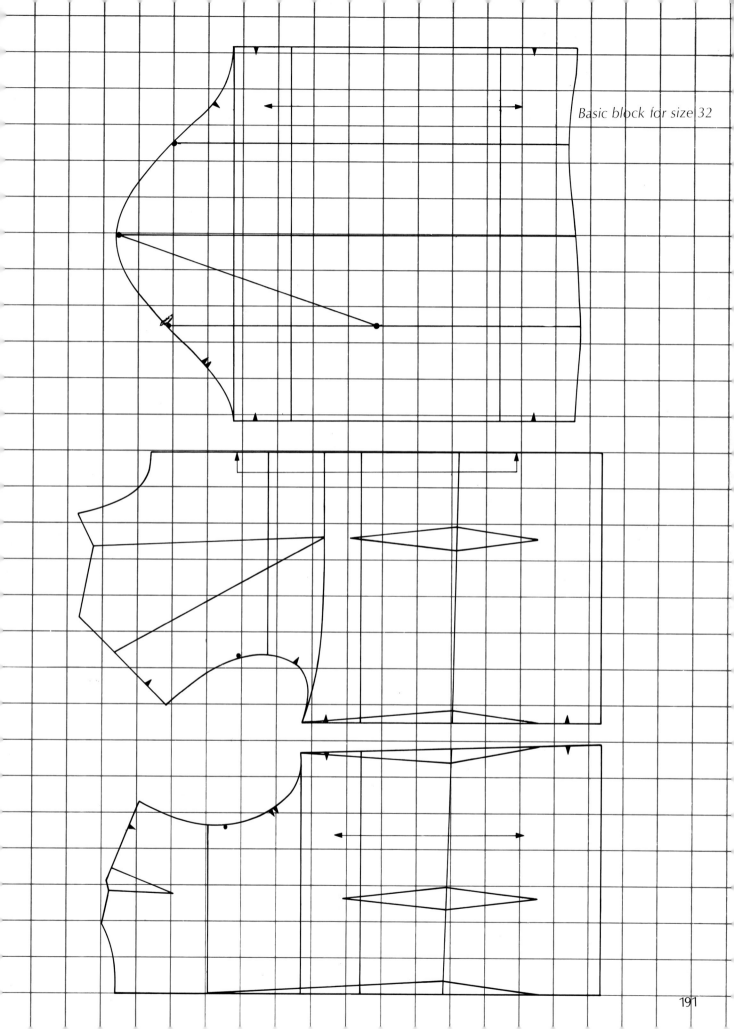

Basic block for size 32

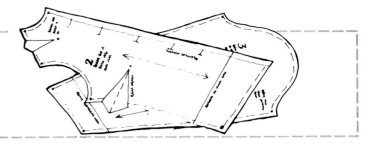

Altering bust darts

Altering the position of the bust dart on a basic block

The basic block for a bodice is usually drawn with the bust dart running into the shoulder seam. Once the correct position of the bust dart has been established it can be moved into various positions or transferred into tucks and gathers.

Underarm dart

This is the most popular dart used on a bodice. Draw a line from the bust point to the underarm seam (figure 1). Cut along this line to the bust point. Crease the pattern on the line nearest to the centre-front (the inside line) of the shoulder dart and fold on to the outside line. Pin into place. The underarm dart will open up automatically. Place a piece of paper larger than the opening underneath and glue into position (figure 2). Remove pins from the shoulder dart and open out flat. Crease the lower line of the underarm dart and pin on to the upper line. Trim off excess paper at the side seam (figure 3). Remove pins and pin the shoulder dart again. The new dart is now completed but it is advisable to move the bust point

approximately 1.3–2cm ($\frac{1}{2}$–$\frac{3}{4}$ inch) towards the centre and re-draw the lines to meet at this point (figure 4). This will allow for the curve of the bust.

French dart

This is more suitable and flattering for a well developed bust. Draw a line half way between the top of the underarm seam and the waistline and complete as above (figure 5). When making a garment with a very low French dart, trim off the turnings to approximately 1.3cm ($\frac{1}{2}$ inch) and neaten the edges together. This prevents pulling on the underarm seam.

Waistline dart

Draw a line from the bust point through the centre of the waist dart to the lower edge of the pattern and cut. Pin shoulder dart. Insert paper under the gap and glue. Trim off excess paper at the lower edge. Mark in balance marks either side of the dart and curve the lines slightly for a more flattering effect (figure 6).

Transferring the dart into the armhole

Draw a curved line from the bust point to just below

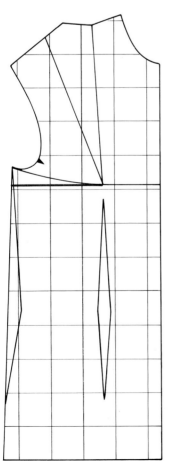

Figure 1

192

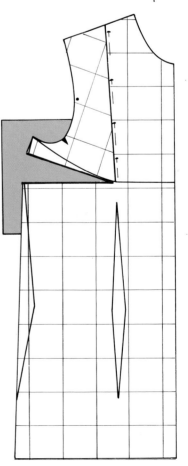

Figure 2

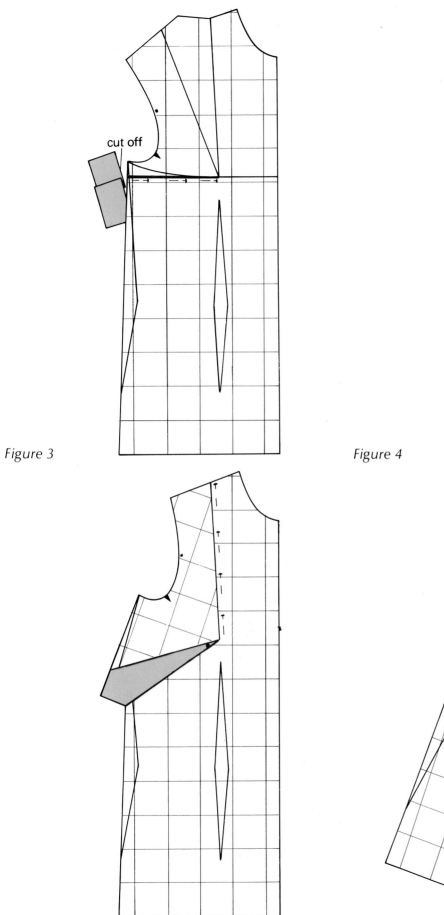

Figure 3

cut off

Figure 4

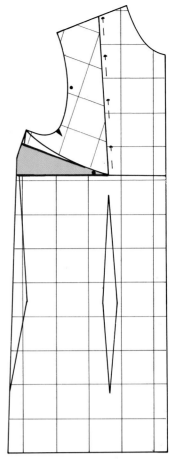

Figure 5

Figure 6

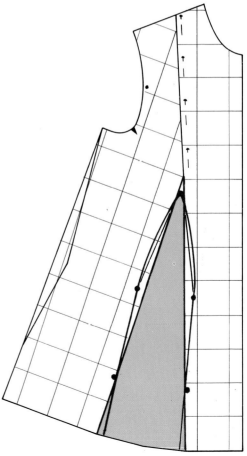

the balance mark on the armhole. Draw in balance marks on the curved line before cutting. Cut, then pin shoulder dart and insert paper and glue (figure 7). When making up the garment this type of dart is usually trimmed and the turnings neatened together and pressed up towards the shoulder.

Transferring the dart into the neckline
Work this in the same way. Usually neckline darts are used as design features (figure 8). After stitching the dart cut the turnings on the fold on the wrong side and press open. Place another piece of fabric over the turnings on the wrong side and from the right side top stitch either side of the dart to the bust point.
When there is a centre-front seam, the fullness from the shoulder dart may be transferred to a ·dart between the centre-front seam and bust point. Use the same method of inserting paper and gluing, but draw the line straight across the pattern or slant it towards the waist (figure 9).

Transferring the darts into tucks
Make a temporary underarm dart without paper underneath. Pin the shoulder dart. Draw the lines of the tucks required so that the centre one is in line with the bust point. Three tucks are usually sufficient (figure 10). Cut along these lines close to the underarm dart, then place paper underneath and work as before (figure 11). The tucks may be stitched on the wrong or right side. If they are stitched on the right side for decoration, the stitching should stop approximately half way between bust point and the beginning of the tuck (A–B).

Transferring the darts into gathers
Draw a curved line along the shoulder seam (figure 12). When making gathers at the waist and centre-front, transfer as for tucks and curve the shoulder seam. When putting gathers into the neckline use the same method as for tucks, but draw a concave curve from the shoulder to centre-front (figure 13).

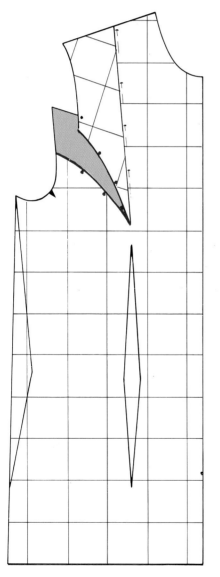

Figure 7

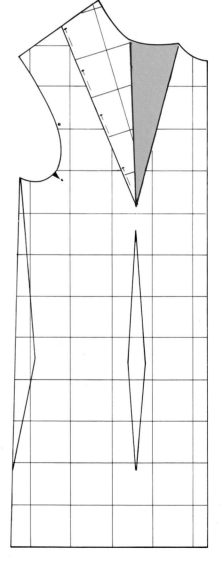

Figure 8

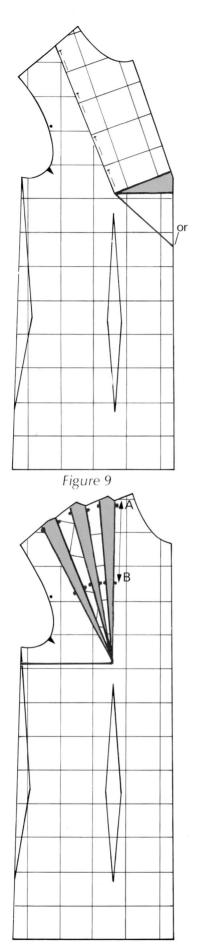

Figure 9

Figure 11

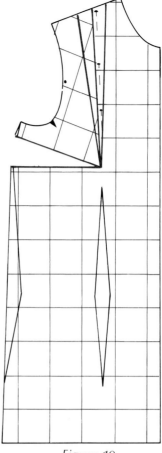

Figure 10

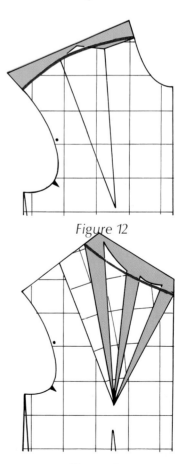

Figure 12

Figure 13

Other ways with blocks

More alterations for your basic block

Once you have made your basic block it is a simple matter to reduce the waistline, lengthen the block pattern and make neck and armhole facings.

How to reduce the waistline

The waistline can be reduced by using extra darts, sloping the centre-front and centre-back on the block, or by increasing the inward curve at the side seams. Measure the pattern on the waistline, omitting the darts. Check with personal measurement and decide which method to use, or combine all three, depending on individual choice and figure type.

Making extra darts On the back bodice divide the waistline into three equal parts and mark with dots. Using the dot nearest the centre-back as the centre of a dart, draw a dart the width of the original dart. Using the other dot as the centre of a dart draw a second dart the same width or narrower than the first. This dart may be the same length as the first one or slightly shorter above the waistline (figure 1).

On the front bodice measure from the original dart towards the side seam approximately 6cm (2½ inches). Draw another dart the same width or narrower. Do not make this as long above the waistline as the original dart (figure 2).

Sloping the centre-front On the waistline measure in from the centre-front 1cm–1.5cm ($\frac{3}{8}$ inch–$\frac{1}{2}$ inch) and mark. Rule a line from just above the level of the bust point on the centre-front to this mark. Rule a line from the mark at the waistline to the centre-front at the lower edge of the block.

The centre-back may be shaped in the same way 'from the waistline to the lower edge of the centre back, but ensure that the pattern is large enough across the front and back at the lower point of the dart. It may be necessary to make a small addition at the side seam to compensate (figure 3).

A small amount can be reduced at the side seam by increasing the curve.

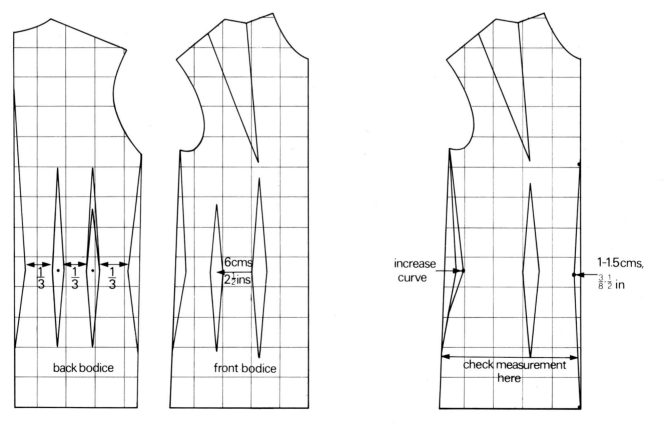

| Figure 1 | Figure 2 | Figure 3 |

How to lengthen the basic block

Place a long ruler along the straight edge of the centre-back and continue the line to the length required. Repeat with the centre-front. Measure from the centre-front and centre-back the width at the lower edge of the block pattern. Draw lines the same length at right angles to the lower edges of the centre-front and centre-back. Complete the rectangles. This will produce a tight fitting sheath type dress.

To flare the side seams measure out from line A approximately 3.8cm–7.5cm ($1\frac{1}{2}$ inches–3 inches) at the hem and draw a line from this point to the side edge above hip level, keeping a smooth line (figure 4A). On an extension of 3.8cm ($1\frac{1}{2}$ inches) curve up the hemline 0.6cm ($\frac{1}{4}$ inch) at the side and on a 7.5cm (3 inch) extension curve up hemline 1.3cm ($\frac{1}{2}$ inch) (figure 4B).

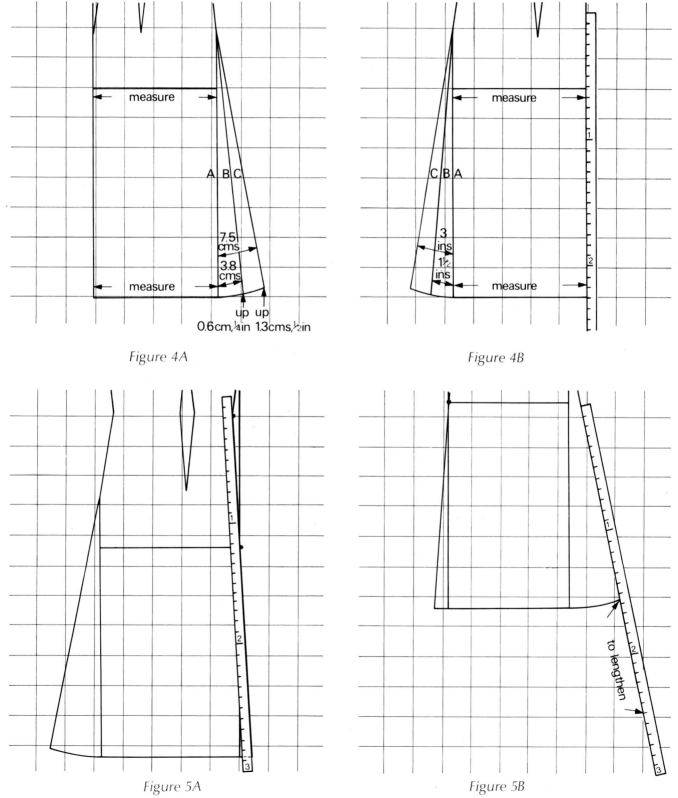

Figure 4A

Figure 4B

Figure 5A

Figure 5B

With a shaped centre-front and back place the ruler along the slanted line, touching the waistline and the lower edge of the block and flare out slightly at the hemline (figure 5A).

To lengthen for evening wear, keep the ruler on the new line and extend to the required length (figure 5B). For a fuller hemline with more waist reduction, extra can be taken out at the centre-front, centre-back and side seams and new lines drawn from these points through the hipline to the hemline (figure 6).

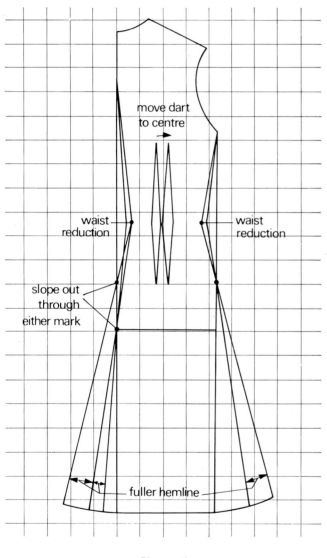

Figure 6

How to make facings for neckline and armholes
Separate facings Draw in turnings outside pattern block. Place the edge of a ruler to the fitting line and, following the curves, mark in lines 5cm (*2 inches*) from this. Draw in balance marks. Place tracing paper over the top and trace off the facing pattern from the original. Draw in a 'Place to fold' mark on centre-front of neck facing and the straight grain line (figure 7).

On a sloping centre-front there will be a seam line

and it will be necessary to write 'Cut 2' on the pattern, to mark in a straight grain line and to add a turning on the centre front edge.

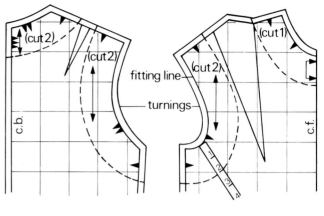

Figure 7

An all-in-one facing is where the neck and armhole facings are not separated. On the front bodice cut across from the centre-front to the point of the shoulder dart. Pin in the dart. On the back cut across from the centre-back to the point of the shoulder dart. Pin in the dart. Draw in a line 5cm (*2 inches*) from the fitting line from the centre-back to the underarm seam, curving it just below the end of the shoulder dart. Draw in another line the same distance from the fitting line from the centre-front to the underarm seam, curving this line approximately halfway between the bust point and shoulder. Trace off the pattern and transfer all markings. Unpin the temporary darts and glue paper behind to keep it in position when the original darts are opened out flat again (figure 8).

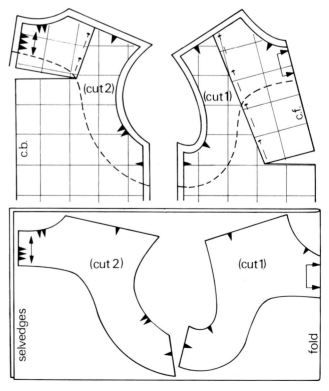

Figure 8

Quick slip pattern

Making a fitted slip pattern from a basic block
You will need graph paper, tracing paper, a long ruler, a short ruler and a pencil to make your pattern.

From the basic block given on page 180, and making any necessary alterations, take a tracing of the bodice as far as the hipline.

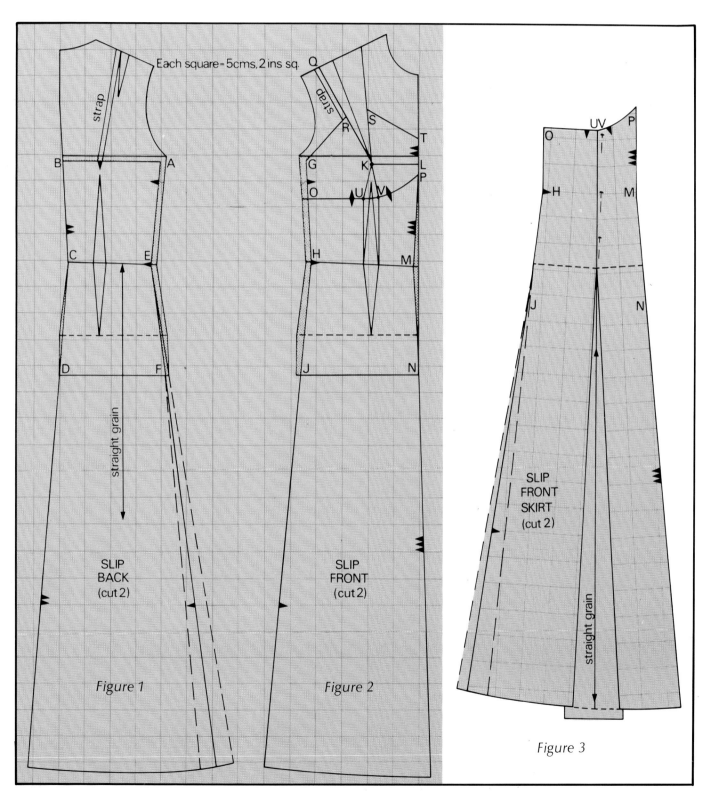

Each square = 5 cms, 2 ins sq.

strap

B A
C E
D F

straight grain

SLIP BACK
(cut 2)

Figure 1

Q
strap
R S T
G K L P
O U V
H M
J N

SLIP FRONT
(cut 2)

Figure 2

O UV P
H M
J N

SLIP FRONT SKIRT
(cut 2)

straight grain

Figure 3

Back

Mark in the waistline CE and the hipline DF. Draw a horizontal line from 1cm ($\frac{3}{8}$ *inch*) below the underarm point to the centre-back. Mark AB.

Place one edge of a long ruler so that it touches the waistline and hipline at the centre-back. Draw a straight line to the finished length.

Draw a line 1cm ($\frac{3}{8}$ *inch*) inside the side seam from A to E. Place the edge of the ruler so that it touches the new line at E and the original side seam line at F and draw a line the same length as the centre-back line. Then from CE measure the required length to hem and draw in the hemline.

Place the ruler from the top of the bodice dart to the inside dot of the shoulder dart. Draw a line the required length for the strap. Mark in the straight grain line and balance marks on the side and centre-back seams (figure 1).

Front

Measure 1cm ($\frac{3}{8}$ *inch*) from the side seam at the underarm point and mark in G. Mark in waistline HM and the hipline JN. Mark a line 1cm ($\frac{3}{8}$ *inch*) in from the original line from G to H. Draw a point 1cm ($\frac{3}{8}$ *inch*) in from the side seam at J and re-mark. Place the edge of the ruler on H and J and draw a straight line the same length as the back side seam.

Draw a line across the bottom of the dart on front and back. Measure the width of both, double this amount and check that the finished measurement is the same as personal measurement. If it is too tight draw the side seam so that the ruler touches the original point J.

Draw a straight line from the bust point to the centre-front, and mark KL. Mark a point on the centre-front 2cm ($\frac{3}{4}$ *inch*) below L, and mark P. Draw a point 1cm ($\frac{3}{8}$ *inch*) in from the centre-front on line HM. Draw the new line P,M, N. Draw in the hemline as for the back. Mark O 7·5cm (*3 inches*) below underarm point G and mark P, 2cm ($\frac{3}{4}$ *inch*) below L. Draw a straight line from O to the centre-front side of the dart and then curve the line up to P.

Measure the width of the dart on the shoulder. Take half the measurement and mark a point this distance from the dart on the armhole side, and mark Q. Draw a straight line from Q to K. Mark two points 10cm (*4 inches*) from K on each line of the shoulder dart. Mark R and S. Mark T 5cm (*2 inches*) up from L on the centre-front line. Then draw in the straight lines TS and RG.

Draw straight lines at right angles from the dart points on HM to meet line OP. Where the lines meet, mark U and V. Draw two lines from U and V to meet at K. Mark the required length of the strap and add the measurement to the back strap measurement. Mark in notches on the side seam to match the back on the centre-front and either side of the dart on the line OP (figure 2).

Cut along OP to separate the bodice and skirt.

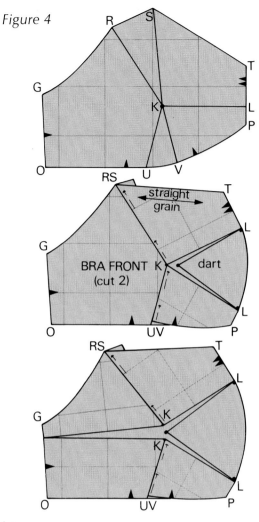

Figure 4

Skirt

Draw a straight line from the bottom of the waist dart to the hemline and cut. Spread out on a flat surface and fold so that U and V meet. Pin the dart from the waistline to UV. Attach paper underneath gap. Draw a straight line from the end of the dart to the centre of the insertion paper. This is the straight grain line (figure 3).

Bodice

Cut along line LK. Fold the darts RS and UV and pin. LK will now open to form a centre-front dart. Draw the lines from two halves of L so that they meet 1cm ($\frac{3}{8}$ *inch*) from K.

For sizes 14 and over, cut from K to the underarm seam. Open up 1–2cm ($\frac{3}{8}$–$\frac{3}{4}$ *inch*) at K and insert paper underneath (figure 4).

Adding turnings and cutting out the slip

After the block is completed, add turnings. The dart on the back is not necessary unless a very close fit is required when a zip may be needed also which should be inserted in the centre-back. When cutting the bodice, it is advisable to place line TS on the straight grain to prevent the neck from stretching. If a non-stretch fabric is being used, the whole slip must be cut on the cross.

Patterns for shirt sleeves

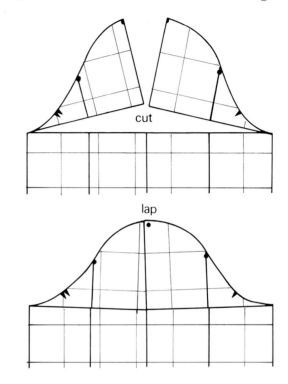

How to alter the sleeve block for basic shirt styles

The basic sleeve block is drafted for an average shirt sleeve plus the length of the cuff. To avoid spoiling the original block, it is advisable when making adjustments to cut two or three sleeves in paper without turnings. Mark in all the lines, as they are necessary for any adjustment if the head of the sleeve requires more or less fullness. The amount of fullness depends on the type of fabric to be used for a garment. Stretch fabrics need less fullness as they will give when the arm is raised. With non-stretch fabrics, there must be sufficient fullness to allow free movement of the arm, otherwise the back armhole seam will split.

Decreasing and increasing the fullness on a sleeve head

To decrease the fullness There are two ways of decreasing the fullness and depth of the sleeve crown. The first is to make a small pleat across the head of the sleeve above the two dots (figure 1A). The other method is to cut the pattern down the centre line to the crown line, then across the crown line almost to the underarm seam. Lap the pattern at the shoulder seam dot and draw a new dot in the centre of the

lapped width. Always leave approximately 1.3cm – 2cm ($\frac{1}{2}$ *inch*–$\frac{3}{4}$ *inch*) ease on the sleeve head (figure 1B).

Figure 1B

To increase the fullness This is usually only necessary for very prominent shoulder bones and sometimes on

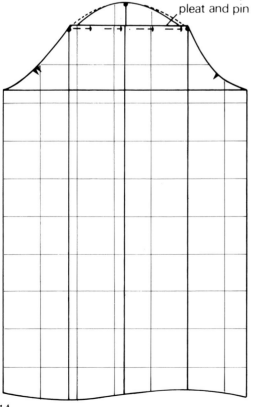

Figure 1A

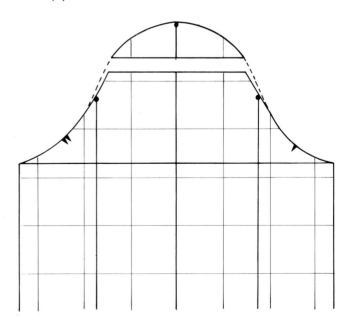

Figure 2A

very round-shouldered figures. Reverse the procedure for decreasing, by method 1A or 1B (figures 2A and 2B).

After any necessary fitting adjustments have been made to the original pattern, the sleeve pattern can be altered for most styles (figure 4).

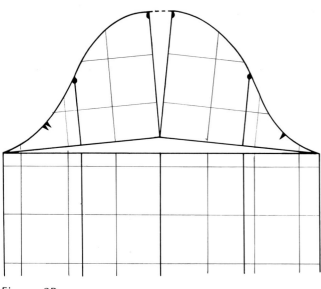

Figure 2B

How to increase width at underarm

Cut through the centre line from the wrist almost to the shoulder seam dot. Open out at the lower edge, insert paper underneath and glue the pattern into place. Draw a new straight grain line and centre line from the shoulder seam dot to the centre of the inserted paper at the lower edge (figure 3).

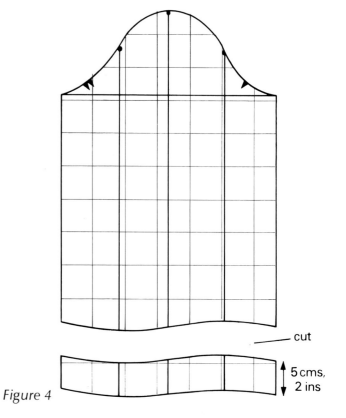

cut

5 cms,
2 ins

Figure 4

Simple shirt sleeve

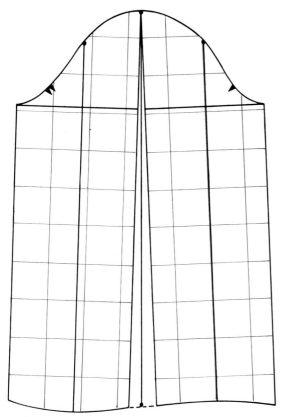

Figure 3

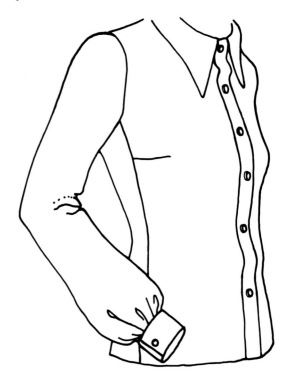

Decide on the depth of the cuff required. Cut this amount away from the lower edge of the pattern, following the curved line.

Cut a piece of paper the length of wrist measurement plus 1.3cm ($\frac{1}{2}$ inch) for ease plus 2cm ($\frac{3}{4}$ inch) for an extension for buttonhole, by double the depth required. This is for the cuff and under-cuff (figure 5A). Add turnings on all sides of the cuff and edges of sleeve (figure 5B).

Bishop sleeve

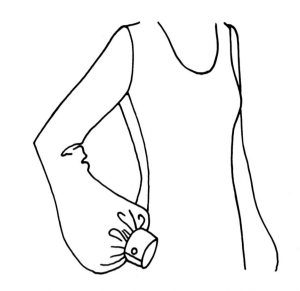

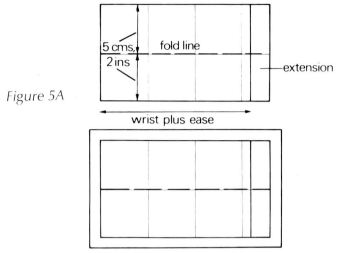

Figure 5A

Figure 5B

This is similar to a shirt sleeve, but much fuller at the lower edge and the fullness drops towards the little finger. Much depends on the effect desired for the finished sleeve, but usually more width is added to the back of the sleeve than the front.

On a pattern without turnings cut on the three vertical lines. Open at the lower edge and insert paper behind the gaps as shown in the diagram. Extra length must be added to allow for the drop of the fullness at the wrist, usually 2.5cm (1 inch) at the front and 5cm (2 inches) at the back.

Mark in the opening. Draw another balance mark in the centre of the cuff and the centre of the middle insertion. This allows for more fullness towards the back of the sleeve. Add turnings as before (figure 7).

The opening for the sleeve should be in line with the little finger. Decide on the length of opening – usually approximately 5cm (2 inches) – and mark this on the back line. The fullness at the lower edge of the sleeve is usually distributed evenly on to the cuff. Mark in balance marks on the cuff and lower edge of the sleeve. The cuff extension wraps over from the front to the back. Mark the front with one balance mark and the back with two (figure 6).

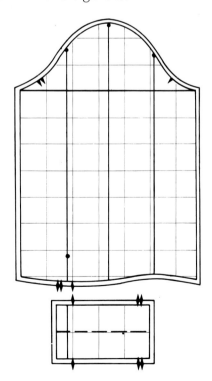

Figure 6

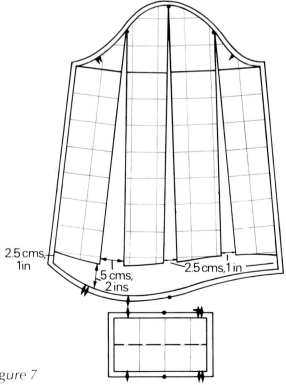

Figure 7

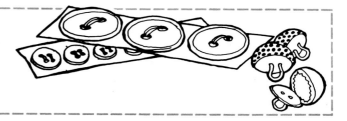

Close fitting sleeves

Adjusting basic sleeve block to make a long close-fitting sleeve

Draw the basic block shape on paper without turnings, but mark in lines A, B and C as indicated in figure 1 to divide the sleeve into quarters. Draw a line horizontally across pattern through elbow dart. Mark in notches 5cm (*2 inches*) either side of this line on the underarm seams. Measure 2.5cm (*1 inch*) from A towards B on the wrist line. Draw a line from this point to meet line A at the armhole (figure 1).

has opened 5cm (*2 inches*) on underarm seam and pin down (figure 3).

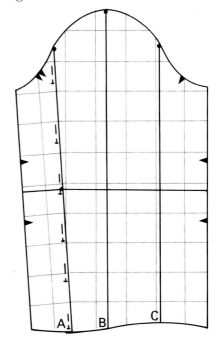

Figure 2

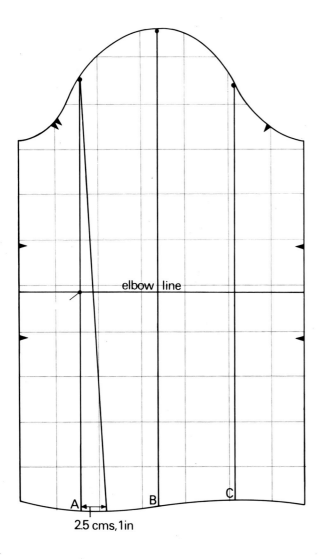

elbow line

A   B   C

2.5 cms, 1 in

Figure 1

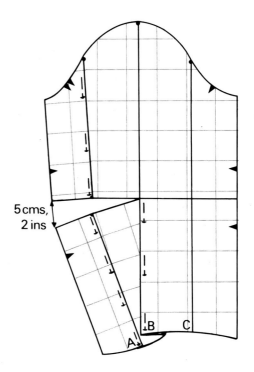

5 cms,
2 ins

A   B   C

Figure 3

Make a crease along line A and fold over to touch the new line and pin (figure 2).
Cut on the elbow line as far as B. Crease line B as far as the elbow line and fold towards line A until the cut

Measure around elbow with hand clenched and arm bent upwards. Add approximately 1.3cm–2.5cm ($\frac{1}{2}$ inch–1 inch) according to the closeness of sleeve required and the type of fabric to be used. Divide this measurement in two and mark in either side of line B on the elbow line.

Mark the pattern where the fold underneath touches it on the wrist line. Measure wrist and divide measurement into three equal parts. Mark in one third from the fold mark towards line A and two thirds towards line C. Approximately 1.3cm–2.5cm ($\frac{1}{2}$ inch–1 inch) ease should be added. Mark this in from the one third mark towards the underarm on line A side.

Place paper underneath the opening at the elbow and glue into position. Draw lines from the underarm point through elbow marks to the marks on the wrist line on both sides of the sleeve (figure 4).

To eliminate the fullness at the elbow, either shrink away the extra fullness, or, work one or two darts – use two darts if there is a lot of fullness as one large dart will make a point in the fabric.

To shrink away the extra fullness, first work a gathering thread between the notches and pull up so that the notches match those on the opposite underarm edge. Then press with a damp cloth and hot iron until all gathers are dispersed. This method will only be effective on certain fabrics.

For a sleeve with one dart, draw a dot in the centre of the inserted paper in line with the original dot or slightly more towards line B. Draw lines from this point to the edges of the opening (figure 5).

Each square = 5 cms, 2 ins

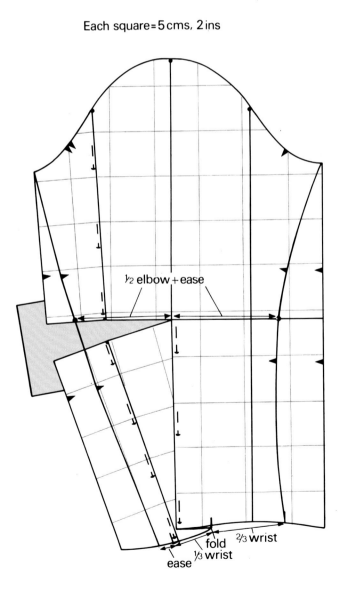

½ elbow + ease

fold
⅓ wrist   ⅔ wrist
ease

Figure 4

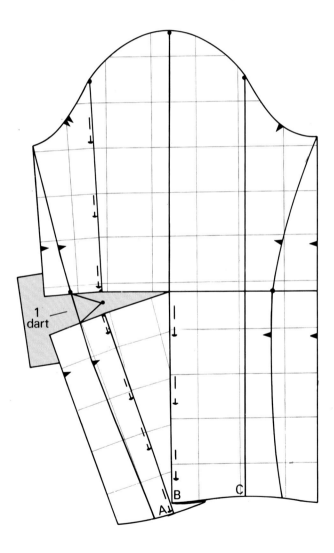

1 dart

A B C

Figure 5

For a sleeve with two darts, measure half the width of the opening on the inserted paper at the underarm seam. Using this measurement, draw a line either side of the opening from the underarm seam to the original dot or slightly towards line B (figure 6).

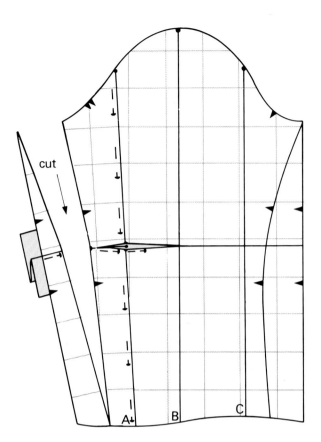

Figure 7

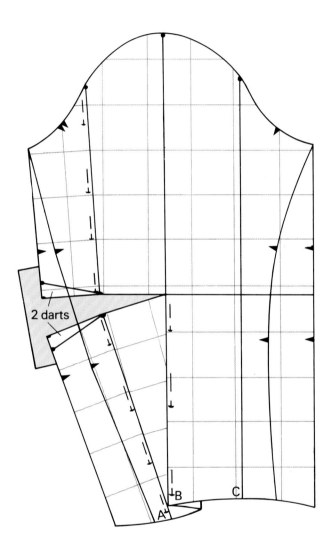

Figure 6

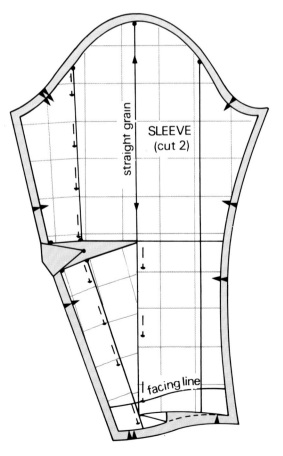

Figure 8

To shape the ends of the darts at the underarm seam, open up fold on line B and pin the new dart with the fold of the paper lying towards wrist line. Cut on new underarm line (figure 7).
Unpin dart and fold again on line B and reshape wrist line. Add seam allowances and notches. This wrist line will require a facing as it is curved. Draw in required depth from wrist line down, and mark notches. Trace pattern off and cut out (figure 8).

Gathered sleeves

Adjusting the basic sleeve block for gathered styles

Shirt or Bishop sleeve

Trace out the original sleeve block, making sure that it is adjusted to your personal measurements, (see pages 180 and following). Mark letters as shown. (*figure 1*). Cut the pattern from E to K, then from K

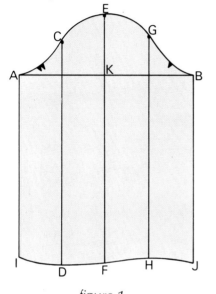

figure 1

almost to A and B. Open on line E–K, moving E and E1 up and out until they are approximately 7.5cms (*3 inches*) apart. Draw a line from E to E1 and mark in the shoulder seam dot halfway add turnings (*figure 2*).

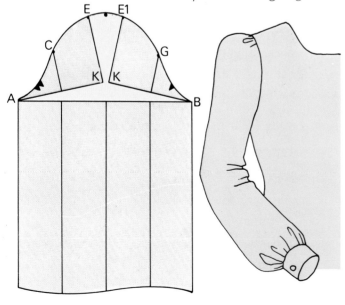

figure 2

When setting this sleeve into the armhole run a gathering thread over the sleeve head from C to G. Pin the sleeve into the armhole with the centre dot to the shoulder seam and with the notches and underarm seams matching. Pull up the gathering thread and distribute the fullness evenly. Tack and stitch on the seam line. Clip the seam allowance at C and G. Trim the turnings to 0.6cm ($\frac{1}{4}$ *inch*) and neaten together. Press the turnings towards the sleeve below the clip and towards the bodice above (*figure 3*).

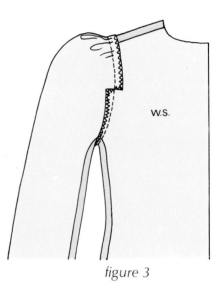

figure 3

For a higher crown (sleeve head), after moving E and E1 out as before, draw a line from C through E to E1 and down to G add turnings and set in as before. (*figure 4*).

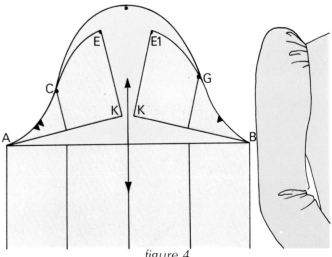

figure 4

Short sleeve with a gathered crown

Trace out the block pattern to the length required and mark in the letters as shown. (*figure 5*). Cut on lines

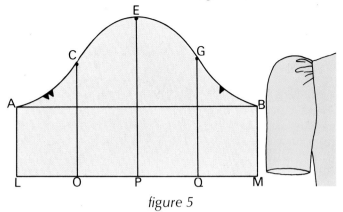

figure 5

C, E and G to approximately 4cms (1½ *inches*) from O, P and Q. Fold three small darts of equal width from the ends of the cuts to O, P and Q, making the line L to M the same measurement as the arm, plus a small amount for ease if required. C, E and G will then open up. Draw a line from C to approximately 5–6.5cms (2–2½ *inches*) above E and E1 to G. Mark the shoulder dot centrally on this line.

The lower edge of the sleeve will be curved and will require a facing of approximately 4cms (1½ *inches*). (*figure 6*). Add turnings and set the sleeve into the armhole as above.

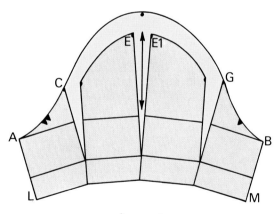

figure 6

Puff or Pouch sleeve

Trace out the original pattern to the depth required and mark in the letters as shown. (*figure 7*). Cut on

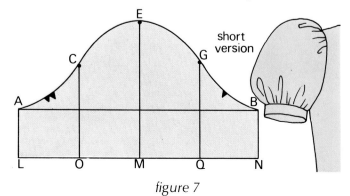

figure 7

lines C to O, E to M and G to Q. Spread the pattern so that there is a distance of 5cms (2 *inches*) between each section. Draw a line from C to 6.5 – 7.5cms (2½–3 *inches*) above E and E1 and down to G. Draw another line from L to approximately 5cms (2 *inches*) below M and M1 to N. (*figure 8*).

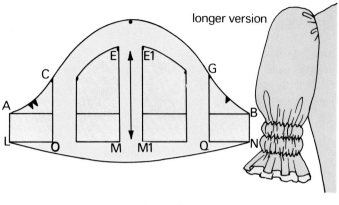

figure 8

Add turnings and set into the armhole as before. The lower edge may be gathered into a band or bias strip binding the measurement of the arm. Alternatively the lower edge may be neatened with a narrow hem or lace attached with zig-zag stitching and rows of shirring worked approximately 2.5–5cms (1–2 *inches*) above the edge, forming a frill.

Flared sleeve

The basic pattern is adjusted in the same way as for puff sleeves, with the line from L to N measuring twice the distance from C to G (*figure 9*).

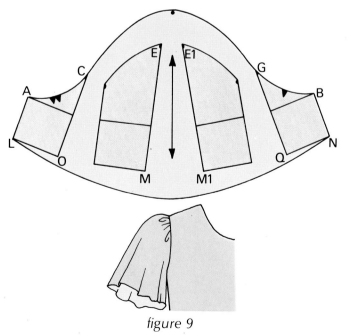

figure 9

Victorian Leg o' Mutton sleeve

Adjust the basic sleeve pattern to a fitted style. Instructions for doing this are on page 204. Draw a line across the pattern approximately 5–6.5cms

(2–2½ inches) above elbow level. Mark in the letters as shown. (figure 10). Cut on line E to P and then from P

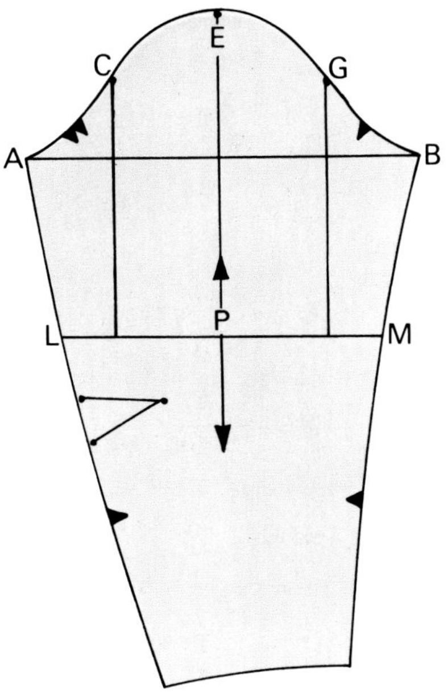

almost to L and M. Raise and open E and E1 until P is approximately 6.5cms (2½ inches) from P1. For a higher crown draw a curved line from C 4–5cms (1½–2½ inches) above E and E1 and down to G. (figure 11). Add turnings.

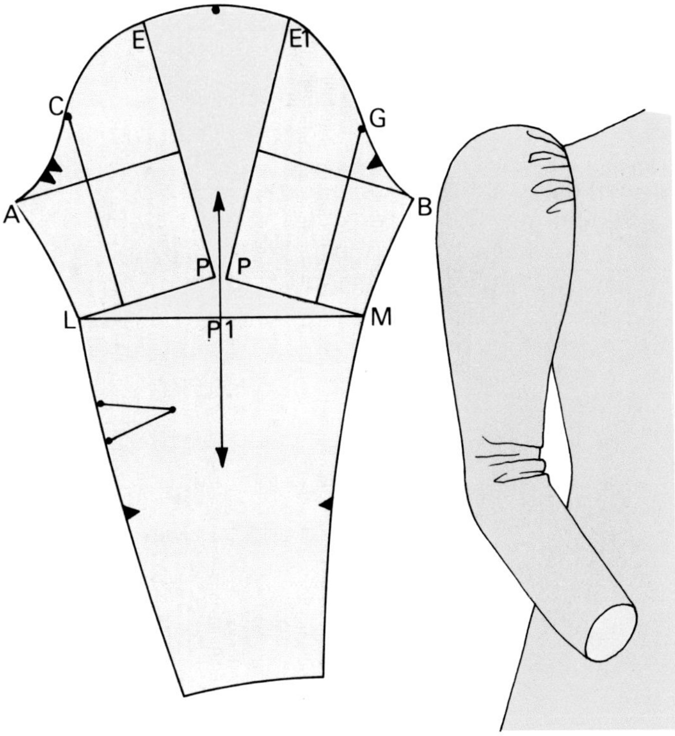

figure 10

figure 11

Two-piece Victorian sleeve
Using the fitted sleeve pattern, draw a line approximately 7.5–10cms (3–4 inches) above elbow level.

Mark with balance marks on this line at O, M and Q. (figure 12). Cut the pattern on this line and adjust the

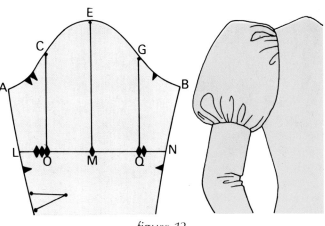

figure 12

top half as for the puff sleeve. (figure 13). Add turnings and cut out.

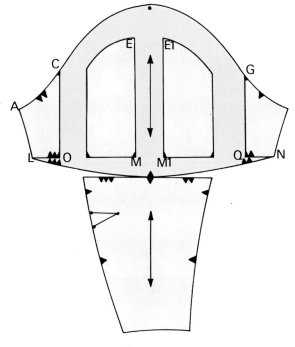

figure 13

Work a gathering thread from O, through M to Q. With right sides together and matching notches, pin the top of the sleeve to the lower half, pulling up the gathering thread and distributing the fullness evenly. Tack and stitch. Trim the turnings to 0.6cm (¼ inch), neaten together and press towards the lower part of the sleeve. Tack and stitch the elbow dart and press towards the wrist. With right sides together and matching seam line and the notches tack and stitch the underarm seam. Press open and neaten. Set the sleeve into the armhole as before.
With most of these styles the appearance is improved with the use of shoulder pads. Instructions for making these for different kinds of sleeves are given on page 82. The pad fits from C to G.

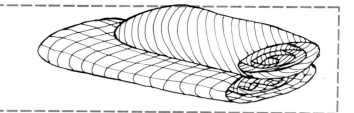

Basic collar patterns

Making simple collar patterns from a basic block

There are two ways of taking measurements when drafting a collar, either by direct measurement of the neck or by using the bodice pattern.

Measure the base of the neck or measure the stitching line of the pattern. Note the measurement from the centre-back to the shoulder and from the centre-back to the centre-front. Using graph paper, draft the collar, adapt to the style required and then add turnings (figure 1).

All the collars in this chapter can be worn buttoned up or open and are suitable for dresses, blouses and children's clothes, but not for tailored shirts.

in one piece add turnings on the neckline and centre-front only (figure 2B). Cut on the cross for a neater fit (figure 2C). If the collar is to be made in two pieces, then turnings must be added to the outside edge.

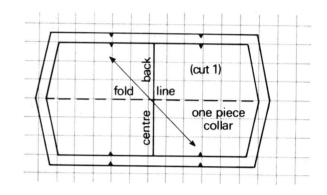

Figure 2B

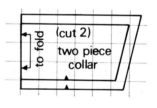

Figure 2C

When this type of collar is cut on the cross no facing is needed on the back neckline of the garment. After stitching on the collar, trim garment and under-collar turnings, turn under the raw edge of the top-collar and stitch to the seam line by hand or machine (figure 3).

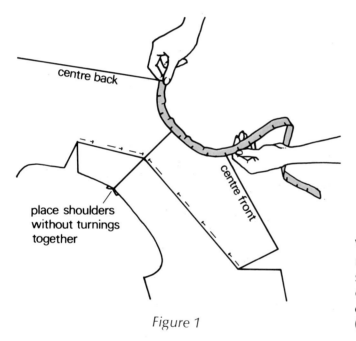

Figure 1

A simple straight collar

Draw a rectangle the length of the neckline by 7.5cm (*3 inches*). One short side is the centre-back and the other the centre-front. Mark in the shoulder seam position on one long side (the neckline edge), and extend the other 2cm ($\frac{3}{4}$ *inch*) on the centre-front. Draw a line from this point to the centre-front of the neckline edge (A-B) (figure 2A). If the collar is to be cut

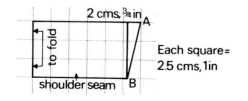

Figure 2A

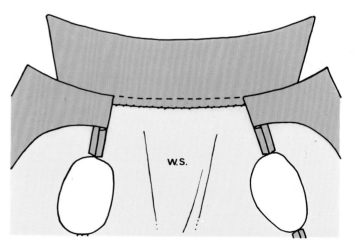

Figure 3

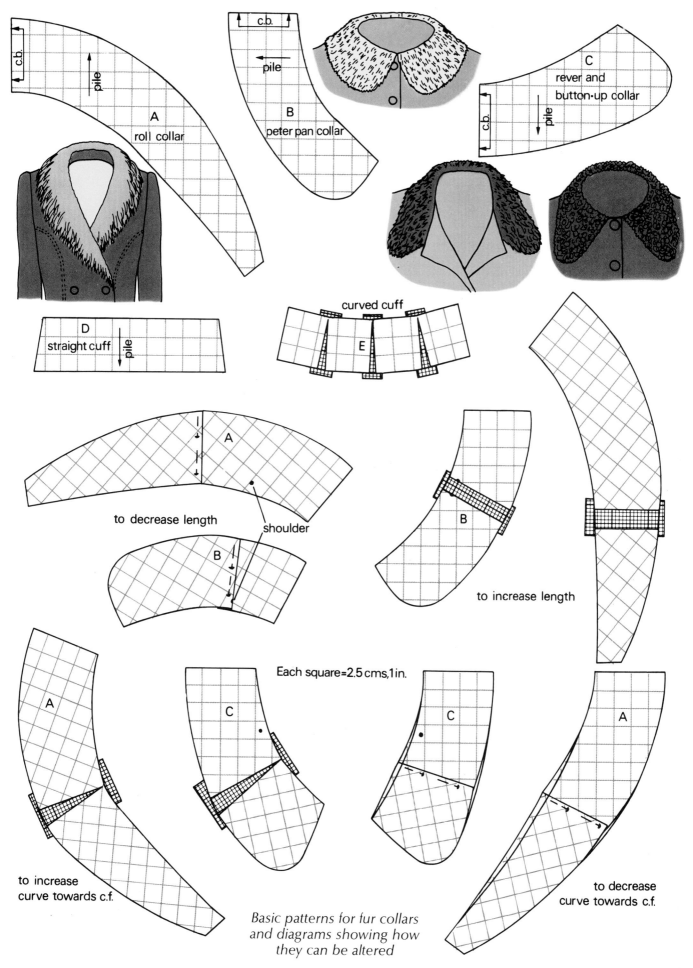

c.b.

pile

A
roll collar

c.b.

pile

B
peter pan collar

C
rever and
button·up collar

c.b.

pile

curved cuff

D
straight cuff

pile

E

A

to decrease length

shoulder

B

B

to increase length

Each square=2.5 cms,1 in.

A

C

C

A

to increase
curve towards c.f.

to decrease
curve towards c.f.

*Basic patterns for fur collars
and diagrams showing how
they can be altered*

A straight collar with a stand

This collar is curved at the neckline so that it will stand up at the back of the neck.

Draw a rectangle as for a simple straight band collar, mark in the shoulder seam position and extend one end (A). On the centre-front mark 2cm ($\frac{3}{4}$ *inch*) up from the neckline (B). Draw a line from A-B-C-D as shown in the diagram. Add turnings on all edges except the centre-back (figures 4A and 4B).

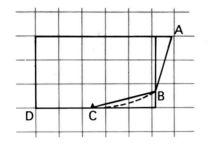

Figure 4A

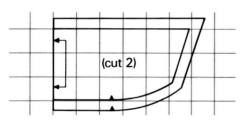

Figure 4B

A straight collar with long points

This is made in the same way as the preceding collar, except that the point is extended by 2.5cm (*1 inch*). Curve the outside edge so that the collar lies flat when attached (figures 5A and 5B).

Figure 5A

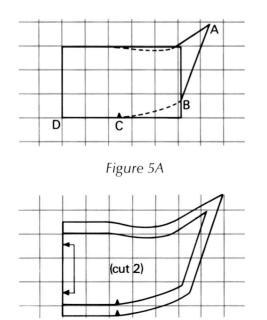

Figure 5B

A shaped stand collar

This collar gives a more tailored appearance. Draw the basic rectangle and shape the centre-front as required. Mark in the shoulder seam position and draw a line from this point to the outer edge. Draw another line approximately half way between this and the centre-back (figure 6A). Cut on these two lines from the outer edge almost to the neckline. Open up the cuts 0.6cm ($\frac{1}{4}$ *inch*) and put another piece of paper under the opening (figure 6B).

This type of collar can be used as it is or a stand can be added to raise the collar around the back of the neck. For a more pointed collar 0.6cm ($\frac{1}{4}$ *inch*) may be taken out on the outside edge approximately half way between the centre-front and the shoulder (figure 6C).

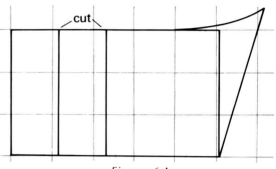

Figure 6A

0.6 cms, ¼ in

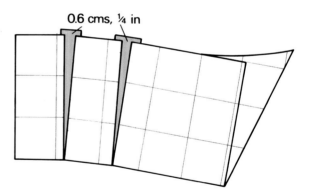

Figure 6B

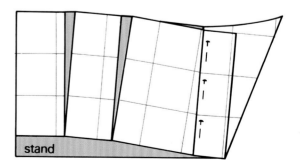

Figure 6C

212

High style collars

More collars to make from a basic block

Upright Mandarin or military collar

This can be cut on the cross from a straight piece of fabric. The measurements are the length of the neckline (as shown on page 210), by approximately 6.5cm ($2\frac{1}{2}$ inches) plus turnings (figures 1A and B). This collar is inclined to hang forward and a curved fit gives a much neater appearance. To achieve this, make the collar 1.3cm–2cm ($\frac{1}{2}$ inch–$\frac{3}{4}$ inch) smaller between the shoulder line and the centre-front. When attaching the collar to the garment stretch it to fit the neckline either side of the centre-front (figure 1C).

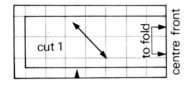

Figure 1A

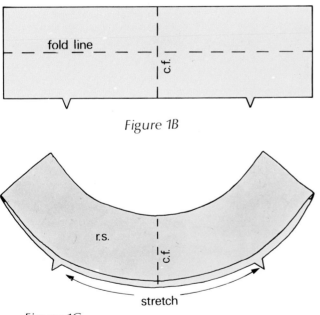

Figure 1B

Figure 1C

Shaped Mandarin or military collar

Draw a rectangle the length of the neckline by 3.1cm ($1\frac{1}{4}$ inches) plus turnings. Mark in the shoulder seam from neckline to top edge. Draw two lines approximately 4cm and 2cm ($1\frac{1}{2}$ inches and $\frac{3}{4}$ inches) in from the centre-front and cut (figure 2A). Overlap these cuts by 0.6cm ($\frac{1}{4}$ inch) on the top edge and re-draw curves where necessary (figure 2B). More or less ease

may be required at the top edge, depending on personal choice and the neck shape. Experiment on a piece of fabric until the fit is satisfactory. Add turnings (figure 2C).

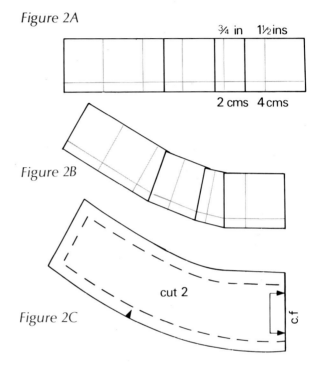

Figure 2A

Figure 2B

Figure 2C

Shaped collar with a centre-front opening

This type of collar can be used where there is a centre-front opening (figures 3A and B), or made in two pieces for a centre-back opening (figure 3C).

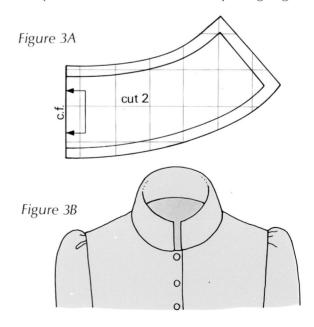

Figure 3A

Figure 3B

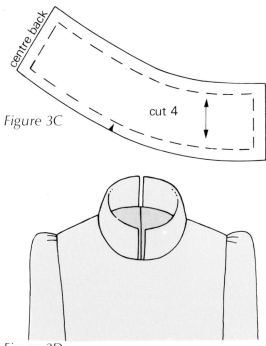

Figure 3C

Figure 3D

Draft as for a shaped Mandarin collar but add turnings to the centre-front as well as the centre-back (figure 3D). It may be necessary to take off another 0.6cm ($\frac{1}{4}$ inch) from the outer edge of the centre-front in order to avoid the two sides overlapping when worn (figure 4A). The corners may be rounded off if preferred (figure 4B).

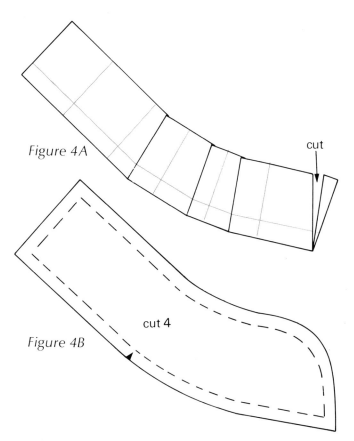

Figure 4A

cut

Figure 4B

cut 4

Roll neck collar

Cut a rectangle on the cross the length of the neckline by double the width required for the stand and roll plus turnings (figure 5A). On certain firm fabrics it is necessary for the collar to be cut slightly longer than the neckline and eased on to it so that the outside edge of the roll lies flat when worn (figure 5B). The collar should be folded over as far as the neckline at the centre-back and held in position with a few stitches or a French tack between the stand and the underside of the roll (figure 5C).

This type of collar can be attached without a neckline facing. With the right side of the garment to the underside of the roll, stitch on the fitting line. Turn on to the wrong side, turn under the seam allowance of the remaining raw edge and hem on to the stitching line. If interfacing is required use a woven type cut on the cross.

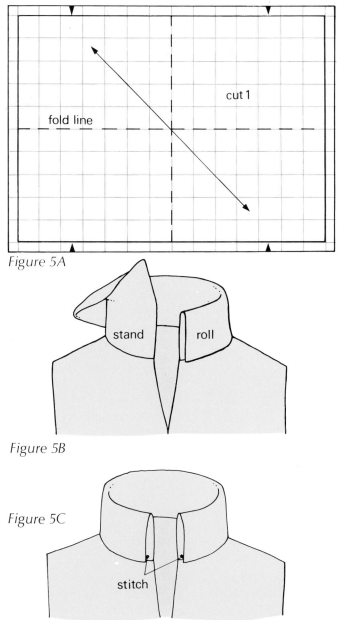

cut 1

fold line

Figure 5A

stand   roll

Figure 5B

Figure 5C

stitch

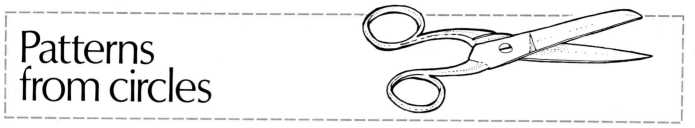

Patterns from circles

Cutting from a circle
Skirts

There are three basic types of skirt which can be cut from a circle: the full circle, half circle and quarter circle skirts. Care must be taken when choosing fabrics as checks and stripes on a half circle will have the pattern running vertically on one edge and horizontally on the other edge.

Making one pattern for all three types of skirt

Draw two lines marked A and B at a right angle on one corner of the graph paper. Place the end of a ruler on the corner and for a full circle skirt draw the radius of one quarter the waist measurement from line A to line B. For example, take a 9cm (3½ inch) measurement from the corner for a 57cm (22 inch) waist. For a 63.5cm (25 inch) waist, measure 10cm (4 inches) from the corner. For a 76cm (30 inch) waist, measure 11.8cm (4¾ inches). Mark the measurement required at intervals between lines A and B. Then draw a curved line through the marks. After drawing the line, place the tape measure on one side and measure the curved line to ensure that the measurement is the same as one quarter the waist measurement. For a half circle skirt draw another line at double the radius from the first line. This is half the waist measurement. For a quarter circle skirt, draw a line four times the radius of the waist measurement (figures 1A and 1B).

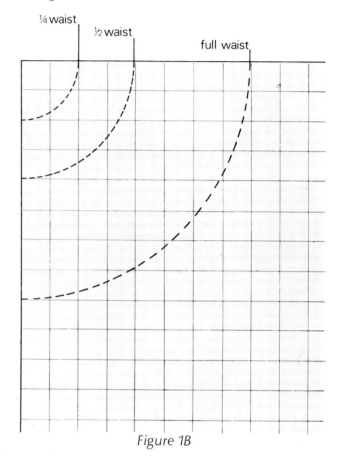

Figure 1B

Length of skirt The hemline should be drawn in, in the same way to the required length. The longer the skirt, the wider the fabric required. Alternatively, if the fabric is not wide enough, a join can be made on the selvedge. Once the pattern is drawn, add turnings and a hem, then cut out.

Cutting out

Full circle skirt Lay the pattern piece on the fabric with one edge to the selvedge. Chalk around the pattern pieces and then reverse, keeping the central line the same. Cut two of these so that the seams are on the selvedges.

Half circle skirt Lay the pattern on to the double fabric. This can be cut on the fold so that there is one seam only at the centre-back or with both edges on selvedges and on single fabric so that there are two seams. If the two seams are to be at centre-front

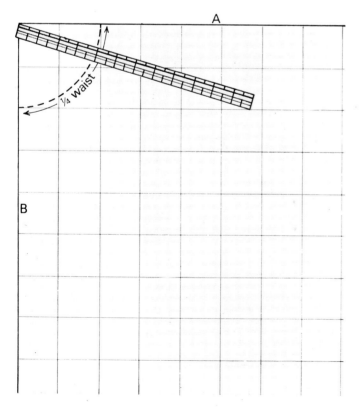

Figure 1A

and back, the fabric used should be soft and heavy so that it falls well over the hips (figure 2).

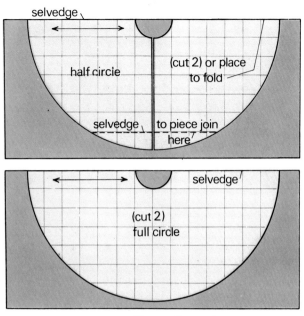

Figure 2

Quarter circle skirt This can be cut in one piece from wide fabric. Take the depth measurement between the waist and hip, and draw in the hipline on the pattern. Put the tape measure on one edge and measure the hipline. If it is not the correct hip measurement, drop both lines until it is obtained. The excess at the waist can then be eased into the waistband (figure 3).

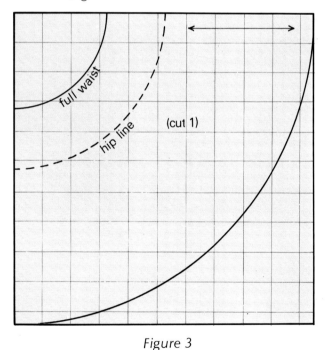

Figure 3

For a fuller skirt a quarter circle can be drawn with the waistline 5cm (*2 inches*) larger. Then draw a line through the centre and take off 1.3cm (½ *inch*) at A, B, C and D. This can now become a two or four

panelled skirt, placing centre front and centre back to the fold or straight grain line (figure 4).

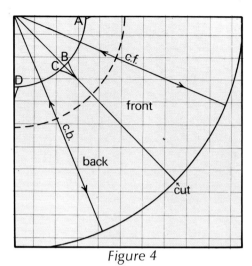

Figure 4

After making up the skirt, it is important to let it hang for at least forty eight hours to allow the hem to drop. Try on the skirt and level the hemline from the floor with a ruler. Make a small hem so that it is not too heavy and does not pull on the skirt.

Traditional bridal veil
Net is used for making a bridal veil and both nylon and pure silk net is available at most large stores from 183cm (*2 yards*) to 366cm (*4 yards*) wide.
For a one layer veil, measure from the top of the head down the centre-back to the required length and add approximately 15cm (*6 inches*) for height behind the head-dress.
For a two layered veil, measure in the same way and add approximately 23cm (*9 inches*) plus one third of the length. Cut a circle to the measurement required. It is not essential to neaten the cut edge, but the edge can be neatened with a narrow lace stitched on the edge or it can be machine neatened with a zig-zag stitch worked over a crochet cord. It is advisable to work a row of stay-stitching around the edge first to prevent stretching (figure 5).

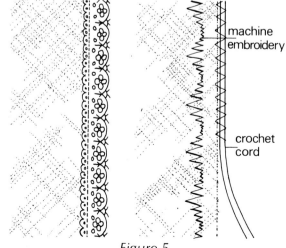

Figure 5

Machine embroidery can be effectively used near the edge of the veil but should always be tested on spare net first using silk or synthetic thread. Motifs or lace can also be appliquéd to the veil, but try on the finished veil first with the wedding dress to ensure that any appliqué will not hide a design feature on the dress.

Attaching a one layer veil to a headdress Fold the circle in half and mark the central line with a tacking thread. Work a row of gathering forming a semi-circle that crosses the line of tacking 15cm (6 inches) below the edge (figure 6A). Pull up the gathering thread and attach the veil to the head-dress on the right side (figure 6B). For a high veil stitch the veiling to the upper edge on the wrong side (figure 7).

Figure 7

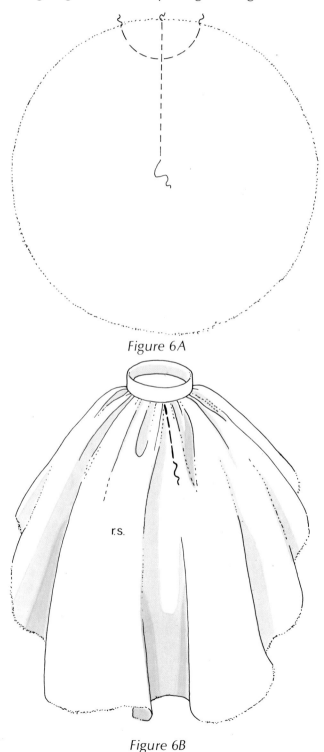

Figure 6A

Figure 6B

Attaching a two layer veil Fold a good third of the circle over. Work a gathering thread and attach to the headdress as for a one layer veil. For a face covering veil it must be attached to the top of the head-dress. A neat effect is obtained by cutting away the net inside the gathering line so that the veil fits the head-dress (figure 8).

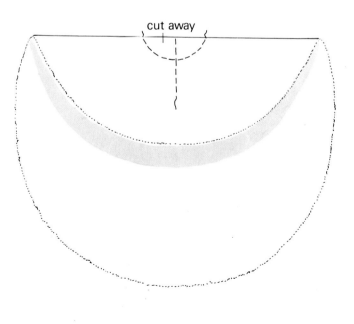

Figure 8

Capes & ponchos

Cutting a cape or poncho based on a circle

Using a basic block that has been adjusted to personal measurements, transfer the bust darts to the shoulder. Instructions for transferring the darts are on page 192. On the front cut a straight line from the lower edge to the bust point and pin the dart. Cut a straight line from the lower edge of the back to the point of the shoulder dart and pin the dart. The fullness is now transferred to the lower edge. To make the neck larger, draw in a line slightly below the original neck-line (figure 1).

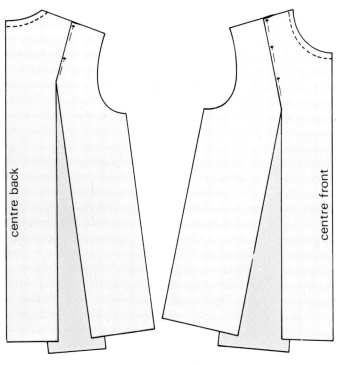

Figure 1

Fold a large piece of paper in half and mark the cross-wise grain. Place the centre-back of the pattern to the straight edge of the paper with the neck point touching the crosswise line. Place the front pattern with the neck point touching the neck point of the back and the centre-front at least 5.4cm (2⅛ inches) from the edge of the paper at the neckline. This is for a 4cm (1½ inch) wrap and 1.6cm (⅝ inch) seam allow-ance. Pin into position. Measure along the centre-back the length required and mark A and B. From the edge of the paper measure the same distance on the crosswise line C–B. From C mark the same length on the centre-front. Draw in the lower edge of the cape from the centre-back to the centre-front. In line with the shoulder point mark D, 6 to 7cm (2¼ to 2¾ inches)

below B and draw a new curve through this to allow for the squareness of the shoulder. Draw in the front wrap and seam allowance. Draw in the facing line. This will be cut separately after the cape has been cut out.

The centre-back may be placed on the fold or the selvedge of the fabric. If placed to a selvedge, turnings must be allowed (figure 2).

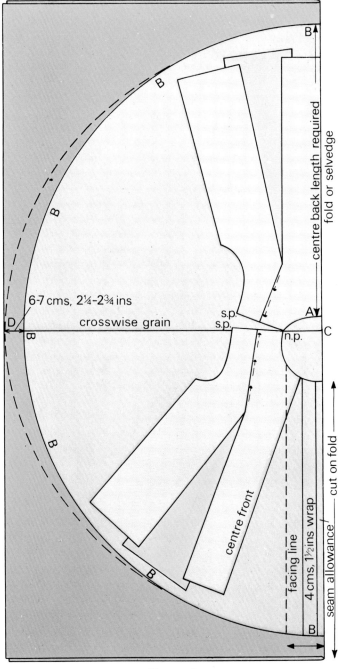

Figure 2

To reduce the fullness of the hem

Draw in a new shoulder point approximately halfway between the original points and mark G. Draw a straight line from the neck points through G to the lower edge and mark H (figure 3). Cut from neck

line and trace through the neckline. Draw in the facing (figure 4).

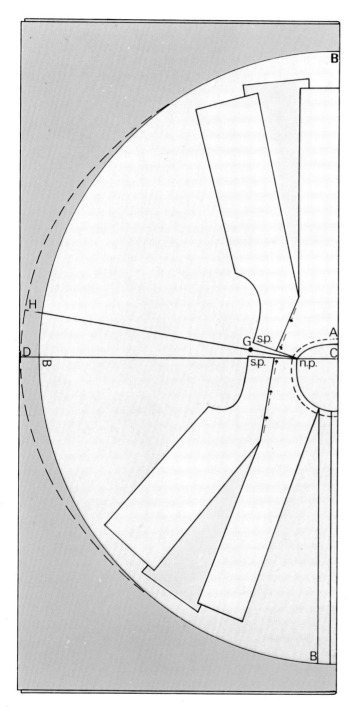

Figure 3

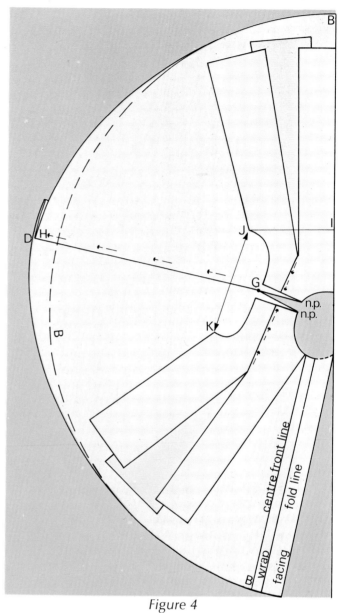

Figure 4

point to G. Crease the paper on line G–H and fold towards D. The fullness depends on the effect required, but the underarm points J–K must be at least half the measurement from I – J to allow for arm movement. It may be necessary to re-shape the lower edge for a good line. There is now sufficient space for the front facing. Fold the paper on the fold

Collars and neckline facings can be cut as shown on page 210. If you want to make a cape that is unlined, the edges should be bound, in which case it will be necessary to cut away the seam allowance on the front edge.

Add turnings to the neckline and hem allowance.

Poncho

The same principle is used but a poncho is usually cut from a square piece of fabric.

Fold the fabric in half diagonally, then in half again to find the bias line A–B. Place the pattern with the centre-front and centre-back to the fold and the neck points touching. Cut out the neckline, allowing for lowering and the seam allowance. Cut on the centre-front fold line to the depth required for the opening. If the centre-front and centre-back are placed to a selvedge turnings must be allowed. The centre-front seam is then left open for the depth required (figure 5).

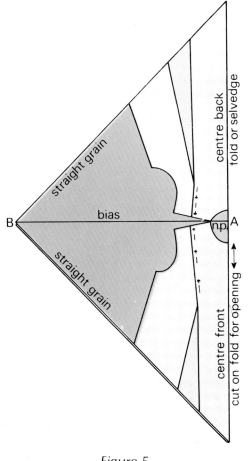

Figure 5

Finishing the neckline on a poncho
Inserted zip
Cut on the fold line the length of the zip below the seam allowance on the neckline minus 0.6cm ($\frac{1}{4}$ inch). Clip diagonally into the corners 0.6cm ($\frac{1}{4}$ inch). Turn the opening edges to the wrong side and tack the fold close to the edges of the zip teeth. Machine stitch on the edge. This zip will be visible (figure 6A).

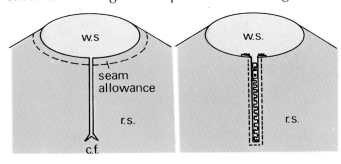

Figure 6A

Where there is a centre-front and centre-back seam, leave an opening at the neckline the length of the zip plus the neckline seam allowance. Tack this together and press open. Place the right side of the zip centrally to the wrong side of the opening and tack into position. From the right side machine stitch 0.6cm

($\frac{1}{4}$ inch) each side of the zip teeth and across the lower edge (figure 6B).

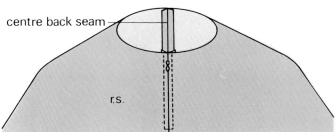

Figure 6B

Faced front opening
With right sides together place a piece of matching fabric on the centre-front line. Stitch 0.6cm ($\frac{1}{4}$ inch) either side of this line and across the bottom the length of the opening required. Cut on the centre-front line and diagonally to the corners. Turn the facing to the wrong side, tack and press. The fronts may be held together with button and chain fastening or frog and toggles (figure 6C).

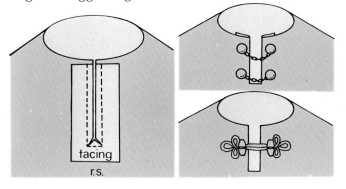

Figure 6C

All-in-one neck and front facing
This can be traced off from the poncho pattern. With right sides together tack and stitch the facing to the poncho around the neckline and each side of the opening position as before. Trim and clip the turnings, turn to the wrong side, tack and press. Neaten the edges of the facing and lightly catch to the poncho (figure 6D).

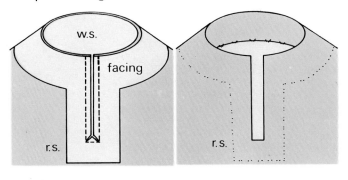

Figure 6D

The edges of the poncho may be finished with a hem or edged with braid or fringing.

Patterns for trousers

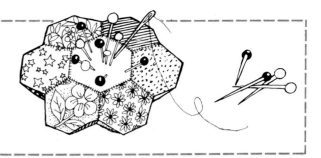

Making a trouser block
You will need graph paper, tracing paper, a long ruler and a pencil to make your block.

Measurements required
Waist, hips, outside leg, inside leg and the depth of crotch.

Front
Draw a horizontal line across the paper 5cm (2 inches) from the top. This is the waistline. Take one quarter of the hip measurement and mark in a point on the waistline this distance from the right hand side. Draw a long vertical line through this point.
Mark A where the vertical line meets the waistline. Take the crotch measurement and mark B on the vertical line down from A. Take the inside leg measurement and mark C on the vertical line at this distance from B. Take half the inside leg measurement and add 5cm (2 inches). This is the knee to ground measurement and should be marked D from C.
Take one third of the quarter hip measurement and add 1cm ($\frac{3}{8}$ inch). Mark E to the left of B at this distance. Draw a vertical line from E to the waist, and mark F. Take one eighth of the hip measurement and add 2cm ($\frac{3}{4}$ inch). Using this measurement mark G below F on the line F–E. Draw a horizontal line across the pattern from G. This is the yoke line.
Mark H from G taking a quarter of the hip measurement.
Draw in I 5cm (2 inches) below G, and J 5cm (2 inches) below H. Draw a horizontal line from I–J which should be one quarter of the hip measurement.
For the waist darts mark points 1cm ($\frac{3}{4}$ inch) each side of A and 10cm (4 inches) down line A–C. Join the points to make a dart. Draw another dart of the same measurements 6cm ($2\frac{1}{2}$ inches) to the right of the first dart.
Take one quarter of the waist measurement and add the width of the darts. Measure this distance from F and mark K on the waistline. Mark L 1cm ($\frac{3}{8}$ inch) above K. Join F to L.
E–M is half of B–E plus 1cm ($\frac{3}{8}$ inch). E–N is half of E–M minus 2cm ($\frac{3}{4}$ inch). Draw a curved line through M and N to I.
D–O and D–P are quarter the knee width minus 1cm ($\frac{3}{8}$ inch). C–Q and C–R are quarter the hem width minus 1cm ($\frac{3}{8}$ inch). Draw a slightly curved line from M to R through P. Draw a curved line from L to Q through K, H, J and O.

Draw a line from R to Q so that it crosses D–C 2cm ($\frac{3}{4}$ inch) above C.

Back
Position and secure a piece of tracing paper over the block already made for the trouser front. Take half of the measurement E–M, add 2cm ($\frac{3}{4}$ inch) and mark S at this distance from F.
S–T is the same as F–S minus 1.6cm ($\frac{5}{8}$ inch) T–U is quarter the waist measurement plus 4cm ($1\frac{1}{2}$ inches). U is on the same level as L. Draw a straight line from T to U.
U is a third of T–U. Mark W 2cm ($\frac{3}{4}$ inch) to the left of V. W–X is one third of T–U minus 1cm ($\frac{3}{8}$ inch). Mark Y 2cm ($\frac{3}{4}$ inch) to the left of X.
Draw in two darts from Y–X and W–V, both 10cm (4 inches) in depth. M–Z is the same as E–M. Draw a straight line through P and O and mark 1E and 1D 2cm ($\frac{3}{4}$ inch) from P and O respectively.
Take the measurement M–P and mark the same distance from 1E to Z. Mark this 1A. Draw a curved line from 1A to I through M and N. Then draw a straight line from I to T. Mark 1B where centre-back line crosses the yoke line.
Take a quarter of the hip measurement and add 1cm ($\frac{3}{8}$ inch) for stretch fabrics or 2.5cm (1 inch) for non-stretch fabrics. Take this measurement and mark from 1B along the yoke line and call this 1C. Mark 1F and 1G 2cm ($\frac{3}{4}$ inch) either side of R and Q.
Draw a curved line from U to 1F through 1C and 1D. Also from 1A to 1G through 1E.

Waistband
This is a rectangle the length of the waist measurement plus an extension of approximately 5cm (2 inches) by double the width required.
The opening can be at the side or in the front. Mark out the waistband in four equal measurements and then add on the extension.
Mark in the notches and the straight grain line. Write 'stretch' between 1A and the first notch, on the inside leg on the back pattern.
Cut out the pattern piece around the outside edge and place on to a piece of graph paper. Pin into position ensuring that the straight grain line lies on a line on the graph paper. Transfer all markings and notches and cut out. Repeat with trouser front.
Add the turnings and the hem allowance. It is advisable to leave extra turnings between U and 1C as this is where alterations can be made if necessary.

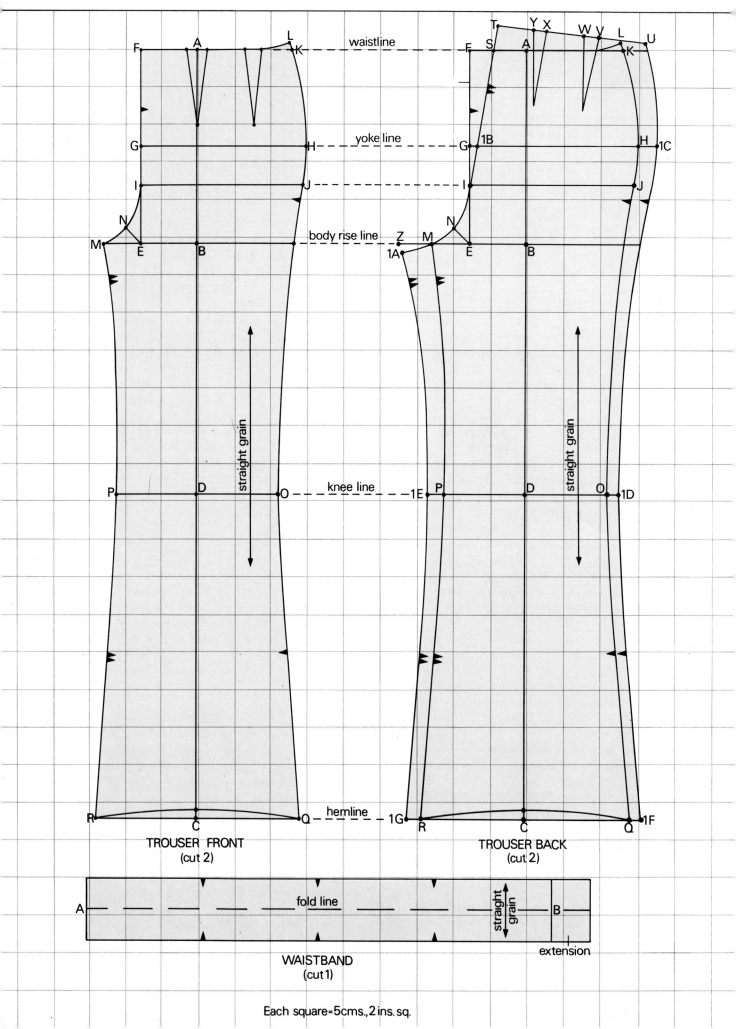

waistline

yoke line

body rise line

knee line

hemline

straight grain

straight grain

TROUSER FRONT
(cut 2)

TROUSER BACK
(cut 2)

fold line

straight grain

extension

WAISTBAND
(cut 1)

Each square=5cms., 2 ins. sq.

Making up trousers

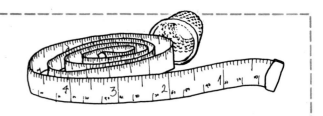

Making up trousers and altering the basic trouser block

Fabric required
1.15–1.40 metres ($1\frac{1}{4}$–$1\frac{1}{2}$ yards) of 137cm (*54 inch*) wide fabric

You will also need
Graph paper for making the pattern, matching thread, petersham the length of the waistband by 4cm ($1\frac{1}{2}$ *inches*) wide, 1 button or hook and bar.

Cutting out the trousers
Fold the fabric and place on the pattern pieces. Take care that the grain line on the pattern lies on the straight grain of the fabric. Pin into place and cut out. Transfer all markings from the pattern pieces to the fabric.

Tacking and fitting
With right sides together tack the darts. With right sides together and matching notches tack the trousers together all around. Leave an opening in the centre-front seam (or in the left hand side seam if preferred) for the zip.

If interfacing is used in the waistband, cut a piece the same length as the waistband and half the width. Tack the interfacing or petersham to the wrong side of the waistband, so that one edge lies along the fold. Tack the waistband to the top of the trousers. Work a row of large tacking stitches down from A–C on both the front and back legs (see figure 8) so that when the trousers are fitted it is easier to see if they hang correctly. In addition these lines of tacking indicate where the creases are to be pressed in. Fit the trousers, then take off the waistband. Transfer any alterations made on the trousers to the pattern.

Making up
With right sides together stitch the darts on the front and back trousers. Press towards the centre-front and back. Stitch the backs together at the centre-back seam and the fronts together at the centre-front seam as far as the dot. Trim turnings and clip at regular intervals. Then press open and neaten. Alternatively trim the turnings to 0.6cm ($\frac{1}{4}$ *inch*) neaten together and press to one side (figure 1).

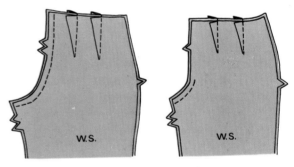

Figure 1

With right sides together and matching notches and crotch seams, pin the front to the back, stretching the back on to the front between the crotch seam and notch. Neaten as before. Tack and stitch the side seams and neaten (figure 2).

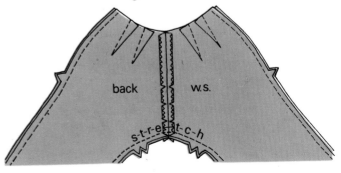

Figure 2

Make a turning of just under 1.6cm ($\frac{5}{8}$ *inch*) on the left hand side of the opening and tack on to the zip so that the fold is close to the teeth. From the right side machine stitch close to the fold. Make a turning on the right side of the opening so that it covers the zip and meets the left fold. From the wrong side tack down the centre of the zip tape through all thicknesses, and from the right side machine over the row of tacking. Curve the stitching at the base of the opening or, if preferred, stitch at a right angle across the base of the zip. Neaten the turnings on the wrong side (figure 3).

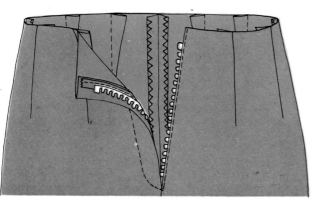

Figure 3

Creases

Fold the legs on the front and back rows of tacking and press. If the rows of tacking have been removed place the seams on top of each other on each leg, at the hemline, kneeline, and base of crotch. Tack creases and then press from the seam lines out towards the creases, avoiding pressing over pins as they leave marks. Remove the tacking, place the legs together and press again (figure 4).

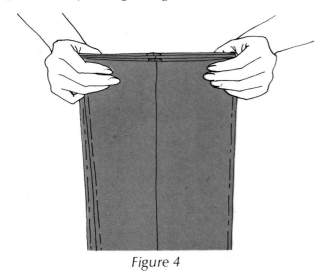

Figure 4

Waistband

With right sides together fold the already interfaced waistband in half lengthways and stitch across the ends and to the dot at one end. Trim turnings and turn through.

With right sides together place the interfaced side of the waistband to the top of the trousers so that the extension is on the left hand side. Tack and stitch. Make a turning of 1.6cm ($\frac{5}{8}$ *inch*) on the free edge of the waistband, turn over and slip-stitch on to the stitch line (figure 5). Work a buttonhole where indicated on the extension and sew on the button to correspond.

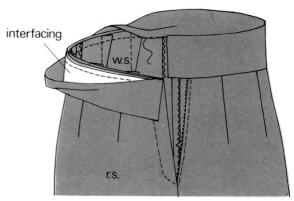

Figure 5

Hem

Try on the trousers with the shoes to be worn and pin up the hem. Re-insert the pins on the hemline. Measure 5cm (*2 inches*) down from the hemline and trim off excess (figure 6).

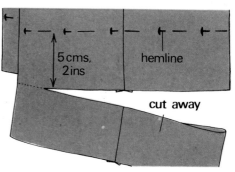

Figure 6

Neaten the raw edge by machine or tape. Turn the hem up on the hemline and slip-stitch into place.
A piece of interfacing may be attached to the wrong side of the hem to add body and help the trousers to hang well. Attach this before the raw edge is neatened.

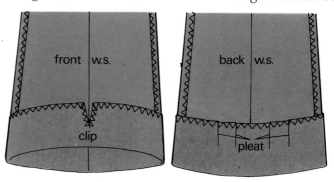

Figure 7

224

If the centre front crease line (A–C) is much shorter than the back crease line (A–C) the hem may need clipping at the front and pleating at the back, so that the hem lies flat: neaten the edges of the clip made and work the pleats either side of the centre-back crease (figure 7).

Altering the shape of the trouser leg

For a straight and fuller leg, on the front trouser block draw a straight line from M to R and H to Q. On the back block, repeat this from Z–1G and 1C–1F (figure 8). The trouser back should always be 2cm ($\frac{3}{4}$ *inch*) wider than the front leg either side of O–P and Q–R.

Close fitting trousers (for example ski pants)

Bend the knee and measure. Measure the ankle also and add approximately 4cm–6cm ($1\frac{1}{2}$ *inches*–$2\frac{1}{4}$ *inches*) to the measurement.

Take half the knee measurement and half the ankle measurement and mark in the new P, O, R and Q on the knee and hem lines of the front trouser. Take the same measurement again and add 1cm ($\frac{3}{8}$ *inch*) tolerance on either side and draw in the new back leg. Ski pants usually reach the ankle bone and need a strap under the foot (figure 9).

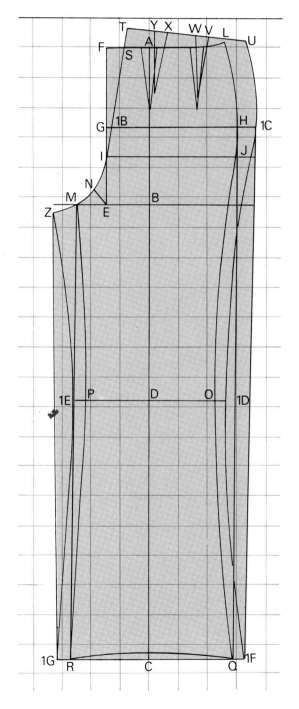

Figure 8

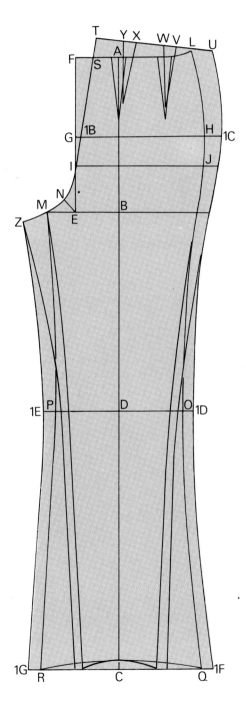

Figure 9

If an elasticated waist is required instead of a zip, F–L and T–U must measure one quarter of the hip measurement. Then make top of the trousers higher by taking double the width of the elastic to be used and adding 0.6cm ($\frac{1}{4}$ inch). Take this measurement and draw the new lines F–L and T–U so that they measure exactly one quarter of the hip measurement (figure 10).

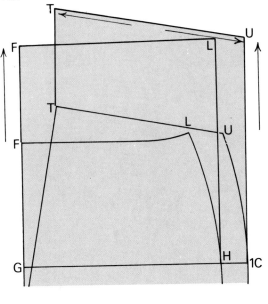

Figure 10

The pattern may be drawn without darts on the front but in this case allow a tolerance of approximately 2cm ($\frac{3}{4}$ inch), which can be eased into the waistband or shrunk away when the waistband is attached. The back trouser can be drawn with one dart on each side instead of two. Both these adaptations will accentuate the curve between L–H and U–1C and care will be needed when drawing to avoid a bulge in the seam (figure 11).

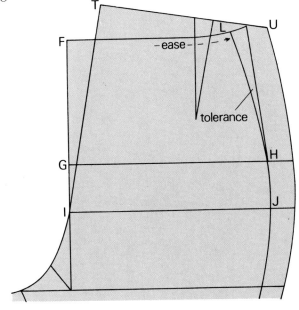

Figure 11

Creases often appear on the front crotch between M and E. To rectify this move T towards U slightly and raise T. Then re-mark U so that the measurement T–U is the same. Draw new lines T–I and U–1C. Use the same method if the garment is too tight on the yoke line, but do not raise T. Try on the trousers and check that the centre-front and centre-back creases hang vertically. If the creases hang towards the inside leg, lengthen the centre-front seam so that F is on the same level as L. Then draw a straight line from F–L (figure 12).

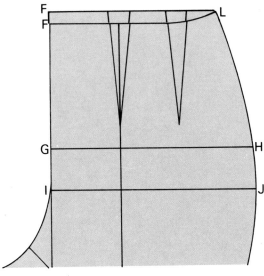

Figure 12

If the creases hang towards the inside leg and the side seam forms a fold below the yoke line, lower L and U to the same level as F and re-draw the waistline (figure 13).

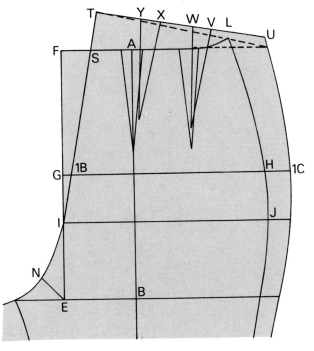

Figure 13

Extra hints for trousers

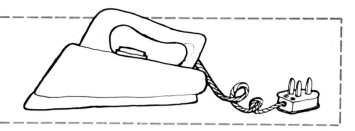

Trouser pockets, turn-ups, and zip openings

Pockets
There are several variations of pocket which are set into side seams just below the waistband.

Making a basic pocket pattern
Use the basic front trouser pattern with one dart on the waistline and move L in 2cm ($\frac{3}{4}$ inch) (figure 1).

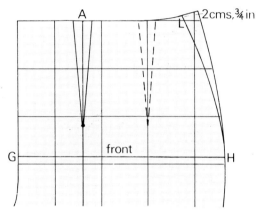

Figure 1

Take a piece of graph paper approximately 25cm (*10 inches*) wide by 20.5cm (*8 inches*) long and fold in half lengthways on a straight line. Place this beneath the trouser pattern so that the lines of the pattern match the lines on the paper with H and J touching the sides and L touching the top. Pin into position and trim off the excess paper at the sides and top. Mark in a dot on the side seam of the pattern and both pieces of the pocket 12.5cm (*5 inches*) below L (figure 2). On the side seam of the back trouser pattern

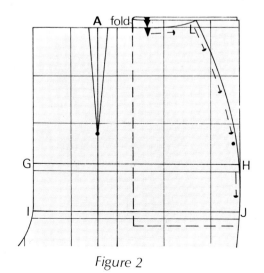

Figure 2

mark in a dot to correspond the same distance below U. Make balance marks (notches) on the waistline and on both pocket pieces underneath.

Remove the pocket pattern and cut through both pieces starting 1.3cm ($\frac{1}{2}$ inch) below the dot, cutting in approximately 2cm ($\frac{3}{4}$ inch) and then round to the bottom edge of the fold line (figure 3). This is the basic pattern that can be adapted to other styles. Turnings must be added as on the main garment.

Making up a basic pocket
This can be made in matching fabric or a light-weight lining with strips of matching fabric stitched to the outside edges. If using lining, stitch strips of matching fabric approximately 5cm (*2 inches*) wide on to the inside of the pocket, turning in 0.6cm ($\frac{1}{4}$ inch) on the edges nearest the fold line (figure 4).

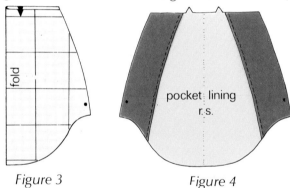

Figure 3   *Figure 4*

With right sides together tack and stitch the pocket to the front trouser from the waistline to the dots. Clip to the dots, trim turnings to 0.6cm ($\frac{1}{4}$ inch) and fold the pocket on to the wrong side at the seam line. Press and work a row of top stitching close to the fold (figure 5).

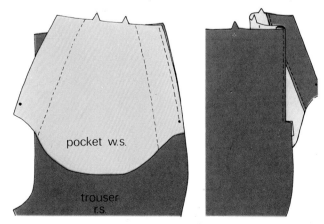

Figure 5

With right sides together tack and stitch the pocket to the back trouser from the waistline to the dot. Clip to the dot. Trim the turnings, press towards the centre-back and neaten together. From the right side work a row of top stitching close to the seam line through all thicknesses (figure 6).

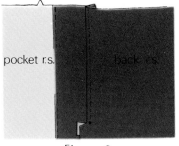

Figure 6

With right sides together tack and stitch the side seam from the dots to the lower edge. Press open and neaten (figure 7).

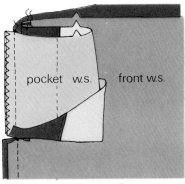

Figure 7

With right sides together and matching dots tack and stitch the lower edge of the pocket from the side seam to the fold. Trim turnings and neaten together (figure 8).

Figure 8

Cut-away pockets

Slanted or curved cut-away pocket Place paper as before and trim off excess. Mark in dot on the side seam. Draw a line from B to 2.5cm (*1 inch*) from the fold line of the pocket at the waist A–C to 7.5cm (*3 inches*) below L. Draw in balance marks between A and B on the front and both pocket pieces. Cut front and top pocket pieces only on B–C. Add turnings as required (figure 9).

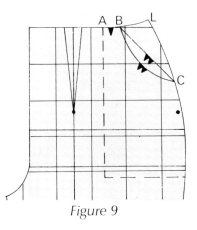

Figure 9

Squared cut-away pocket Work as before but draw a straight line 4cm (*1½ inches*) long down from B–D. Mark C 5cm (*2⅜ inches*) below L and draw a horizontal line from D–C (figure 10).

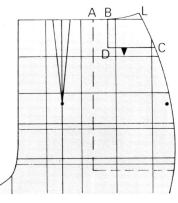

Figure 10

Cut-away pockets can be made in matching fabric or in lining with strips of matching fabric attached. If using lining the strip for the top pocket should follow the shape of B–C and be approximately 2.5cm

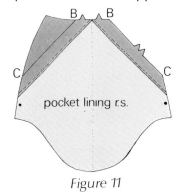

Figure 11

(*1 inch*) in depth. The strip for the under-pocket should be the same shape as the pocket and at least 2.5cm (*1 inch*) lower than the top pocket fitting line. Stitch the matching strips on to the right side of the pocket, turning in 0.6cm ($\frac{1}{4}$ *inch*) as before (figure 11).

Making up cut-away pockets

With right sides together tack and stitch the front pocket to the trouser front. Trim turnings and clip curves or corners. Turn to the right side, tack the edge and press. Work a row of top stitching 0.6cm ($\frac{1}{4}$ *inch*) from the edge. Pin on to the under pocket so that balance marks and dots match. Turn to the wrong side and stitch the pocket from the dots to the fold line. Trim turnings and neaten together (figure 12).

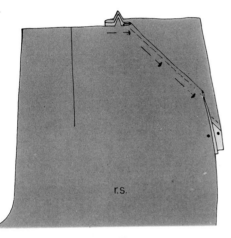

Figure 12

With right sides together and matching dots and balance marks tack and stitch the side seams from the waist to the hem, stitching through all thicknesses where the pocket crosses the fitting line. Clip across the front seam allowance below the pocket. Press the pocket seam towards the back and the rest of the seam open and neaten. Sew the clipped edge to the pocket turning. For extra strength, work safety bars at the ends of all pockets (figure 13).

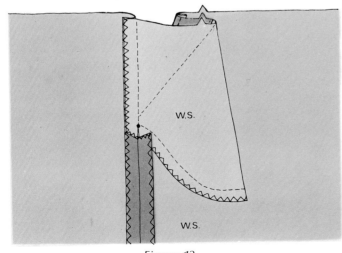

Figure 13

Turn-ups

These are added on to the pattern at the hemline and are usually 4.5–5cm (1$\frac{3}{4}$–2 *inches*) wide. The amount to be added is double the width of turn-up required plus approximately 2.5cm (*1 inch*). Draw in the lines as shown in the diagram, but do not cut out (figure 14).

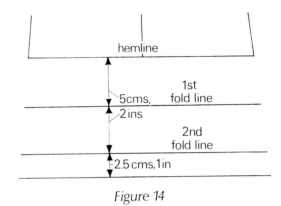

hemline

1st fold line

5cms, 2ins

2nd fold line

2.5 cms, 1in

Figure 14

Fold upwards on the hemline, down on the first fold line, then on to the wrong side at the second fold line. Cut on the original line through all thicknesses of paper (figure 15).

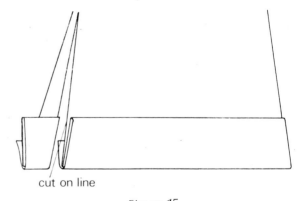

cut on line

Figure 15

Making up turn-ups

Try on the trousers after the creases have been pressed in. Turn up to the correct length on hemline and on to the right side. Measure up from the hemline the depth of turn-up required, fold down again towards the hemline and turn the remaining fabric under to the wrong side. Trim off any excess fabric, neaten the raw edge and slip-hem into position. Press on the right side and work a French tack or a few back stitches through the trouser leg and underneath the turn-up to hold in position 1cm ($\frac{3}{8}$ *inch*) from the top of the turn-up.

Fly zip opening
Method 1

The length of the zip must be sufficient to allow the trousers to pass over the hips without strain. Place the zip on to the centre-front of the pattern with the top 1.3cm ($\frac{1}{2}$ *inch*) below the waist line and mark a dot on the pattern at the end of the teeth. Place a piece of graph paper beneath and mark the dot through to this. Draw in a curved line from 2.5cm (*1 inch*) below the dot up to the waistline 5cm (*2 inches*) from the centre-front (figure 16).

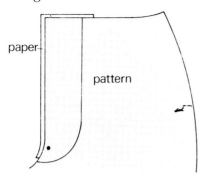

Figure 16

Remove the paper and cut on this line. Add turnings to the centre-front and waistline as required. Cut out three pieces to this shape, once with fabric double and once singly so that the right side of the fabric is in the correct position for facing the upper fold of the front. If a curved zip is used, as on men's trousers, the opening should face towards the right and if a straight zip is used the opening should face towards the left. Iron or tack a piece of interfacing to the wrong side of the single piece. With right sides together join the front facing to the centre-front from the waistline to the dot. Clip to the dot, trim turnings and press towards the facing. Work a row of top stitching on the facing through all thicknesses. Turn facing to the wrong side, tack the edge and press (figure 17).

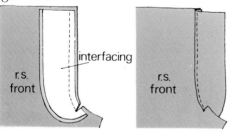

Figure 17

On the other trouser front clip almost to the dot. Roll a fold from the dot to the waistline 0.3cm (*⅛ inch*) beyond the centre-front and tack on to the zip tape, close to the teeth. With right sides together tack

Figure 18

and stitch the zip guard 0.6cm (*¼ inch*) from the outside edge. Turn to the right side and top-stitch the edge (figure 18). Place the guard beneath the zip tape and work a row of stitching through all thicknesses from the waistline to the dot. Stitch as near to the teeth as possible (figure 19).

With right sides together tack and stitch the centre-front seam below the dots. Press open and neaten. Place the faced centre-front so that it touches the original fitting line and pin into position (figure 20).

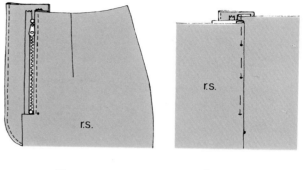

Figure 19   *Figure 20*

Turn to the wrong side and, working through the zip tape and facing only, stitch from the lower end of the zip to the waist line approximately 3cm (*1¼ inches*) from the edge. Make sure that the zip guard is kept free (figure 21).

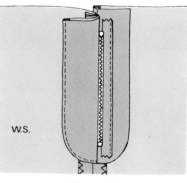

Figure 21

Neaten the raw edges of the zip guard and facing and sew the end of the guard on to the seam line on the wrong side. Work a safety bar at the end of the zip (figure 22).

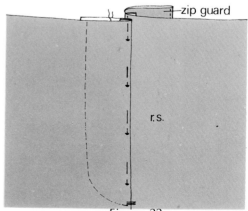

Figure 22

Index

Advanced machine techniques	55	Drawn thread	58	Pleats *cont.*			
Appliqué with lace	152	Dressmaker's stand	27	knife	137		
				Pockets	119, 123		
Back stitch	51	Easy care fabrics	20	concealed	125		
Basic blocks	166	Equipment	7	patch, welt	121		
for bodice and sleeve	180, 184, 188			piped	124		
for skirts	167, 170	Fabrics (for the figure)	23	Poncho (pattern for)	219		
pleated	174, 177	fur	155	Pressing equipment	14		
for sleeves	201	sheer	148	collars, gathers, seams	15		
bishop	203	striped and checked	45				
close fitting	204	Facings	67	Quick slip pattern	199		
flared	208	Fastenings	112	Quilting	59		
gathered	207	Flared collars	81	by machine	59		
Basic seams	50	Flounced collars	74	shadow	60		
Basic sewing techniques	46	French cuffs	92				
Basting	49	Frog fastenings	114	Rouleau	139		
Belts	105						
Belt carriers	109	Gathering	47, 56	Seams	50		
Bias binding	101	Galloon lace	153	basic, flat, channel, French, double			
Binding	46	Godets	135	tucked, single tucked	51		
Blind hemming	55			Mantua	52		
Bodice toile	30	Hemming	56	Sheer fabrics	148		
Bodkins	13	Hems	131	Shell hemming	57		
Bows	102	flared	132	Shirring	46		
Braids	142	faced	134	Skirt toile	33		
Broderie anglaise	113	Honeycomb stitch	65	pleated	174, 177		
Buckles	113	Hooks	112	Sleeves	82		
Buttons	113			dolman, kimono, raglan	83		
Buttonholes	115	Invisible zips	99	Sleeve blocks	201		
Buttonhole maker	13			bishop	203		
		Jersey polyester	144	close-fitting	204		
Cable stitch	63			flared	208		
double	65	Kimono sleeves	83	gathered	207		
Cape (pattern for)	218			Sleeve openings	90		
Casing	47	Lace	151	Sleeve pad	28		
Casing	47	Cluny, guipure	152	Smocking	63		
Channel seam	50	Leather	159	Stay stitch	49		
Cluny lace	152	Linings	127				
Collars	71			Tailor's chalk	12		
(patterns for)	210	Machines	9	Tailored collars	74		
Commercial patterns	35	Machine edge stitching	48	Tailor tacker	12		
altering	39	Mantua seams	53	Tassels	141		
cutting out	37	Measurements (how to take)	25	Ties	103		
fitting	37			Toggles	114		
laying out	35	Necklines	75	Tracing wheels	12		
marking and tacking	37	Needle and thread chart	8	Transparent ruler	12		
Corselet belt	105			Transfers	63		
Cotton fabrics	16	Open end zip	99	Trellis stitch	63		
Cravats	103			Trousers	221		
Cuffs	86	Petersham	96	making up	223		
circular	87	Pinking	49	Tucking	57		
wrapover	86	Pin tucking	57	Tucks	135		
Cummerbund	110	Piping	46				
gathered	111	made from bias	101	Vandyke stitch	65		
		Plackets for sleeves	90	Velcro fastening	112		
Darts	48	for zips	97	Velvet	163		
Decorative zip	99	Pleats	135				
Diamond stitch	66	box	136	Zips	97		
Distance piece	62	fan	137	curved seam	98		
Dolman sleeves	83	fish tail	138	decorative, invisible, open-end	99